Critical Perspectives on Further Education and Training

Edited by
Camilla Fitzsimons and Jerry O'Neill

ANTHEM PRESS

Anthem Press
An imprint of Wimbledon Publishing Company
www.anthempress.com

This edition first published in UK and USA 2024
by ANTHEM PRESS
75–76 Blackfriars Road, London SE1 8HA, UK
or PO Box 9779, London SW19 7ZG, UK
and
244 Madison Ave #116, New York, NY 10016, USA

© 2024 Camilla Fitzsimons and Jerry O'Neill editorial matter and selection;
individual chapters © individual contributors

The moral right of the authors has been asserted.

All rights reserved. Without limiting the rights under copyright reserved above,
no part of this publication may be reproduced, stored or introduced into
a retrieval system, or transmitted, in any form or by any means
(electronic, mechanical, photocopying, recording or otherwise),
without the prior written permission of both the copyright
owner and the above publisher of this book.

British Library Cataloguing-in-Publication Data
A catalogue record for this book is available from the British Library.

Library of Congress Cataloging-in-Publication Data
A catalog record for this book has been requested.
2023948247

ISBN-13: 978-1-83998-915-5 (Hbk)
ISBN-10: 1-83998-915-7 (Hbk)
ISBN-13: 978-1-83998-916-2 (Pbk)
ISBN-10: 1-83998-916-5 (Pbk)

This title is also available as an e-book.

CONTENTS

List of Figures and Tables   v

Acknowledgements   vii

Preface: 'Done with Prefabs'   ix
    Sarah Sartori and Students from Dunboyne CFE

Introduction: Critical Perspectives on FET in Ireland   1
    Camilla Fitzsimons and Jerry O'Neill

Chapter 1.   Philosophical Foundations: Applying bell hooks' Engaged Pedagogy to FET Contexts   17
Camilla Fitzsimons

Chapter 2.   Engaging Holistically with Curriculum and Assessment   29
Sarah Coss

Chapter 3.   Why We Need to Talk about Race in Further Education and Training   45
Lilian Nwanze

Chapter 4.   Neurodiversity and Inclusion in Further Education and Training   63
Jane O'Kelly

Chapter 5.   Adult Learning in Groups: 'A Practice of Freedom'   79
Bríd Connolly

Chapter 6.   Towards Critical and Postcritical Global Education   93
Eilish Dillon

Chapter 7.   A Winter Sun: Creative Reflexivity as Practitioner Research   107
Jerry O'Neill

Chapter 8.	Older than the Internet: Digital World Literacy and Adult Learning *Leo Casey*	123
Chapter 9.	Towards a Grounded Practice: Community Education in Ireland Today *Eve Cobain, Susan Cullinane and Suzanne Kyle*	135
Chapter 10.	Identity (Trans-)formation in Second-Career FET Teachers *Brendan Kavanagh, Francesca Lorenzi and Elaine McDonald*	151
Chapter 11.	A Precarious Profession *Camilla Fitzsimons and Jerry O'Neill*	169

'Afterwords': A Concluding Conversation   183

About the Authors   201

Bibliography   207

Index   233

LIST OF FIGURES AND TABLES

Figures

2.1	The product and process models of curriculum development	32
7.1	A triskelion reflexive flux	112

Tables

6.1	Three types of global education	98
10.1	Mezirow's ten phases of transformative learning. Adapted from Mezirow and produced in Kitchenham (2008, 105)	161

ACKNOWLEDGEMENTS

First and foremost, we want to thank everyone who has ever been in a group with us or with any of the authors featured in this book. Sometimes this would have been as a student in an FE College, university, community education, within a campaign group or perhaps a community of practice. Maybe we met via Zoom or Teams, in classrooms, staff training rooms or some other space temporarily transformed into an adult learning environment. Thanks also to those of you who we often find ourselves sitting with for long periods in our own staff room as we contemplate some of the big questions that feature throughout this book.

This contribution has undoubtedly been a collective effort, so a huge shout out to all of the contributors: Bríd, Brendan, Eilish, Elaine, Eve, Francesca, Jane, Leo, Lilian, Sarah C., Sarah S., Susan, Suzanne and the students from Dunboyne College and their tutor Aoife O'Dwyer. We know we pestered you all along the way but we are grateful for your thought-provoking contributions. Thanks also to those of you who helped out in other ways: Ann, Anna, Anne, Bríd, Bernie, Ciara, Gareth, Gina, Kevin, Lilian, Nuala, Stephen and Ted. You know what you did.

In Anthem, thanks to Courtney Young who sent the initial email that we responded to with our idea and to Jessica Mack, Brinda Ponni and Jebaslin Hephzibah who took an interest in our work and kept things moving along. You were always so attentive and careful in your dealings with us – thank you. Thanks to Balaji Devadoss for his careful and keen eye in proof editing.

Finally big thanks and love to partners, children, parents, aunts, siblings, friends, cats and dogs that gave us space and time when we should have been paying more attention to you.

Go raibh míle maith agaibh go léir,

Camilla and Jerry

PREFACE: 'DONE WITH PREFABS'

Sarah Sartori and Students from Dunboyne CFE

Sarah Sartori ... with Michelle Power, Sarah Duke, Jake Rutherford, Amy McDonagh, Dean Smyth, Darren King, Manahil Hussain, Jack Hamilton, Ronan Marsh, James Brennan, Luca Kavanagh, Katie Park, Sylvia Tone, Caoimhe Hayes, Julie Plunkett and Caitlin O'Brien Killeen.[1]

We settle into a space together ... circling questions that touch on the thoughts and words of the writers that stretch across these pages ... but mainly, in this moment, we are thinking about what is it like to be an FE student scattered among the units of an industrial estate ...

Our conversation pushes and pulls across the space ... across the page ...
I make a start...
    So ... tell me ... what's it like here ... how are you getting on?
There's a long pause ... but I am happy with silences ... and slowly, sure enough, the
                  responses come ...

                                                        Well...
                                        It's not like secondary school ...
                        ... more subject choices ...
... the classes aren't too big...
                ... so you can still get one-on-one help ...
And continuous assessments ...
                They lay out assignments easily for you, like, you know... so that you're not doing it wrong ... I needed a lot of guidance ... which is good.

---

1 This preface was crafted from conversations with students from Dunboyne College of Further Education who contributed to two discussion sessions centred around the emerging themes of this book. These conversations were facilitated, harvested and edited by Sarah Sartori and coordinated by Aoife O'Dwyer, Academic Support Coordinator and Tutor and Coordinator on the Level 5 Pre-University Access Course in Dunboyne CFE.

But the whole place ... the FE space is ...
                                                ... kind of like a middle ground ...
like university ... but with prefabs
... a bit like secondary school
                              I thought we were done with prefabs ...
                   ... so, yeh ... a middle ground ...

I let the conversation trail off and we move on ... we talk a bit then about their tutors ... their teachers ... how do they see them?

They have to be passionate ...
                        They probably want to help out
                                          .... to make a difference ...
They obviously have a passion for it ...
                        They draw you in
                              ... ask you questions
    ... involving you in the topic
                                  ... you're learning for yourself
They don't make you feel as if you're below them ...
                                    ... we're all on the same ground
                          ...even though we're not
                                ... but it feels different here ...

Again I pause and survey the room ...
        I wonder about the critical dimensions of their learning ...
So, what about the world outside the class here ... what's going on with the planet ... the big picture stuff ... do you get into that here?

              We never really talk about what's going on ...
                  We've done ... like a ... day where we're talking about diversity ...
                                  ... different races and all that ...
And how was that?
                   Well ... you have to be careful ... you don't want to offend ...

So you don't like talking about racism?
                         No ... we don't have any problems with that ...
                         it's just we don't really have to think about it ...
It's not an issue for us .... It's not really in our head ...
        We want to be teachers ... and it's usually people from the same background ...

They pause ... is it uncomfortable? ... I remember the coloured post-it's on the tables ... We stay in the silence as they scribble their thoughts and stick them onto the whiteboard ...

PREFACE: 'DONE WITH PREFABS'

Isn't really discussed ....

Not spoken about ...

Isn't talked about ...

There is restlessness as we settle back in the space ... we're coming to a close ...
What about reflection, I ask finally. What about time and space to reflect?

It's helpful to look back ...

You understand yourself ... the way you think ...

In what way, I wonder. Do you think differently?
Again, there is a long moment of thoughtful silence ... I let the space between the talking do its work ... until ... one voice simply, but carefully, shares ...

I have changed.

INTRODUCTION: CRITICAL PERSPECTIVES ON FET IN IRELAND

Camilla Fitzsimons and Jerry O'Neill

In 2024, around 150,000 adult learners will sign up for some sort of programme of learning somewhere across Ireland's expanding Further Education and Training (FET) sector; that's over three times the amount of people who start university for the first time.[1] Some of these adult learners will have finished school the year before and will be enrolling in a year-long (or sometimes two-year-long) 'Major Award' at one of the many Further Education (FE) Colleges that are scattered across the country. Some will sign up for a blended 'on-the-job' and 'off-the-job' apprenticeship programme. Others will study a diverse and growing selection of programmes including – to name just a few, childcare, sound engineering, hairdressing, sports coaching, event management or computers. Some of those who graduate will then get jobs in the relevant field. Others, especially those who sign up for one of the growing number of 'pre-university' courses, do so in the hope that doing well in this course will improve their chances of getting into Higher Education (meaning university).

Many students won't be school leavers but will be older adults who will enrol in FET for a variety of reasons. Some will be hoping to prepare themselves to go back to paid work after time away, for example, if they were a full-time carer in the home. Others will want to learn new skills for the jobs they are already doing. Many more will be there for personal reasons. They might want to learn how to cook, paint or play a musical instrument. Maybe they want to expand their knowledge of liberal arts or social studies or perhaps they will

---

1 FET figure is taken from 2020 enrolment number as published on https://www.solas.ie/research-lp/fet-statistics/. Accessed April 4, 2023. According to https://hea.ie/2022/09/12/higher-education-key-facts-and-figures-2021-2022/, around 45,000 new students enter university each year.

sign onto a programme specially designed to improve their reading, writing or IT skills. Many will sign up for a course so that they can meet other people, have some fun and just get out of the house. There will also be thousands of recently arrived refugees and asylum seekers who will attend one of the dozens of English for Speakers of Other Languages (ESOL) courses that are available nationwide.

Mostly, these people will hugely benefit from these courses. Many will meet their vocational or future educational goals and will likely find personal fulfilment, expand their social circles and enjoy themselves. Perhaps people will change their outlook on themselves and on the world in which they live. Some will struggle along the way, especially with the demands placed on them to produce academic essays, complete work placements and attend to the many other requirements of increasingly bureaucratized education frameworks. And some will drop out, unable to juggle the many responsibilities and commitments they have with the extra load of learning or maybe because they discover that they are not that interested in the contents of the course they signed up for. Many might be justifiably bored and frankly uninspired by the style of teaching they encounter.

The Purpose of Education

For those of us who teach (or, in our cases, taught) in FET, how we approach this work will be guided by the assumptions we carry about the purpose of education: Is it about fostering people's capacities to be as individually successful as they can be? Or is it about serving the economy by collectively enhancing our national skills base through training? Or do we see that there is a role for education in helping people to enhance their reading of, and relationship to, their social and environmental worlds?

The case we make in this book is that we must draw this often-marginalized latter purpose into the core foundations and perceptions of education. FET can continue to foster people's individual capacities and it can enhance their skills in a way that supports personal transformation. But it can also encourage people to go deeper and can support the social, political, and environmental transformations required to create a world that badly needs our critical attention and care.

You may have already raised an eyebrow at the mention of 'social, political and environmental transformation' as part of the work of educators and as something very separate to our work. For example, let's think about a classroom where an adult educator is teaching future childcare workers about organizing a play activity for young children. You might wonder, what this could possibly have to do with politics?

So, maybe this is a good place, right at the start, to be clear about the purpose of this book. As its title suggests, and whilst appreciating the personally transformative potential of education, we argue that it is our responsibility to better understand, and respond to, how existing political and social systems, including the education system, have shaped the lives of these imagined childcare students and indeed the lives of the children that they will care for.

The theoretical preference that speaks to this perspective is often called *critical pedagogy* – a problem-posing philosophy of education, with the principle of praxis (meaning informed activism) at its core. This perspective assumes, as its starting point, that our world is fundamentally shaped by asymmetries of power and privilege. Critical pedagogy is first and foremost about asking 'why?' For example, why do many more people from areas described as 'affluent' go to university when compared to those living in 'disadvantaged areas' (Higher Education Authority 2022). Or why do so few Travellers complete secondary school when compared to their non-Traveller peers?[2] Furthermore, why do so many of the people described above who sign up for courses to combat loneliness and social disconnectedness likely experience these symptoms as a direct result of the intense focus on competitiveness and individuality in our social world (Becker, Hartwich and Haslam 2021)? And why does the system that creates these difficulties for people then defund public mental health services and local community supports while a privatized, 'wellness industry', that is often too expensive for most people to access, is allowed to thrive? What about asking why the many fine graduates of further education courses in childcare, healthcare or retail skills, despite holding vital skills, will likely end up in precarious jobs that often pay little more than the minimum wage? The coronavirus pandemic of 2020–2022 showed just how fundamental these frontline workers are. Furthermore, given that, increasingly, many of these frontline workers are migrants, what is our responsibility as educators when it comes to questioning the economic, social and environmental reasons why they took such huge risks to leave their countries of origin or how immigration policies treat them when they arrive? Where do we discuss the racial injustices many experience as part of their everyday lives if not within adult learning environments?

But critical pedagogy goes further than just asking us to open conversations about these issues. We agree with the Brazilian educationalist Paulo Freire's

---

2 The most recent official figures available are from the 2011 census which measures just eight percent of Travellers as having completed to Leaving Certificate, compared to 73 percent of non-Travellers.

strongly argued assertion that the education system is part of the system that creates and upholds these inequalities by functioning as a site for domestication where 'schools [and adult, community and further education] become easy spaces for selling knowledge which corresponds to capitalist ideology' (Shor and Freire 1987, 8). As Richard Shaull writes in the foreword to *Pedagogy of the Oppressed*,

> There is no such thing as a neutral education process. Education either functions as an instrument which is used to facilitate the integration of the younger generation [or adult learner] into the logic of the present system and bring about conformity to it, or it becomes 'the practice of freedom' the means by which men and women [sic] deal critically and creatively with reality and discover how to participate in the transformation of their world. (in Freire 1972, 13–14)

Usually, this isn't intentionally done but unless educators appreciate this wider function of education, they risk 'serving only to dehumanize' (Freire 1972, 48) at the expense of potential liberation.

We contend that it is more urgent than ever that this often invisible, but culturally dominant, purpose of education is brought to the fore and problematized so that we might continue to nurture individual development and foster active, engaged and even disruptive citizenship as well. People may then become critically literate and compelled to take action in a social, political and environmental world that is increasingly shaped by escalating levels of crises and social injustices. To borrow words from the cultural critic and critical pedagogy proponent Henry Giroux,

> It is crucial to develop pedagogical practices that address the underlying causes of poverty, class domination, environmental destruction, white supremacy, and a resurgent racism. It is essential to develop a discourse that extends the possibilities of critique to a wide variety of issues in order to analyze that threads that weave through them. (Giroux 2021, 36)

Shifting Ground, Structures and Names

Before going any further, let's deliberately return to the not unproblematic term 'FET' that we have used both in the title and in the opening line of this book. When we both began our careers in the 1990s, the term didn't exist. One of us, Camilla, started out in community education working with women's groups in North Dublin. The other, Jerry, worked initially in further education colleges in Scotland and, then, in community and work-based adult education in Ireland. Our critical and pedagogic curiosities have led us to a variety of educational spaces: we have worked in adult literacy centres, community development projects, adult education centres and further education colleges. We have organized, developed and facilitated courses in voter education, housing activism, local leadership, environmental awareness, human rights, social analysis, access courses, reproductive rights, social activism, work-based learning and a wide variety of vocational programmes where we always attended to the social and emotional dimensions of learning that, strictly speaking, fall beyond the so-called work-readiness that many of these programmes were geared towards.

If we were to begin our careers again today, these diverse fields of practice would be categorized within the relatively newly named 'FET' sector – a concept, term and acronym created and adopted by policymakers in the early part of the 2010s to name and, possibly, tame a hitherto heterogeneous field of practice which included all aspects of adult, community, vocational and further education.

The creation of 'FET', both as a name and a political aspiration for adult education, didn't happen in a vacuum. It is not an acronym that is used widely outside of this country although there are shades of reference in it to the long-established FE sector in the UK, which is quite distinct from the community education field. At the same time, 'FET' also resonates with the acronym 'VET' (Vocational Education and Training), the term used across many mainland European countries to describe the lifelong vocational educational space that stretches from the latter stages of school, through to vocational education and employment.

Just like education itself, the act of naming our world, and in particular, renaming a social something – whether that be a person, group, region, country or field(s) of educational practice – is also not a neutral act. There are questions of power for us to consider in this Irish context that will likely resonate with experiences in other parts of the world also. Who is doing the naming? Why is this educational space being (re)named at all? And what are the connotations and the suggestions associated with the new names that we give our fields of work?

One starting point in getting to the 'why' behind these questions is to pay close attention to a significant ideological, political, structural and policy shift that has been ongoing within the broad field of adult education since the start of the twenty-first century, if not earlier. Certainly, in an Irish context, it was around the start of the 2010s, that the state, energized by an earlier European-led employability discourse (Murray et al. 2014) and an increasing fixation on standardization and quality across education systems (Fitzsimons 2017a, 133–161), initiated a structural and ideological re-imagining and re-forming of adult, community and further education.

This motivation to 'reform' aspects of provision was certainly not lessened by a series of crises including public outcry about management cultures within certain areas of vocational education at the time. Indeed, the need to reinvent, and rename, the then vocational and training authority known as FÁS was fuelled, in no small part, by a public scandal in 2008 that initiated a government investigation into the use of public funds for first-class foreign travel and lavish accommodation by senior members of the organization. This scandal was just one of many involving public and political figures at the time across Ireland, including two long-running political and planning scandals that contributed to a general distrust of high-level public servants and politicians.

There are a couple of ways of viewing moments of disorientation that happen in times of significant and widespread structural crises and shifts. A positively inclined perspective might see junctures of disorientation as an opportunity, as Jack Mezirow (1990) might suggest, for significant transformative learning for individuals, groups and organizations. But being disorientated in itself is not enough for such learning to occur – what is also needed is the creation of time and space for authentic and meaningful critical reflection. On the other hand, such moments of structural disorientation also present another possibility as outlined by Naomi Klein in her book *Shock Doctrine* (2007). Klein argues that the great psycho-social disorientation created by national crises, like a recession or even a pandemic, can become, for those that way inclined, opportunities to strip and restructure existing socio-economic systems with the relative satisfaction that there isn't a public appetite to discuss the values or motivations driving such rapid restructuring and repurposing. The rationale of such actions, Klein argues, is to deliberately accelerate a particular *neoliberal* version of advanced capitalism that seeks to reinvigorate the accumulation of capital by placing all of our trust in a return to free-market economics.

Neoliberalism is a word and idea that you may encounter quite a bit in this book and it has certain characteristics that are important to comprehend. These include a hollowing out of the state through privatization, high levels of deregulation (including rules about the control and transfer of money) and a political model that is committed to reducing national budget deficits through austerity measures, rather than interfering with a supposed 'free market' by, for example, limiting profits. For public services, such as adult, community and further education, that are not formally privatized, a neoliberalized path is laid out for them which imports business models and practices that both mimic, and service, the market economy.

So, although there isn't much evidence of a Mezirowean response to the systemic disorientation in the adult, community and further education fields in the early 2010s, the rapid and widespread sectoral restructuring undoubtedly has hints of a shock doctrine dynamic. Regardless of how we interpret the power and politics at play, it was within this moment of fundamental systemic disorientation that SOLAS was quite suddenly presented to a disillusioned public as a brand-new national oversight organization that was given responsibility for all publicly funded adult, community and further education, with a training element (previously the work of the now disbanded FÁS) built in.

It is our assertion that the processes and politics of adult education's structural and ideologically neoliberal re-forming and renaming in this period formed part of the wider de/reconstruction project by Ireland's political class. As is typical with processes of neoliberalization, the justification for the resultant changes was cloaked in the often reasonably sounding language of transparency and accountability (Fitzsimons 2017a, 13–14). This created a sense in the public and sectoral imagination of 'cleaning the houses' and starting afresh.

In terms of adult education, a significant part of this restructuring exercise was how SOLAS's first national strategy, *The Further Education and Training Strategy 2014–2019* (SOLAS 2014), which was produced with minimal if any consultation, merged 'adult and community education' with 'further education' – two fields of practice that had, prior to this merger, often been considered quite separately. In renaming this new, all-encompassing educational space, 'adult' and 'community' were dropped and replaced with 'training' to create 'Further Education and Training'. Regardless of its name though, the task for FET was to dedicate itself to all aspects of adult, community and further education including, to give a flavour, personal development, leisure-based learning, citizenship education, vocational education and training including apprenticeships, and all post-compulsory education outside of Higher Education (HE).

This wasn't the first time such a reconfiguration had been initiated from above. In the late 1990s and early 2000s, and coinciding with European policy discourse of lifelong learning (Fitzsimons 2017a, 136–140), *The Green Paper: Adult Education in an Era of Learning* (Department of Education and Science, hereafter referred to as *The Green Paper*) and the highly regarded *Learning for Life: White Paper on Adult Education* (Department of Education and Science 2000, hereafter referred to as *The White Paper*) also transformed domestic policy. Together these policy interventions created significant change. The needs of the economy and employers were included within *The Green* and *White* papers (and have always been part of adult and community education provision), but they were balanced alongside personal and civic considerations. The most visible outcome of these policy interventions was the appointment of Community Education Facilitators (CEFs) across the country.

Importantly, though, the process that led to this earlier realignment was characterized by high levels of consultation not only with adult educators but also with adult learners. In fact, Appendix 2 of *The White Paper* lists the authors of 184 written submissions the government received across community groups, public sector providers (e.g. FÁS), employer groups and individual members of the public. Appendix 3 lists 64 oral submissions from across public providers, charities, advocacy organizations (e.g. Age Action and the Irish Traveller Movement) and again, community groups and employer organizations.

It is worth emphasizing the impact of the many submissions that were made by existing adult and community education providers that had emerged in the 1980s and 1990s as part of a bottom-up response to the needs of communities and social justice movements. One of the contributors to this book, Bríd Connolly (2005), has consistently highlighted the importance of community-based, politicizing education as part of a 'women's movement' that was characterized by ways of working that were underpinned by the principles and practices of critical pedagogy. Connolly has described how these community education spaces allowed 'women to see themselves as active participants in Irish society, women who might otherwise, through socialisation, perceive themselves as operating within the private sphere only' (Connolly 2001, 1). In seeking funding for the work that they were doing, these groups banded together with other community-based initiatives, in particular, an anti-poverty focused 'community development movement', forming a vibrant and often oppositional independent Community and Voluntary Sector (CVS). As a result of this historical process and community focus, many early community education practitioners emerged from the population groups where adult education was practised (Fitzsimons 2017a, 88).

Where the *White Paper* and *Green Paper* reflected a balance among personal, political and vocational needs, the initial reinvention of adult, community and further education as FET unapologetically prioritized the vocational and employability dimension that best services the market economy. This reorientation was alongside a substantial downsizing of the CVS through forced mergers and harsh funding cuts that resulted in the closure of over 160 Community Development Projects nationwide, most of which were directly involved in providing community education (Fitzsimons 2017a, 82–87). The activist and community worker John Bissett (2015, 174) describes this downsizing as a neoliberal 'strategic turn ... which signalled a sharp authoritarian turn in the state's position vis-à-vis the community sector'. Some groups did survive but did so under different managerial structures and often because they altered their practice so that they could avail of the limited employability-oriented funding opportunities that were available (Magrath and Fitzsimons 2020, 42–43).

Just as many adult educators emerged from their communities, so too, in vocational education, practitioners often emerged from their professional and occupational communities such as hairdressing, plumbing, the business sector or childcare. Often these practitioners worked within the aforementioned, and quite structurally and pedagogically separate, national training body, FÁS. But many also worked within vocational colleges which have been historically called PLC (Post-Leaving Certificate) colleges; some of which date back to the 1930s. These colleges, which resemble the FE sector in the UK, were collectively managed across 33 county-based Vocational Education Committees (VECs) nationwide. In 2013, these VECs were restructured into 16 Education and Training Boards (ETBs) and integrated FÁS centres within this new national structure. Within this contracted model, PLC colleges, offering mostly vocational and access to university courses, began to identify as 'Colleges of Further Education'.

But beyond these more recognizable training centres and colleges of further education, there are so many other places all over the country where publicly funded adult education happens almost invisibly to the general public across a wide range of smaller-scale adult and early school-leaver education centres and projects. What happens in these spaces is often, although not always, determined by the employability vision laid out in policy.

Yet, looking more broadly, there still exists a rich diversity when it comes to the provision of learning programmes within adult, community and further education across Ireland. A quick internet search uncovers pretty much anything you can think of from 'account administration' to 'Zumba dancing' with thousands of options in between. Mostly, these courses are free of charge and most people sign up voluntarily.

However, we can't always assume that adult learners are always voluntarily engaging. Some adult education provision is *de facto* compulsory: for example, when adult learners are required to attend courses to keep their full social welfare benefits. Or when young people are enrolled on early school-leaver programmes. Or prisoner education – another space where one could contest the degree of learner autonomy to engage, or disengage, without judgement by official others. And then there's an ever-increasing influx of migrants, some of whom arrive quite suddenly because they are fleeing from conflicts and/ or environmental catastrophes. Some have little choice but to sign up for an expanding provision of language classes as they negotiate life in a country whose public services and supports over-rely on the English language. It is also the case that some migrants who hold professional qualifications from countries outside of the European Credit Transfer and Accumulation System

(ECTS) end up in FET where they enrol on vocational courses that prepare them for lower-paid roles. For instance, it is not unusual for nurses registered in other countries to retrain as lower-paid healthcare workers.

There is, then, a lot going on, and a lot we can get involved in, to claim, define and purpose the rough ground of this, at least historically, neglected domain of the educational landscape.

Towards a Coherent and Equitable Tertiary Education System

One earlier signposted aspect of this top-down, strategic intervention in adult education which originated in the early 2010s has been the creation of a new and distinct government ministry dedicated to further and higher education. The first minister of this new department, 'The Department of Further, Higher Education, Research, Innovation and Science' (DFHERIS), was Simon Harris, a high-profile senior political figure who many believed had a solid track record in his previous senior role as Health Minister. Since his appointment, Harris has consistently used his role to highlight the value and potential of further education. When Ireland's second national strategy for further and adult education, *Future FET: Transforming Learning* 2020–2024 (hereafter called *Future FET*) first appeared, it was clear that both its process and contents were different than its problematic predecessor. Not only was its release preceded by extensive nationwide consultation, but there is a sense that significant thought and work had gone into revisiting the idea and purpose of FET that was more attuned to a more expansive role beyond education for work readiness. In the foreword, written by Harris, FET is described as being 'at the heart of communities across the country' and that its purpose is 'to repair, repurpose and revive our economy and our communities' through the principle of 'building skills, fostering inclusion and facilitating pathways' (SOLAS, 3). This high-level attempt to balance hitherto dominant economic imperatives with the needs of communities is a tension that reflects much of the diversity of positions, practices and purposes of both programmes and practitioners across the heterogeneous landscape which FET, as a rapidly developing national policy space, seeks to hold. Yet, it is heartening to see *Future FET* (SOLAS 2020) attempt to reconcile that tension and it does go some way to address concerns about the absence of community in the first strategy. Indeed, and with the acknowledgement that it could almost be missed, *Future FET* identifies social justice as one of the four core values of FET alongside lifelong learning, active citizenship and economic prosperity (SOLAS, 36).

Of course, *Future FET* is just one of several adult education priorities laid out in the programme for the government. There are also plans to streamline, and make more visible, pathways into, through and out of further and higher education as the term 'Tertiary Education' seeks to gain purchase and bridge the traditional sectoral divisions between further and higher education (Department of Further and Higher Education, Research, Innovation and Science (DFHERIS) 2022).

Although we welcome closer collaboration and more clarity on pathways between FE and HE, it is also important to acknowledge that FE is a distinct and valuable educational and community space in its own right which provides rich spaces for many thousands of adults who are not interested in progressing to university. We also have a new ten-year strategy for *Adult Literacy, Numeracy and Digital Literacy 2021–2031* (Government of Ireland 2021) as well as an ongoing commitment to fund community-based education through *The Reach Fund* which was introduced at the height of the COVID-19 pandemic but renamed and sustained in an acknowledgement that there was an ongoing need for such support (SOLAS 2022). There are also plans to regenerate or relocate many of the buildings FE Colleges currently occupy. For example, in 2021, a €30 million expansion plan was unveiled for just one of these Meath-based colleges transforming it into one of Ireland's first 'College of the Future'.

If we take all of these developments together, one could argue that the future looks bright for adult, community and further education in Ireland. The concern though is that, although financial investment is certainly welcome and necessary, there is ongoing financial precarity for smaller, locally based education providers who spend considerable amounts of their time and energy chasing multiple funding streams to stay afloat (Magrath and Fitzsimons 2020). Moreover, strategizing a collective and clear response to a growing political clamour about the important role of further education in creating a socially inclusive, economically vibrant Ireland feels completely out of step with some of the harsh employment realities for the workforce who are expected to facilitate such a transformation and whose lives are often shaped by stubbornly high levels of precarity. The casualization of work goes far beyond FET and is much more than an Irish problem. Rather, it too is one of the recognized symptoms of neoliberal free market economics (Jaffe 2021; Horgan 2021). A highly casualized education workforce not only undermines individuals' right to decent work but also inhibits the development of the high-quality and sustainable professional practices and cultures which are needed for adult education to flourish (Finnegan and O'Neill 2020; Fitzsimons, Henry and O'Neill 2022; O'Neill and Fitzsimons 2020). Furthermore, the move towards a 'unified tertiary education' system adds to an already strong sense of ambiguity around professional equity for FET educators and where government responsibility lies for qualified FET teachers and educators, many of whom are registered with The Teaching Council of Ireland, the professional standards authority for the teaching profession.[3]

A most fundamental and connected concern is the broader track record of the neoliberal free-market economics that inform current policy direction. What guarantees do we have that this more egalitarian policy directive of *Future FET* is anything more than lip service? How do we reconcile a government discourse that claims social justice as a cornerstone of *Future FET* but at the same time persists with neoliberal politics that have failed to deliver the trickle-down economic benefits it promised?

What we do know is that FET operates within social parameters where there are unprecedented levels of income inequality as a small number of individuals have been allowed to accumulate vast amounts of wealth. Such is the scale of this income inequality that, according to the World Inequality Report for 2022, the richest 10 percent of the population currently take in 52 percent of all global income whilst the poorest half earns just 8.5 percent (Chancel, et al. 2022). In the Republic of Ireland, the number of Irish people with individual wealth of over €46.6 million has more than doubled in the last ten years with the richest 1 percent gaining 70 times more wealth than the bottom 50 percent (Oxfam Ireland 2023).

This wealth for a relatively small number of people contrasts with precarious lives for others, not least because of the neoliberal privatization of social housing provision, without a framework of tenants' rights, which has directly resulted in a previously unimaginable housing and homelessness crisis (Hearne 2022). In June 2023, there were c12,000 people living in emergency accommodation in Ireland and over 20,000 living in for-profit Direct Provision Centres which provide accommodation for people seeking international protection under asylum rights (Fletcher 2023). Previously, community development initiatives have centred on and won certain housing rights (Dorman 2007; Bissett 2008). However, since this great realignment, the independent community organizations that hired the workers to coordinate this work no longer exist.

Again, you may be wondering why a book about FET has strayed into a discussion about global economics and homelessness. But it is now well documented that these factors – housing circumstances, financial poverty,

---

[3] Historically, the Teaching Council's relationship has been with the Department of Education, but how will these two government departments collaborate to ensure that distinct FET teaching professionals can be afforded the same professional rights and opportunities as their primary and post-primary colleagues?

generational educational disadvantage, family status, minority ethnicity, perilous citizenship and/or disability – significantly impact a person's performance in educational systems (Lynch 2022) and their likelihood to enrol in FET. As adult educators, we must take account of the micro and macro contexts of people's lives.

But even if the policy change promised in *Future FET* turns out to be rhetoric, this shift back, in policy *vision* terms at least, to the more socially orientated goals of adult education is a welcome one and one we have a duty, as critical scholars and practitioners, to hold and nourish whatever our roles in the field. The negative impacts of neoliberalism run deep, but the magnitude of today's crises brings opportunities to re-imagine our futures and get to grips with the kind of society we want to live in. This is the challenge we set ourselves as we too reframe FET in Ireland.

Outline of the Book

This book began with the voices of students from Dunboyne College of Further Education who, through a process facilitated by Sarah Sartori, provided their own perspectives and reflections on the themes of the book.

This introductory chapter you have been reading has served a number of functions. It briefly described the landscape of a complex, heterogeneous FET sector and outlined our perspectives on the potential of adult, community and further education in Ireland. It introduced the concept of neoliberalism having a detrimental impact on adult and community education in Ireland before identifying spaces of optimism by acknowledging a welcome government commitment to the continual expansion of FET in Ireland for a diverse range of educational purposes.

Following on from this introduction, Chapter 1 (by Camilla) on 'engaged pedagogy' is philosophically oriented and seeks to provide practical examples of how we might make political demands of adult education by finding and expanding spaces where we can critique structures of power and privilege amidst curricula that often seem quite far removed from the neoliberal global landscape that is being painted.

In Chapter 2, experienced further and higher education practitioner, Sarah Coss offers a practical and thought-provoking account of the challenges of working creatively and dialogically with FE curricula while at the same time attending to the many bureaucratized demands of Ireland's National Framework of Qualifications (NFQ) and corresponding European Credit Transfer System. She discusses the difference between the assessment *of* learning rather than *for* learning and challenges common myths about educator autonomy. She also prompts us to think about curricula more broadly and the unseen power of the hidden curriculum in determining our actions and beliefs. Sarah encourages us all to approach curriculum and assessment collaboratively, critically and creatively.

Chapter 3, written by Lilian Nwanze, builds a case for the importance of discussions about racism and white privilege. She draws widely from her experiences as a racialized Black female educator who has worked across FE and HE. She focuses on how Irish immigration laws and policies ensure that a large number of non-EU migrants, a cohort more likely to be racialized, inevitably end up in FET and proposes concrete actions an FET practitioner can do as they strive to embody an anti-racist approach, the last of which is an emphasis on love.

In Chapter 4, Jane O'Kelly presents a reflexive exploration of neurodiversity in adults and prompts us to consider whether their needs are recognized and accommodated in FET settings. The chapter defines neurodiversity in adults, current debates on neurodiversity in the literature and in neurodiverse communities and the challenges facing neurodiverse people in adult and further education.

In Chapter 5, Bríd Connolly explores a feminist egalitarian groupwork stance, with a focus on the possibilities of groups in social movements and their influence on adult and community education. She critiques both psychological and business approaches to groups and reframes them in the light of thinking about 'soft skills', increasingly seen as a work-related set of attributes, rather than as sites for emancipatory human and social interaction. Bríd argues FET pedagogy needs to be able to draw on these aspects of groupwork in learning environments for FET to become a key actor in challenging the status quo of education as a social institution.

In Chapter 6, Eilish Dillon reflects on why a critical approach to global citizenship education (GCE) is so important for adult, community and further education today. She focuses on how GCE has come to the fore internationally (most visibly through the UN's Sustainable Development Goals) as a response to contemporary global challenges (e.g. climate change, inequality, violence, populism, racism and different forms of exploitation and oppression). Eilish highlights ongoing concerns that understandings and practices around it are not as critical or transformative as they need to be and introduces some debates about how GCE is understood and what this means for different forms of practice.

Much has been written about the centrality and value of reflective practice as a core component of educator professional competence and development. In Chapter 7, Jerry performs, as much as talks about, reflective practice by drawing on a moment of pedagogic inertia with a group of emerging FET educators to critically, and creatively, reflect upon his own, always developing practice.

His partially poetic chapter demonstrates a creative and critical approach to individual and group reflexive practices which, he argues, is not just central to the ongoing professional development of all FET practitioners and the sector itself, but can also be seen as a form of practitioner-based creative research in itself.

Leo Casey follows in Chapter 8 by exploring some of the overlooked connections between adult learning and digital literacy. In offering a critique of functional, skill-deficit models of literacy as espoused in human capital policies, he reflects how, typically, these policies characterize literacy as an individual deficiency in relation to employability and economic potential. Leo argues that there is a need for educators to question the disproportionate emphasis on policies based on models of human capital and the interests of big technology in determining the learning needs of our students and proposes that teaching and learning for Digital World Literacy can provide an alternative framework based on the values of lifelong learning and adult education.

Chapter 9, *Towards a Grounded Practice: Community Education in Ireland Today*, is written by Eve Cobain, Suzanne Kyle and Susan Cullinane, who are all experienced community education practitioners and leaders in networking community education. They link community education to social movement theory and expand on connections between community education and Ireland's community development, and anti-poverty movement of the 1980s and 1990s. They analyse the experiences of practitioners as they navigate the very different contemporary landscape and illuminate the impacts on the personal and professional identity of community educators and the knock-on consequences for the potential of community education to challenge structures that perpetuate inequalities and injustice.

In Chapter 10, Brendan Kavanagh, Francesca Lorenzi and Elaine Macdonald explore the process of teacher identity and (trans)formation of what they term 'second career teachers' within further education colleges whose work principally involves the delivery of major awards at levels 5 and 6. This exploration provides a sharp lens through which to view contested and vexatious concepts and particularly the conceptualization of FE as a 'second chance' and 'alternative' pathway.

In Chapter 11, we (Camilla and Jerry) conclude by highlighting in more detail the very real challenges facing educators working in a field that is characterized by high levels of precarity. We consider the extent of casualized working patterns and its impact on the national and European-led drive to enhance the status, quality and the 'professionality' of adult education as a career. We raise some serious questions about the contradictions of enhancing the sector while ignoring the consequences of casualized work practices on opportunities for professional growth. We argue that any move towards realizing a high-quality critical and sustainable distinct professional pathway for emerging educators must become a policy priority for any government that is serious about recognizing the value and potential of the FET sector.

In the methodological spirit of adult education, we close this contribution by bringing the authors from all of the chapters together for some 'Afterwords' as we reflect on the process of compiling this book and, as we look forward to the work to be done, to consider our hopes for the future of FET.

Chapter 1

PHILOSOPHICAL FOUNDATIONS: APPLYING BELL HOOKS' ENGAGED PEDAGOGY TO FET CONTEXTS

Camilla Fitzsimons

I sometimes find it hard to fit into formal education environments. This was brought home to me a couple of years ago when I went along to an open-forum seminar at the university where I work. The event was for lecturers and PhD students and was advertised as an informal, participatory, yet scholarly affair. The format was an opening introduction by the host, then two speakers – one academic and one student – each of whom troubleshooted a research conundrum with a wider audience of around fifteen people. The atmosphere seemed collegial and friendly and words of support and encouragement framed the event. After a while, I began to feel a little uncomfortable as, for me, the seminar descended into a space where academics, and occasionally students, appeared to compete with each other in putting forward the cleverest, most cutting-edge response. I spoke at one stage. I wasn't my most articulate self as I wasn't sure about how I was going to express my thoughts before the words left my mouth. As I remember things, my point was to question the futility of much curricular reform and to inquire as to whether tinkering around within the confines of existing school accreditation structures was the best use of our time as academics. 'Maybe we should be more ambitious', I suggested, 'and stick to the script that we need to revolutionize the school curriculum altogether – a ground zero approach', I lamented. I suspect I didn't make my point as clearly as I would have liked.

Later into the seminar, I was directly challenged by a more senior academic who, although not entirely dismissive of my ideas, was less pessimistic about the potential for schools to infuse criticality without making any fundamental changes to the way they are. They sounded cleverer and more fluent and named me in positioning their assertions in direct opposition to my apparent naivety. There was learning in the contents of their words. But this was overshadowed by the feelings stirred up within me as, almost immediately, I felt deflated and a little foolish. The lesson I learned that day was that despite how the event was billed, this wasn't the space to explore ideas and take risks. I disengaged and haven't returned since.

Finding one's self in a space that is shaped by hierarchy and where, as I did, people feel alienated isn't unusual in universities and colleges. In fact, it is quite common. bell hooks (1994) describes these as educational arenas that personify an all-too-common disconnect between the mind and the soul. The alternative she suggests is what she coined 'engaged pedagogy', an expression that often swills around in my head and that regularly guides my practice. Are my students engaged, I frequently ask myself, or do they look disengaged or uncomfortable? Are they shuffling in their chairs hinting that they need a break or surreptitiously browsing on phones for something more interesting than what is going on around them? Sometimes I apply the Freirean metaphor of 'banking' to these on-the-spot evaluations as I navigate the tensions of encouraging free-flowing dialogue, my own desire to instil the ideas I prefer and/or the pressure to instrumentally 'teach to the assessment' so that people do well in their exams. These crude, although not entirely redundant, determinations do help, but they are not enough to sufficiently guide my attempts to create the sort of learning environments hooks proposes – ones that are stimulating, relevant, responsive and inclusive of a range of ways of knowing and being. And all of this within a world that is increasingly shaped by economic insecurity, racially motivated violence and dire predictions with respect to the health of our planet.

The Philosophy Behind My Practice

The philosophical orientation that most clearly guides these ambitions is what is commonly termed *critical pedagogy*, an approach to education that particularly draws from values and methods attributed to the Brazilian educationalist Paulo Freire and further expanded on by others including bell hooks, a prolific critical pedagogue and feminist writer in her own right. If you read on to other chapters in this book, other writers draw from these ideas too. By way of summary, Freirean philosophy argues education is never neutral: it either maintains the capitalist status quo or seeks to transform it. Critical pedagogy challenges the aforementioned 'banking approach to education', which is described as a way of working where seemingly passive learners sit quietly and ingest a dominant fixed knowledge that is fed to them by the 'expert' educator, be they a schoolteacher, adult educator, lecturer, union official or a workplace instructor. hooks describes this depository model as 'based on the assumption that memorizing information and regurgitating it represented gaining knowledge that could be deposited, stored and used at a later date' (hooks 1994, 5). Banking techniques aren't just tired teaching methods, they represent an approach to education that often ignores student well-being, and that provides fertile ground for instilling capitalist ideology as common sense, making it almost impossible for us to imagine living any other way.

Yet despite the significant influence of critical pedagogy within the curricula of most university courses on education, the banking approach that hooks and Freire dissuade us from using continues to dominate in most of the Further Education and Training (FET) classrooms I have visited over the years as part of my work as a supervisor to student FE teachers as part of their training. One especially influential reason for this is that many educators, especially those who haven't explored philosophies of education, instinctively draw from their own experiences of attending school or college. And so, a cycle continues where the expectation for many learning environments is that they are tightly controlled, seemingly objective and where there is a strong emphasis on the unproblematic transfer of canonical knowledge (or fixed truths). If you studied or read into philosophies of education, this would most likely be labelled as a 'behaviourist' approach – an orientation where the methods that dominate are uncritical reinforcement and recall and the intended outcome is measurable change (Fitzsimons 2017a, 107).

When adult educators seek to avoid behaviourist patterns, they most commonly lean towards *humanistic* models as an alternative. This is a person-centred philosophy that seeks to nurture and guide each student so that they can self-direct in becoming the best version of themselves that they can be. The influential psychologist and scholar Carl Rogers calls for 'unconditional positive regard' from educators; an embodiment of care and respect that enables people to find the right frame of mind to unlock 'vast resources for self-understanding, for altering his or her [or their] self-concept, attitudes, and self-directed behaviour' (Rogers 1989, 135). Humanistic education can encourage critical thinking and can motivate people to make important changes in their lives. They can also be very supportive spaces to be in and they frequently include opportunities for people to share learning-related anxieties and repair the trauma of previous negative educational experiences (Heron 1999, 55).

At a glance, it can be hard to see any downside. After all, these are environments that epitomize a congruence between the heart and the mind. People can feel very supported and can be empowered to achieve great things. But there are important differences between this and the engaged pedagogy hooks avows which not only sets out to transform individuals but to also transform society itself. This can seem like an enormous undertaking for an educator and you might not think this has anything to do with your day-to-day work, but bear with me for a while, and I will explain why the social relations of power both inside and outside the classroom walls, and the interconnected experiences each person brings, have particular pedagogic value.

To begin, a critical pedagogic critique of person-centred education challenges the very idea that there is such a thing as an autonomous 'self'. None of us live in a vacuum. Our lives are fundamentally shaped by what hooks repeatedly describes as 'the imperialist white-supremacist capitalist patriarchy'. She calls on us to embody a way of working that raises people's consciousness about the structures of society and which offers new and different ways to think and be.

As introduced in this book's opening chapter, the ideology that dominates within today's 'imperialist white-supremacist capitalist patriarchy' is neoliberalism, which is best understood as an economic and cultural model of free-market economics. Neoliberalism prioritizes market well-being over citizen well-being and divests control of public facilities like transport, education, housing and even welfare to private interests. The reason given for this privatization is that these essential services can run smoothly and without the burden of bureaucracy and old-fashioned trade union agreements. The role cast for ordinary people is to work hard enough to take our share. If we do this, the fruits of our efforts will enable us to catch the slipstream of entrepreneurial success.

Movements for equality are also said to be possible within neoliberalism. For example, if women are to overcome patriarchal structures of male privilege and female subordination, they are encouraged to 'lean in' and push forward so that they can share the spoils of a flourishing market and take their rightful place at the tables of power (Sandberg 2013). Supporters of neoliberalism might also acknowledge racism, ableism and other forms of inequality, but the solutions they posit favour individual growth where the root problems are located within unenlightened people and not the structural and economic foundations of society.

The problem with these assertions is that neoliberalism hasn't worked; in fact, it has made things more and not less unequal (Allen 2013, Coffey et al. 2020). Humanistic education isn't to blame for this but, according to Paulo Freire, claiming people can significantly improve their life chances through self-actualization is mythical because it ignores the central features of race, gender and class in people's lives (Freire 1972, 116). Teaching individual women to become more assertive and forthright might help some people get ahead. But it does nothing to threaten the structures of patriarchy, a system with a particular function within 'the imperialist white-supremacist capitalist patriarchy', namely to essentialize gender roles in a way that naturalizes men as courageous, competitive and good leaders and women as nurturing, caring and empathetic. Or, to borrow words from Sarah Jaffe, it is the space where we are taught that 'the work of cleaning, cooking, of nursing wounds, of teaching children to walk and talk and read and reason, of soothing hurt feelings and smoothing over little cries comes naturally to women' (Jaffe 2021, 23).

So long as we continue to perform gender in these ways (Butler 1990), social reproduction work, meaning the essential labour that we expend to sustain us as social beings (Ferguson 2019, 86–87), will remain devalued. This is the work we do to prepare food and maintain our dwellings. It is the labour expended in caring for the young, the old, the sick and others who need care. It is also the work we do to build communities. Amidst patriarchal capitalism, this essential work is mostly offloaded to women and mostly within the heteronormative family which, despite the romantic overtures that often dominate, is first and foremost an economic system. Such is capitalism's dependency on this labour for its survival, the charity Oxfam estimates that the unpaid care work carried out by women and girls adds up to at least $10.8 trillion each year, and that's when it's costed at minimum wage (Oxfam International 2021). Advanced capitalism also grossly manipulates social reproduction labour to have the minimum impact on profits.

Many women do succeed within neoliberal society, including me. I have a permanent job with high levels of autonomy where I get paid to think. I have a good salary. But my successes cannot be decoupled from the many advantages I enjoy as a middle-class, white, cis-privileged woman. According to Arruzza, Bhattacharya and Fraser (2019, 11), the gains of privileged women like me are because we get to *lean on* the labour of other women, most of whom are migrant and working-class. Sometimes this is easy to spot. For example, in Ireland, migrant women are more likely to work in the low-paid domestic and care wage economy (Migrant Rights Centre Ireland 2015, 14), and indeed they often train for these jobs in FET settings. This allows middle-class women to outsource what used to be their own domestic and care labour. The taken-for-granted nuclear family I spoke about above only took hold for property-less families in the last couple of hundred years and only because imperialism in the first instance denied payments to those they enslaved (Ferguson 2019, 18) through structural racism and has continued to suppress wages in sectors of the economy dominated by migrant and ethnic minority workers. Other times, women (and everyone) living in the Global North fail to tune into the extent to which we lean on structural racism. How much do we care about the ongoing exploitation of labour in the Global South, for example through the fast-fashion textile industry where millions of women and girls endure terrible terms and conditions of employment under trade deals with multinationals that are anti-union. This same industry wreak havoc on the environment and is second only to the oil and gas sector as the most polluting industry.

These are just some examples of why any suggestion that there is a shared sisterhood of female experience is 'a false and corrupt platform disguising and mystifying the true nature of women's varied and complex social reality' (hooks 1984, 41). No one form of oppression exists on a single axis. Rather, they are *intersectional* (Crenshaw 1991). This explains why the workplaces and life chances open to men and non-binary people are equally dependent on racial, class, cis and hetero hierarchies and the absence of disability.

So What Should We Do?

These are big ideas to process, and you might still be wondering what any of this has to do with your job as an adult educator. But if these factors, many of which directly impact the lives of our diverse student groups, aren't talked about in educational spaces, then where are they talked about? Certainly, it might feel overwhelming to even think about doing something structurally significant about intersectional inequality in our day-to-day work and might feel well beyond the job description of an adult, community or further education practitioner. But I encourage you to look carefully at the moments when this is possible. Where can you encourage *conscientização* (Freire 1972), which translates as consciousness-raising or, to put it more simply, finding opportunities where you crack open relations of power in a way that is relatable to the lives of people in the room, and the topic you are discussing?

There are spaces within adult, community and further education where we can infuse critical conversations. Take a 'communications' module as a case in point. Most of the time, students are asked to demonstrate proofreading and editing. There is nothing to stop an educator from choosing wisely when selecting the text to be reviewed. What about picking something from the website of a trade union, a leaflet from a migrant advocacy group or a blog post about feminism? Whatever you choose, this can be used in a way that moves us away from descriptive memorization towards critically interpreting its underlying significance and the relationship between language and power (Freire and Macedo 1987, 32–33). Or if we are teaching a module on 'spreadsheets', why not give people a global debt database and ask them to enter data and move information around on this? They might be surprised to learn that the countries with the highest levels of debt are mostly in the Global North. Care-related courses, be these childcare or healthcare, can explore the feminized nature of this work. They can also ask why is it – increasingly – migrants who end up in low-paid precarious roles and why people of colour are often discriminated against when they seek higher-paid work (Akinborowa et al. 2020, 129). What about asking why domestic violence work has been co-opted into the seemingly neutral role of social care, thereby stripping it of its radical feminist roots (Wilson 2022)? Even our focus on global conflicts should be examined to ensure that equal attention is given to the imperialist actions of the United States including their ongoing support of Israel's illegal and bloody occupation of Palestine (Makdisi 2010).

These changes are doable but maybe the question I inarticulately raised in that seminar space about a ground-zero approach is also worth contemplating. Revolutionizing our learning environments takes deeper work that begins with questioning the very contents that many of us still teach across FET (and Higher Education) programmes. Most curricula are deeply biased towards the normative nature of 'whiteness', something Ruby Hamad (2021) describes as a shifting, political concept that refers to certain privileges enjoyed by people whose identities most resemble Western European heritage. For example, the ethnic minority status of Irish Travellers was only acknowledged in the Irish school curriculum in 2018 and only after a lengthy campaign by Traveller-led organizations. Instead, their nomadic lifestyle has been aggressively curbed for decades through a series of assimilationist policies. Their ongoing oppression is the perfect example of how 'whiteness' goes deeper than skin colour alone. Have FET curricula made similar deep-seated adjustments in incorporating the role of Mincéir outside of the deficit models that dominate? What about the way much 'history' erases the experiences of working-class communities (Wrigley 2017, 539) and how most subjects consistently paper over the catastrophic impacts of 'western' ways of living on the Global South (Salem 2018, Vergès 2022)? No subject is without the need for a rethink given that even the seemingly neutral disciplines of maths and science remain gendered, classist and west-centric (Powell and Frankenstein 1997, hooks 2010, 49).

It's not helpful for me to throw stones at FET from an ivory tower without looking inwards too. University curricula about critical pedagogy can be equally problematic. It is impossible to ignore how many of its 'accepted truths' were produced and legitimated amidst conditions where women were unproblematically depicted as subordinated. For instance, in his much-referenced text *Pedagogy of the Oppressed* (1972), Freire draws solely from a male interpretation of the world and only describes men's realities. Although some feminists excuse his earlier work as typical of the time and praise him for retrospectively acknowledging his gender-blindness, he continued to claim universality and to underplay the specificities of women's lives in later works (Jackson 1997, Ryan 2001, 67). One of his most notable critics is bell hooks herself who repeatedly highlights the sexism in his writing. 'There has never been a moment when reading Freire that I have not remained aware of not only the sexism of the language' she writes, or 'the way he ... constructs a phallocentric paradigm of liberation — wherein freedom and the experience of patriarchal manhood are always linked as though they are one and the same' (hooks 1992, 147). Despite the anguish this causes her, she asks us to 'take the threads of Freire's work' (hooks 1994, 52) and develop the engaged pedagogy this chapter is encouraging.

But many academic texts on critical pedagogy continue to be authored in a way that normalizes white-western ways of being and that ignore, for example how female academics do more occupational housework and student care than their male counterparts to the detriment of their own research-led, academic career making (Mirsa et al. 2011, Thamar et al. 2017). Moreover, how many critical pedagogues working in universities do anything tangible to address high levels of occupational precarity within universities and further education spaces, something that is more likely to impact women (O'Keefe and Courtois 2019)? It is also the case that the accreditation frameworks Higher Education currently serve are, at times, instrumentalist, highly bureaucratized and a potential barrier to responses by critical education, in real time, to the urgencies of social justice demands.

What Else Can We Do?

It is also worth pointing out that creating spaces that model the politicizing aspirations of critical pedagogy aren't necessarily spaces where people feel safe and supported and where the humanistic aspects of a Freirean philosophy are important to hold (Aronowitz 1993, hooks 1994, 14). Take my own example of feeling foolish and unsupported in the group I described at the outset. Some minor but important changes would have greatly helped. There could have been a dedicated time for people to introduce themselves by name and say a little about why they were there. This would have lateralized a strong power imbalance between tenured staff who knew each other and students who were newer to the institutional culture. Other strategies would have greatly helped too, including arriving early to make sure the chairs were arranged in a circle and not in rows. That day, there had been a hasty attempt to organize the room that way whilst most people were already present. More broadly, I encourage a facilitative rather than lecture-style approach. We can also regularly check in with our students by simply asking them how they are getting on, in a way that leaves dedicated time for people to authentically respond.

We must also bear in mind that, when we introduce radical ideas and create conditions for people to speak authentically, they can react strongly and angrily about the circumstances of their lives. This can cause conflict in educational environments where we are conditioned into thinking these spaces should be calm and non-combative. But the goal of educators shouldn't be to maintain a conflict-free space, something bell hooks talks about at length in her book *Teaching Critical Thinking*. She writes,

> Unfortunately, it is often professors and not students who want to maintain the 'safe' classroom because it is simply easier to demand that students cultivate an atmosphere of seamless harmony in the classroom and harder to teach them how to engage in meaningful critical dialogue. (hooks 2010, 88)

Creating false notions of safety that prevent dialogic exchanges is, hooks argues, an exercise in silencing people.

There are other changes we can make in our teaching to ensure the environments we create are as inclusive as possible. In particular, it is our responsibility to adapt to advances in gender theory most recognizably captured through the ideas of Judith Butler in their contribution *Gender Trouble* first published in 1990. Butler describes how gender isn't something that is fixed and binary, it is created through repetitive behaviours, performed time and again where, as they (1990, 3) put it, 'the feminist subject turns out to be discursively constituted by the very political system that is supposed to facilitate its emancipation'.

Butler teaches us how, if we continue to perform gender in accordance with dominant cultural contexts, our worlds will continue to conform to masculinist norms. This 'troubling' of subjectivities challenges each of us to risk the uncertainty of our gender identity and reflect on how we too perpetuate the social constructs we seek to dismantle.

Again these can be difficult ideas to grasp but as Butler's ideas permeate, many trans and non-binary people are finding the strength to emerge from the margins of west-centric societies where they have been particularly oppressed (Fausto-Sterling 2000, Gill-Peterson 2018). Again, educators can struggle to know where to start. Clare Tebbutt (2022) offers some practical advice, namely that we should openly disagree with homophobic comments, draw from queer examples of ordinary life and allow people to self-identify their names and pronouns rather than rely on class lists. Tebbutt also challenges us to concentrate our efforts on authentically listening to queer experiences, including how they intersect with race, class and ableism. This can spark other non-queer students to critically analyse the privilege they hold in the context of growing transphobia and homophobia.

We must also be prepared to recognize, and act on, other privileges that we may hold. Taking myself as a case in point, as well as my own cis-privilege, I also cannot divest myself from my whiteness, or the class benefits that I hold which have definitely set me on the path I am currently on despite doing badly at school. What I can do is labour to create conditions that disrupt how these are upheld. For example, I can problematize the Eurocentric nature of what I teach (Zakaria 2021, 14–15) and amend my own citation patterns (Ahmed 2017, 14), and I can amplify the contributions of those whose writings are traditionally under-explored or simply ignored.

I can also seek to rectify my own daily micro-actions that undermine or erase the actions of others. I can get better at listening, asking questions and creating spaces for other voices to be amplified. If I declare myself an 'ally', I must reflexively ask if this is truly the case. Queer activist Benny Le Master shares their own 'healthy cisspicion' (italics in original) and alerts us to the 'ally industrial complex' amidst broader organizing structures (2019, 155). Le Master locates some blame on the ongoing roll-out of 'diversity training' across many education providers where the model used is frequently reductivist and mostly excludes those at the centre of a phenomenon. The result, they claim, is 'a conceptual, fragmented, and immaterial framing of transness as oppose to a sustained dialogic engagement in and through transness in its perpetual becoming across contexts' (Le Master, 155–156). Others too have problematized current practices under the guise of equality, diversity and inclusion where the undergirding continues to be white, masculine signifiers. Sara Ahmed notes,

> Many practitioners have a critical awareness that much of what counts as diversity work for organizations is not about structural transformation: diversity is often a technique for rearranging things so organizations can appear in a better or happier way. [...] Diversity is a way of rearranging a series that does not disrupt that series. (Ahmed 2017, 98).

But again, I must proceed reflexively. In other words, I must turn inwards and attempt to see ways in which I unwittingly create these structures despite them being in opposition to my own values. Simply centring those most impacted by a particular phenomenon can be performative and damaging. Olufemi Táíwò (2022) is particularly concerned about a current trend of what he calls 'passing the mic' (71) where giving voice to people historically rendered voiceless has become an end in itself for dominant groups to the detriment of the urgent need to dismantle oppressive structures.

And What about Praxis?

Táíwò's observations raise important questions about what happens outside the classroom walls, something that has always been a central feature of critical pedagogy. As bell hooks (1992, 146) explains,

One of the concepts in Freire's work and in my own work that is frequently misunderstood by readers [...] [is] many times people will say to me that I seem to be suggesting that it is enough for individuals to change how they think. [...] Again and again Freire has had to remind readers that he never spoke of conscientization as an end itself but always as it is joined by meaningful praxis [...] praxis is not blind action, deprived of intention or of finality. It is action and reflection.

But how do we incorporate praxis into our everyday practice especially when we consider the omnipresence of neoliberal capitalism and how overwhelmed many of us can often feel? In another publication (Fitzsimons 2017a, 233–235), I make concrete suggestions on how to do this:

- create communities of practice that are less controlled by institutional and policy constraints,
- showcase politicizing practices and
- be active participants in direct action campaigning when its intentions are to question neoliberal policies and seek egalitarian change.

For example, when Maynooth University (where I work) announced that construction of a promised new student centre was to be terminated despite thousands of students paying a levy to fund the project for many years, on-campus protests were immediately called by the student's union. Some lecturers acted in solidarity by stopping their classes and joining students in a demonstration outside the President's Office. But advising practitioners on how to proceed is not straightforward and I should trust people's own capacity in knowing the best next steps to take as each of us work in the cracks of an often precarious working environment as discussed in Chapter 8.

In conclusion, this chapter was intended as a catalyst to encourage us all to create adult learning environments where people feel safe and secure, both individually and collectively and where we are brave enough to ask critical questions about the nature of the world that we live in. The choice hooks' engaged pedagogy presents is to either integrate people into the logic of 'the imperialist white-supremacist capitalist patriarchy' or see our work as a practice of freedom where people come together and actively shape history. The task for adult, community and further education practitioners who are drawn to this philosophy is to infuse the principles of equality and social justice throughout our work and be the change that we want to see in the world. No mean feat, but worth a try.

Chapter 2

ENGAGING HOLISTICALLY WITH CURRICULUM AND ASSESSMENT

Sarah Coss

I had been teaching in Further Education and Training (FET) for more than a decade when I sat down to plan for an upcoming accredited module in *Communications* benchmarked by Quality and Qualifications Ireland (QQI) at Level 5. I began as I always do by reviewing the module to decide how to approach it this time around. My initial interest was piqued by what had been titled Section 2 'Reading and Writing'. 'How can I creatively provide people with space to explore and improve their reading skills?' 'What will I do?' I asked myself, before fondly remembering a particularly creative and energetic primary school teacher from my own life. 'I'll create a newsroom,' I decided and enthusiastically set about sourcing a good old-fashioned scrapbook and glue sticks. I wrote a set of simple instructions for the group. We would read. We would all read. I started on day one with my scrapbook in hand and my own choice of readings to get us going: a newspaper article on a current nurse's strike, a satirical article about the same strike, a poem by the revered poet Patrick Kavanagh and a picture.

Practically speaking, I divided the class into working groups and, over the course duration, each group took turns to choose materials that appealed to them. Our reading activity at the start of each class was integrated with other requirements of the module which included group work, negotiation and the practical application of information and communications technology (ICT). Alongside reading, students emailed, texted and printed – essentially, they communicated with each other. Each week learners added their own choices of articles, poems, stories and images which we stuck into the scrapbook as a record of our reading experience together – everything was going so well! As we progressed, we also explored what it was like to read aloud. This started accidentally at first but at the end of sixteen weeks, each person had the opportunity, confidence and support to read aloud.

Organically, this emerged as a skill the learners valued as many of them hadn't read aloud in many years or had never done so in the English language. I was conscious that the skill of reading did have to be assessed, but my initial goal was to bring energy and enthusiasm for reading. Each week as we participated together in class, we were also meeting, to use the official language, the 'intended learning outcomes' for the course. I observed my group achieving the expected skills (skim content, obtain an overview, select a text, read the text, identify key points and finally, discuss and critique a wide range of materials).

Skip forward to assessment time which drew me back to the course guidelines outlined in my centre's *programme module* (which I'll explain more about below). These guidelines asked each learner to provide 'evidence' of their reading skills by writing a 300-word summary and completing a worksheet. While this assessment design did meet the criteria set out by QQI, I was left with a nagging discomfort that there were so many more creative and meaningful tasks that would also allow my learners to, to quote from the programme module, 'use reading skills appropriate to a task'.

So I followed my centre's guidelines and set an assignment that I knew from experience would appease the next stages of assessment, namely the compulsory and, mostly, welcome internal and external quality assurance processes. In the Irish FET context, this meant negotiating three stages: internal verification (IV), external authentication (EA) and Results Approval Panel (RAP) processes. However, I felt caught up in a system that required me to assess my student's reading with an individual assessment through a written summary and a series of comprehension questions on a worksheet. Under pressure to comply with my provider's guidelines, I set my group six questions and allotted three marks to 'understanding of the material' as stated in my provider's marking scheme. This meant each question was worth 0.5 marks.

Despite being prepared for the task at hand, my usually cheerful learners were noticeably stressed and were complaining, yet they took on the task and battled through it. When the time came for me to mark their work, my heart sank. The first learner had not answered question one fully, leaving me to calculate what proportion of the 0.5 marks I should award based purely on her work produced on that day. 'Oh, what had I done?' I had turned our creative, encompassing and vibrant weekly social reading activity into a reductive and quantitative measurement. As I continued grading, our scrapbook filled with poems, comic strips, pictures, newspaper articles and a crumpled copy of a child's school newsletter sat in my floral bag at my feet. Perhaps most poignantly was an article from *The Irish Times* chosen as their first reading task – picked by the group because it beautifully detailed the journalist's renewed resolution to read extensively and voraciously. My students all passed, but by grading their reading skills using an individualized task with little real-world application, I couldn't shake the feeling that I had failed them.

Thinking about Curriculum

Sharing stories and experiences is a technique outlined by Stephen Brookfield as an interesting way to contextualize theory. This opening vignette is just one example of my experiences that is intended to prompt you to look for your own 'connecting points and generalizable insights' that link to your practice (Brookfield 2017, 180). My reason for starting with this particular example is that it provides a useful starting point to unpack the various required elements when we consider curriculum design and assessment within the overarching qualification frameworks typically applied in FET contexts.

The point this story emphasizes is that, too often educators enter the classroom and join with their learners in creative and dynamic activities only to experience the sense of feeling blocked, restricted or constrained by their understanding of requirements placed upon them by the curriculum, or more often, the assessment process. This chapter provides a practical standpoint to explore issues of curriculum design, particularly assessment design, and offers suggestions on what creative, bench-marked practice might look like. My hope is that it gives you the confidence to be as innovative as possible in working with assessment and curriculum in your practice.

But before we dive into some of the everyday detail, challenges and opportunities of assessment and curriculum for practitioners, it's important, first, to step back and think for a moment about what we might mean by curriculum in the context of FET. A good place to start is to acknowledge that the term 'curriculum' itself is a contested concept meaning different things to different people in various domains of education. Unsurprisingly, curriculum is also linked to philosophical and political notions about the purpose of education. If, for instance, we believe that FET principally exists to enhance individual employability, then we will probably lean towards curricular models and practices which are defined by prescribed content and skills that are developed with employer groups or their government and/or policymaking allies. If, on the other hand, we believe that adult education's purpose is to enhance critical thinking for personal and social transformation, then our curriculum will likely draw from the experiences of participants and prioritize the 'process' within learning. Geraldine O'Neill outlines several different curricular models that broadly fit along a product–process continuum (O'Neill 2015, 28) (Figure 2.1). Of course, the tension for many FET educators is that they are drawn to process ways of crafting a curriculum in, or so it often feels, a product-obsessed curriculum world.

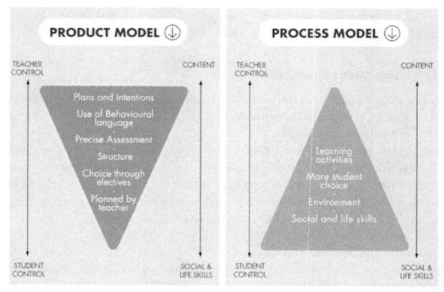

Figure 2.1 The product and process models of curriculum development (O'Neill 2015, 28).

Another point worth reflecting upon is that, when we talk about curriculum, we tend to think about the formal or prescribed curriculum, whether this is mandated by a national curricular body or explicitly articulated in some other, usually text-based, form. But if we take the broad view of a curriculum as the sum of experiences of people across their learning, then we must also consider the unintended learning experiences that occur – the unintended curriculum. These less explicit, but often long-lasting, learning experiences are often referred to as the 'hidden curriculum' which can be understood as the unwritten or implicit sociocultural lessons learned as we pass through a particular educational system or institution (Lynch 1989). For example, what we learn about what and who is valued in society can often be reinforced and reproduced through the language we use, our reading lists, the case studies we present, the posters on the corridor walls, the awards and prizes that are offered or the way we arrange our classrooms.

What's more, much of what we understand as the curriculum is, or has been, defined by Western European and non-indigenous North American practice and literature. This is beginning to be pushed back in some parts of the world – especially in places, such as Australia and Canada, where official curricula have been complicit in the denial of traumatic colonized pasts. Yet we are starting to hear the voices of indigenous educators who ask all those engaged with curriculum making to be sensitive to the diversity of knowledge and approaches to learning that exist and, instead, invite us to think, for example, about the role of land-based and intergenerational knowledge in the formation of curricula (Antoine et al. 2018).

If we take that invitation, then to look at the land and, indeed, the living world in its broadest sense, it seems timely to acknowledge just how much our advanced industrialized knowledge has contributed to a climate emergency that is threatening our existence as a species. If we haven't learned, yet, from our collective experience as a species how to thrive without killing the planet, then we may need to consider widening our perspective on knowledge sources beyond the human perspective. Maybe it is time to consider, as some urgently urge us to, thinking and learning more collaboratively with other living species on a planet that is suffering from the dominance of centuries of focus solely on human development and growth (Sidebottom 2021).

Bearing in mind, then, that the very notion of an objective, stable, fully visible, even human-centred curriculum is something that we should start to question and, additionally, to heed Dempsey's (2023, 50) call for us to recognize our own responsibilities in constantly asking what, how and why in our curriculum making, I'll return to my own story.

Aligning Curriculum and Assessment

As can be gleaned by the reading exercise described at the outset of this chapter, there are many moving parts when we design and assess learner evidence of achievement. These include the tasks assigned to the educator and the over-arching role of the positioning of these with the wider landscape of assessor(s). At first glance, it seems hardly surprising that some tensions have emerged for many educators, in part because of the, at times, overwhelming level of administration and bureaucracy (Fitzsimons 2017b, 23–26). Drawing from the experiences of over 130 FET practitioners, Fitzsimons argues this tension revolves around issues of contested control, inhibition of innovation, unsynchronized processes, burdensome workloads and unnecessary requirements that can stifle the educator's desire and ability to be innovative and responsive for fear that 'taking a gamble' on assessment could have consequences for the learner. Often, their concern, as was mine, is that higher up the chain of the assessment hierarchy someone who is not in the classroom will impose a different understanding of what is best for the group.

For most FET practitioners, the requirements we work to are set by the aforementioned awarding body QQI with each award mapped to

Ireland's ten-level National Framework of Qualifications (herein called NFQ).[1] This NFQ describes what learners should 'know' or 'be able to do' based on a given qualification and shows learners the pathways to move from one qualification, or qualification level, to another (NFQ 2015). John Biggs (2012) describes this 'aligned' teaching and learning (or learning outcomes approach) as a system where clear objectives are set regarding what should be learned and assessment tasks are chosen that allow learners to coherently and meaningfully demonstrate their achievement of these objectives. Part of QQI's job is to maintain and develop the NFQ and 'quality-assure' service providers to guarantee they are meeting this requirement.

At the time of writing, QQI has as many as 1,738 distinct Level 1–6 awards across the common awards system (CAS) classified as 'Minor' (component) Awards or 'Major' Awards (the culmination of achieving set credits from component awards) as well as Special Purpose and Supplementary Awards. In the aforementioned research with practitioners, Fitzsimons found 'frequently, the NFQ's learning outcomes approach is singled out for causing tensions between the needs of individuals and the pressures to teach to a restrictive curriculum' (2017b 21).

Ireland's NFQ is not stand-alone but it internationally aligns with the European Qualifications Framework (EQF). One consequence of this wider alignment is that the mostly neutral language used to describe our NFQ is employed to ensure there is consistency with this wider framework. The language of standards, consistency, clarity and transparency while 'allowing scope for programme diversity, innovation and flexibility' across comparable qualifications (QQI 2022, 2–3) are commonplace across many countries that use similar structures. Servicing these frameworks often creates enormous amounts of administrative work for FET practitioners without a benefit to the students or a dividend for society more broadly, something critics align with a growing managerialist culture associated with the neo-liberalization of education (Hussey and Smith 2008; Biggs 2012; Allais 2014; Bailey and Colley 2015; Fitzsimons 2017a). However, it is my contention that it is possible to remain adherent to these overarching frameworks while also being creative in content, delivery and assessment.

So, in the midst of these frameworks and criterion, what role did QQI play, as guardian of the NFQ, in the choices I made when teaching the Level 5

---

1 Within the NFQ, Level 1–6 standards are reserved for primary, secondary and further education settings Level 6 operates at FET (Advanced Certificate) and Higher Education (National Certificate), while Levels 7–10 are the domain of Higher Education Institutions (HEIs), mostly universities and technical universities.

Communications component specification (coded as 5N0690) that I described when opening this chapter? What is their role in deciding how to assess this group of adult learners who were immersed in a creative, thought-provoking flow of learning? The answer is that they are actually much less involved in the specifics of curriculum and assessment design than many people think. Certainly, they led the consultation and development of the module and they did sanction the eleven predetermined learning outcomes as well as the assessment techniques which are listed as 'portfolio/collection of work' worth 50 per cent of the marks, and 'skills demonstration' also worth 50 per cent.

It is also the case that the FET provider where I worked must apply to the QQI for award validation using this above-cited specification when they are proposing the much more detailed module programme of learning and assessment that I was using as the blueprint for the course. This does create limits on the way I can work. To demonstrate (again using the same award), although QQI do instruct that half of the overall assessment is by 'a portfolio/collection of work', they equally state that '*All providers* are required to submit an assessment plan as part of their application for programme validation. Assessment Plans include information relating to scheduling and integration of assessment' (italics added).[2] What this means, and what people often don't fully understand, is that it is the validated service provider (the FE colleges or education centres where we work) and not QQI that created the curriculum we deliver. Or maybe we can imagine, as Priestley et al. (2022, 13) suggest, that curriculum making happens at a range of levels across the educational spectrum: in the classroom; within educational institutions; through national bodies, legislation and policymakers; and by influential and powerful international bodies such as the EU, UNESCO, The World Bank and OECD.

Navigating Awards Frameworks and Service Provider Requirements

So where can I, if I am a curriculum-maker, apply innovation, diversity and flexibility? Let's continue to draw on examples from the NFQ, this time a Level 6 award called *Menu Design and Applied Nutrition* (coded as 6N2097). This has seventeen prescribed learning outcomes each of which must be assessed across two predetermined assessment techniques of a project (worth 40 per cent) and an exam (worth 60 per cent). This seems straightforward enough and immediately lots of ideas spring to mind. But this isn't the only document I must contend with as the centre where I work will have created a more

---

2 All awards are listed on the QQI website https://qsdocs.qqi.ie/.

comprehensive set of instructions when they applied to have the programme validated by QQI. This document (or curriculum) gets called different things by different providers – I'll use the term *programme module* as it's what I'm most familiar with. It is the existence of this programme module that can cause confusion. Yes, the NFQ has provided consistency in learning outcomes and assessment techniques. But, typically programme modules contain indicative contents that match each prescribed learning outcome. This content is usually suggested by subject experts.

Sometimes educators are under the impression this content must be delivered verbatim. This is not the case, *indicative* means that the educator can expand, change or update as they see fit once this falls in line with the prescribed learning outcomes. Indeed, different providers often have different ideas about how to meet learning outcomes. For example, when assessing 'the effect of additives … on nutritional value of food', one provider might welcome using artificial additives in menu preparation, while another might see this as anathema to good menu design. This example demonstrates how attempts to define quality and standards in education ignore the contested nature of knowledge and how no one person or institution gets to definitively determine universal standards and truths (Fitzsimons 2017b, 17).

Another aspect where there is scope for flexibility and differing interpretations is when considering what emphasis to give each learning outcome. For example, when delivering 'Functional Maths (coded as 4N2138)', one educator might investigate Learning Outcome 1, 'Explain how mathematics can be used to enable the individual to function more effectively as a person and as a citizen' in their opening session. A second learning outcome, 'use a calculator with confidence …', might be attended to in every session with each person's skills building week by week. These decisions are commonly made in an educator's outline scheme of work (or schedule) – a broad strokes overview of how you intend to meet the required learning outcomes over the stated time you are with the group. Most providers will require, as part of their quality assurance (QA) procedures, that you submit your scheme of work in a timely fashion, usually before the course starts or very soon afterwards.

The Assessment of Learning

Programme modules must also 'map' how each learning outcome will be assessed using the appropriate technique(s). In my experience, this mostly takes the form of sample assessments that were sent to QQI when the programme was originally validated. Their purpose was to prove to QQI that we had the capacity to comply with quality assurance policies day to day. Sometimes programme modules also include marking schemes. If I imagine it is my first time teaching Functional Maths, I would likely welcome the fact that I can work from these supporting documents:

- A pre-existing programme module with contents mapped to learning outcomes.
- Pre-prepared assignment briefs that match learning outcomes.
- A marking scheme that breaks down how marks should be awarded.

I should also step back from the paperwork and remind myself that this formal assessment of learning is often loaded with emotion – we learn very early in life that an A grade is better than a D.

But it is also important that I think expansively about assessment in the learning process. Boud and Soler (2016) argue that assessment is best understood as an active part of the curriculum that enables students to achieve particular outcomes; not just a means of ascertaining whether outcomes have been achieved or not but as an integral part of learning in its own right. The best way to understand 'assessment' is as a tool by which we measure and recognize a person's achievements. There are three accepted functions of assessment: (1) assessment *of* learning, (2) assessment *for* learning and (3) assessment *as* learning (QQI and I acknowledge that there are benefits to each of these approaches). Assessment is a necessary and often beneficial aspect of learning rather than an obstacle to learning. Yet the example I described when opening this chapter happened despite my knowing what I know about assessment.

So, what is an educator's role as the first assessor? What freedom do I have to choose another technique than the one outlined in the component specification? Can I pick something other than a 'portfolio/collection of work'? The answer to this last question is 'no'. This is one of the essential requirements that I don't have flexibility on. These techniques were chosen by QQI as the optimum approach (although QQI allows for alternative assessment techniques in exceptional circumstances).

But can I develop my own assessment materials for my group that fit within this technique? Can I collect evidence every time I observe each learner's reading skills in line with what is required? Can I use audiovisual aids to evidence their skills when reading and analysing material? Could we submit the scrapbook itself with an explanatory note as evidence or some combination of all of these assessment tools? The short answer here is 'yes'. As the first assessor, my role *should* allow me to make these decisions once I stay within the agreed parameters. QQI confirms this in the component specification when they write,

The *assessor* is responsible for devising assessment instruments (e.g. project and assignment briefs, examination papers), assessment criteria and mark sheets, consistent with the techniques identified […] and QQI's assessment requirements. (QQI 2012, 3 emphasis added)

Elsewhere, QQI defines the assessor as 'a qualified practitioner' who 'may be the teacher, trainer or lecturer, workplace supervisor, manager or team leader' (QQI 2018b, 7–8). In other words, me.

But think back to that complex relationship between the other assessors that I referred to as the chain of assessment hierarchy earlier on. There is also the internal verifier(s) – typically a colleague, and an external authenticator who is approved by QQI and appointed by my employer. What are their roles in determining if learning outcomes have been suitably assessed?

Well, sometimes their role, or their power, is more firmly located in the heads of practitioners like me than anywhere else. After all, it was more my thoughts, my worries about these overarching quality assurance structures and processes that, eventually, determined the methods I used to assess my group. I allowed these thoughts to usurp my sense that the reading skills employed and evidenced each week by my adult learners were robust and substantial: they chose materials; skimmed for content; extracted key points; read together; and analysed and critiqued all the poetry, comics, broadsheets, tabloids, graphic communication and vocational texts they encountered over the course. Yet, I still knew if I had decided independently to submit my scrapbook alongside a marking scheme verifying the extent to which learners had met the learning outcomes, they would not have fulfilled the criteria expected of them as outlined in the programme module. I was just one part of the assessment chain, just one small cog in the curriculum-making machine, and I knew from practice that the 'local changes' that I was contemplating submitting, no matter how small, would not be accepted. The internal verifier would have enforced this. In short, I was constrained by internal regulations that prescribed a rigid 'one-size-fits-all' approach to assessment and the marking scheme, despite QQI's assertion that standards '[…] vary in their specificity allowing scope for programme diversity, innovation and flexibility […]' (QQI 2022, 3). This isn't a unique situation, rather Biggs (2012, 47) maintains that, in a criterion-referenced system (such as the NFQ), 'we frequently express one meaning of understanding but assess another'. Thus, the educator gets caught in a system where they are compelled to engage in assessment activities that are at odds with their pedagogy.

So how do we create an environment where the first assessor is trusted to have the best grasp of what is most appropriate for a group? After all, trust is named in the QQI *Green Paper on Assessment of Learners and Learning*

(QQI 2018a, 21). The Green Paper also alludes to an overall progressive and learner-centred approach when it states,

> Effective learning involves not only the receipt of information by the learner but processing that information, engaging with it [...], linking it with prior learning, and reflecting on whether and in what ways they have been transformed. (QQI, 17)

However, closer inspection of the document reveals that, broadly, it mostly leans towards the assessment *of* learning as its principal focus. It is our responsibility as educators to ensure balance across these domains and we should ask ourselves the following questions:

- In what way do I approach the assessment as being *of* learning, that is, a summative task designed to measure and map achievements along a predetermined scale?
- In what way do I approach assessment as being *for* learning, that is, as a learner-centred and meaningful discovery that is an integral part of programme delivery?

In keeping with the spirit of this book, one could also ask in what way do my assessment techniques best support practice that might align with Freirean theories of praxis. Are we as educators perhaps unwittingly undermining the adult education principles and practices we work so hard to develop as soon as it comes to assessment time? Are we complicit in acts of creating the hidden curriculum?

My own observations are that there are two factors worth re-emphasizing that tend to impact our capacity to embody creative group work and to enhance transformative learning. First, there is the need to conform to a learning outcomes approach that, by its nature, excludes unanticipated and delayed learning outcomes and which underappreciates the many facets of learning that are not easily captured as an end result (Hussey and Smith 2008; Allais 2014). Second, and not unrelated, there is a growing cultural and institutional interpretation of what 'learner evidence' should look like. Taken together, these factors contribute to the dominant practice of the assessment *of* learning. The alternative, formative assessment is articulated by Luckritz Marquis (2021, 52) as 'a two-way street between educator and learner' explaining,

> In general, formative assessment allows both educators and learners to understand better where learners are in the learning process within the context of a particular course or discipline. Such understanding can help learners

and educators alike modify their plan either for learning (in the learner's case) or facilitating learning (in the educator's case) based on feedback. And, since the learner receives information about their own learning from such assessments, such feedback is invaluable as they become self-regulating and reflective learners.

Formative assessment is possible once there is alignment between the needs of the learners, the vision of the assessor in meeting those needs and a supportive overarching system that allows trusting relationships to flourish. As stated in the Green Paper, 'fundamentally, qualifications are tokens that depend on trust relationships underpinned by valid and reliable assessment' (QQI, 20). Formative assessment can align with accreditation systems and can include reflection, portfolios, projects, peer learning, peer assessment, dialogue, feedback and so on (see Fitzsimons and Dorman 2013 for an interesting discussion about NFQ Levels 2–4 in particular). Techniques such as projects and research activities can be designed in such a way that students produce their own evidence as they create knowledge and develop skills in an explicitly personal and social manner. Group work can assess rich collaborative learning and can frame learning as a social endeavour rather than an individual task. I believe collaboration and sharing are more valuable life skills than competition and that the process of group work is important, if not more than the product. However, the standpoint of QQI is that, in each of their component specifications, it states that 'group or teamwork may form part of the assessment, provided each learner's achievement is separately assessed'. Discussions on how we can use group assessment activities should be encouraged rather than simply dismissing this as too difficult.

Part of the picture is that stories from the field regularly point to issues of mistrust – particularly mistrust of the educator – often leading to overly detailed production of evidence to justify marks awarded (Fitzsimons and Dorman 2013, 53; Fitzsimons 2017a, 181–189; Fitzsimons 2017b, 24).

In fact, a culture has emerged where there is a desire for full accountability on behalf of the educator/assessor. Marking schemes are becoming more and more prescriptive and detailed for fear that those with the power to evaluate standards and quality both locally (the IV – Internal Verified) and externally (EA – External Authenticator) won't 'sign off' on a first assessor's work. Somehow, we have created a system that seems to be more focused on producing evidence, often mapped to decimalized marking schemes that have lost sight of the holistic benefits of assessment *for* learning. Camilla Fitzsimons (2017a) interprets the structures that we have created for ourselves as 'a process of self-regulation where the structures of education are imposing rules and regulations that are above the actual demands of the accrediting body' continuing, 'instead of laying all the blame with internal verifiers and external authenticators another vantage point is to draw from Foucauldian logic on the nature of power' (Fitzsimons 2017a, 180). As educators seek to get students through at all costs (Bailey and Colley 2015), Fitzsimons argues the additional administrative labour created is an end result of the internalization and amplification of often inaccurate demands of the regulator, something that is only made possible when there are chains of command created around us.

Thankfully, change is underway with the arrival of Broad Awards Standards.[3] QQI states that the Broad Award Standards are an elaboration of the generic descriptors of the NFQ and will guide programme developers in the development of minimum intended programme learning outcomes (MIPLOs) and minimum intended module learning outcomes (MIMLOs) when revalidating programmes (QQI 2022, 6). This allows providers to design and develop awards in a timely manner and to respond to the changing needs of their learners.

One example of the use of MIPLOs and MIMLOs is in the overhauled Early Learning and Care (ELC) qualifications at NFQ Levels 5 and 6 – a departure from the common award system. Under this revised system, awards standards are not designed to be used as detailed programme specifications. Instead 'a diverse range of potential programmes and intended programme learning outcomes is compatible with these Awards Standards' (QQI 2019, 1). It remains to be seen the level of flexibility that will emerge from the hierarchical structures' characteristic of many providers. Unless we address issues of trust, diversity and contextualized learning, my concern is we risk the potentially responsive and flexible nature of the Broad Awards Standards falling into the same traps I have identified to this point and therefore curtailing the activities of the learners and educators in the classroom.

Creative Ways to Assess Learning

For the final part of this chapter, I will turn to my principal goal – to encourage people working in FE settings to push the boundaries of what are often self-imposed limitations on curriculum development and assessment so as to create the best learning experience possible for our learners in engaged, stimulating learning environments. This doesn't negate the need for standards – it is important that we are clear on what we want students to learn and that we

---

3 At NFQ Levels 1–4, these awards cover ten core competencies, aligned with the 2018 EU Competences for Lifelong Learning (and subsequent EU competence frameworks) and ten vocational awards standards (QQI 2022).

assess them accordingly in an aligned system of instruction (Biggs 2012, 44). While awards standards do determine learning outcomes and assessment guidance, educators can and should be led by their own philosophical orientation in setting diverse and context-specific guidelines for how learners might achieve the assessment criteria. 'Sustainable assessment' (Boud and Soler 2016) should meet the needs of the here and now *and* prepare students to meet their own future learning needs.

To be creative means to create. To lean on your own skills, talents and interests in making materials that support the co-creation with students in environments that are facilitative, empathetic and accepting (Rogers 1989). Schemes of work can be kept flexible, open-ended and broad enough to allow the local, contemporary and individual knowledge and interests within each group to emerge.

Banking methods can be interrupted by getting to know our students and allowing them to learn about us in an effort to bring the curriculum alive. Some of my most dynamic and memorable classes have included adults sharing stories about themselves, their workplace, their community or frequently about family – the personal stories about themselves with their parents, partners, toddlers and teens! These funny, typical, challenging, ordinary, everyday stories when discussed through the prism of the topic at hand and the theory and practice of the educator bring new ideas to life allowing people to experience those 'a-hah moments' of clarity. Part of our job as educators is to also know our subject well enough to contemporize, customize and localize our curricula and, indeed, to see the confluence of our learners' experience and the content we offer as a richer curricular offering. This means having the confidence to deviate from set class plans, not relying on the same materials year in and year out, and contextualizing assessment guidelines for learners.

Certainly, there are challenges to finding the right resources and it is time-consuming to not work verbatim from the programme module, or to solely work from readily available manuals or textbooks. However, the most valuable resource you have is the group of people you are working with and participatory, dialogic, hands-on group processes are possible whether we are delivering theoretical or practical courses (see Chapter 5 for more on this). In my own practice, the book *The Partners Companion to Training for Transformation* (2001) by Maureen Sheehy is my most dog-eared and coffee-stained resource. This draws from the 1995 *Training for Transformation* books by Anne Hope and Sally Timmel which are underpinned by Freirean approaches that understand learning as a dynamic of action and reflection that is unpredictable and unique to each situation. Additionally, at the point of planning your course, tools such as the simple 'Why? and How?' exercise outlined by Rogers and Horrocks

(2010, 168) are invaluable in determining the rationale for learning outcomes and how you intend to meet them. I encourage you to find your own core texts, creative exercises or professional development opportunities that support the embodiment of education theories of participation, reflection, problem-posing and critical thinking.

Sometimes students resist group work and dialogue. Many people have been taught to expect a more traditional approach. Educators thus need to work with and facilitate their groups to explore the style of teaching and learning that works best for them. Explaining your philosophy can help. Moreover, while small group work and paired learning can allow learners to explore and engage with their topic when they might feel lost in a larger group, it is important to be wary of tokenistic group work such as dividing your learning group into smaller groups and pairs without a clear rationale or direction in mind. As Bríd Connolly reminds us in Chapter 5, Adult Learning in Groups, intention is everything when it comes to effective group work.

In situations where you deem paired work or small group work to be unsuitable, meet your students where they are at by carrying out ongoing observations and listening surveys (Sheehy 2001, 71) to inform and guide your materials and content, thereby ensuring your learner's experiences and interests are embedded in the course design. Knowledge of contemporary social and political practices such as anti-racist practices (Brookfield and Hess 2021; Fitzsimons and Nwanze 2022), valuing diversity in learning groups (Coss 2022) and issues of equity in the classroom and wider society are relevant to all learning groups.

All the while, build assessment into these practices. For example, some ways of working that have stayed with me long past the end of a course include the following:

− A Level 5 *Human Growth and Development* module that used role-play and lots of laughter to explore Marcia's four stages of identity development (used as a learning activity).
− A Level 8 *Group Work Certificate* where learners chose poetry, music and dancing to Y-M-C-A to explore stages of group development (a particularly memorable interpretation by a group of students used as a learning activity).
− A Level 3 *Child Development* class exploring the benefits of play where a group of women from the Traveller community recalled the games they played as children and then organized a 'play day' for adults in their service (used as a learning activity and an assessment piece).
− A Level 3 *Social Studies* Youth group who chose to explore issues relating to 'joyriding' because this was a feature of their lives (used as a learning activity and as an assessment piece).

- A Level 7 Certificate where learners used a 'body sculpture' exercise based on the Theatre of the Oppressed (Boal 2002) to explore their educational histories (used as a learning activity and reflective assessment). This was particularly transformative for those who had positive educational experiences allowing them space to witness and understand the negative experiences of others in the group.
- A Level 5 *Intercultural Studies* class where a learner independently chose to evidence the learning outcomes required in a project by sharing food and artefacts with the group. During this, she informally chatted with her group about her own culture in comparison to her research undertaken on this second culture, underpinning the discussion with theory (used as a learning activity and an assessment piece).

Conclusion

The challenge this chapter has set for educators is to continue to push for creative and engaging group activities to be recognized and valued as assessment tools. There is a social and personal benefit to replacing many individualized tasks in favour of critically relevant assessments where learners engage in group discussion, practice a skill, produce an artefact or present information to each other about what they have learned. I argue that this is a more accurate method to assess learning than any complex system that includes using points and decimal points for each mark allocated. Educators may be teaching with the needs of their students in mind, but unless work is actively supported through meaningful assessment practices, their good intentions can be inhibited (Boud and Soler 2016, 401). When facilitating accredited learning, we have to work harder if we are to preserve our integrity as creative and critical educators.

Working holistically is an area of practice I am continuing to explore and develop. Furthermore, I am relying on these aspects of my pedagogy more than ever with the advancement of A.I. and large language models, such as ChatGPT. Dynamic curricula and meaningful assessments are the sites where educators in FE can bring themselves and their courses to life and they keep our work relevant, engaging and valuable in a changing world.

Chapter 3

WHY WE NEED TO TALK ABOUT RACE IN FURTHER EDUCATION AND TRAINING

Lilian Nwanze

In recent times, especially since the murder of George Floyd in May 2020, there has been an increase in activism and discussions about racism. In Dublin, an unprecedented 5,000 people came out in protest at Floyd's murder under the auspices of the Black Lives Matter movement (Pollack 2020). There have also been countless webinars and panel discussions, some of which I have been an invited contributor to, organized by various stakeholders on issues bordering on anti-racism, diversity and inclusion. In this chapter, I build a case for the importance of starting and continuing these discussions specifically within further education. I draw widely from critical race theory (CRT), my experiences as a Black female academic, my own research and other research done around the subject matter.

Classrooms are not neutral spaces (Freire 1972). They do not exist in isolation either. They are in fact microcosms of the larger society. The systems and structures that prevail in any society will inevitably replicate themselves in the classroom unless actively interrupted (Darder and Torres 2003). So, rather than beginning my discussion from the classroom, I start with Irish society. And by arguing that Irish immigration laws and policies are structured in such a way that a large number of non-EU migrants, a cohort that is predominantly Black, inevitably end up in further education as students. I also rely on the argument that Further Education and Training (FET) in Ireland (like nearly all education in the world today) has undergone an evolution of its previously multifaceted ethos and has moved towards a 'performance based and employment oriented' ethos (Grummell 2014, 122). It is consequent upon these two arguments that I hinge my call for serious, consistent and concerted discussions about racism in FET; an area where there is scant research on learner and practitioner experiences in Ireland to date.

I go on to explain white supremacy and racism, again with a historical focus, before proposing six things an 'FET practitioner' can do as they strive to embody an anti-racist approach. The last of these six proposals is an emphasis on love.

As Camilla and Jerry detailed in the introduction to this book it is worth reiterating that the politics and practice of FET in Ireland is fraught with various and competing philosophical and ideological approaches to education (Murray et al. 2014). Looking both at extant policy and what obtains in the field, two main approaches stand out. On the one hand, there is a historically grounded, radical, Freirean 'learning to be' (Biesta 2006, 172) approach where the multifaceted needs of learners are prioritized and consulted and where education is 'the practice of freedom' (Freire 1972, 69). On the other hand, there is a more recent neoliberal agenda of 'learning to be productive and employable' (Biesta 2006, 172) that frequently adopts what Freire describes as a *banking* approach to education and where the pedagogic focus is on a measurable end result. My own philosophical orientation is towards the former and, as this book demonstrates, there are undeniable tensions in holding this ontology amidst recent FET policies and discourses that use language that is evident of a governmental neoliberal agenda for FET in Ireland (Grummell 2014; Fitzsimons 2017a). Other chapters have debated these approaches. It is enough grounding for me to simply acknowledge that these tensions exist. From my experience in teaching in FET, you could walk into two different classes within the same centre and see both ideological approaches on display, sometimes even when the same module is being taught. Whichever ideological or philosophical leanings a practitioner or a provider tends towards, it has become imperative, with the change in racial demographics in Ireland in the last twenty to thirty years that, amidst these ideological differences, racism and the impact it has on the sector and society more broadly, be brought to the fore.

Ireland: Migration Patterns

Every time I facilitate a class on race and racism in Ireland, I include a 'gallery walk' activity where I put up different sentences on the wall about race and racism and ask students to walk around the room, take a look at the sentences and converge around one they feel strongly about. A lot of times, especially with my undergraduate students, there is almost a consensus around one of the sentences – *There is racism in Ireland but the racism in Ireland is not as bad as it is in America*. I ask the students to discuss among themselves why they have chosen this sentence and then to feed their discoveries, or findings, back to the class. About eight times out of ten, the students tell me that from what they see in the media, racism is worse across the Atlantic than it is in Ireland. I then ask them the basis of their comparison or the indices they used to ascertain how racism is worse in one place than it is in another. Usually, the class goes silent.

Even though racism is a global phenomenon, there is a danger in discussing racism generally and without reference to particular social and historical contexts. Critical Race Theorists (a theory that originated in the 1970s from the US) discuss this danger as a core part of their theory and argue that every attempt to discuss racism without particular recourse to the history and conditions of a particular geographical territory will end up perpetuating oppression and inequality (Bonilla-Silva 2015).

In her book *Why I'm No Longer Talking to White People about Race* (2017), Reni Eddo-Lodge argues that countries must examine their own histories on race and not simply rely on American-centric accounts. From an Irish perspective, even though there were foreigners in Ireland before the 1990s (Garner 2004), the period between the mid-1990s and the late 2000s heralded an unprecedented increase in migration from countries all over the world. This sudden influx of migrants was not unconnected to the advent of a period of rapid economic growth and prosperity that was fuelled by foreign direct investment and that is popularly referred to as the Celtic Tiger. Ireland, a country known globally as an emigrant nursery (Lentin and McVeigh 2006), suddenly became a choice migration destination. People from countries in the European Union (EU) as well as from other continents flocked inwards to take advantage of the blossoming economy. With the change in demographics, pervasive global issues of difference and 'othering' became inevitable. The categorization of these migrants is important – generally organized across four classifications (Fanning 2002). These are the following:

1. Irish citizens who were emigrating from the diaspora back home.
2. Nationals of EU member state nations.
3. Immigrant workers from non-EU countries who were granted and issued work permits.
4. People seeking international protection (asylum seekers).

The first two categories arrived in Ireland with automatic rights to reside as well as unrestricted access to education and the labour market. The case was different for the third and fourth categories and some analysts have argued that Irish immigration policies, targeted at the last two categories of migrants, position Ireland as a 'racist state' (Lentin and McVeigh 2006; Lentin 2007). Government policies have always been designed to limit the number of people coming into the country seeking asylum. The landmark 2004 citizenship referendum, which led to the amendment of the citizenship-by-birth practice that was previously in force, was organized in response to migrants whom the state accused of flocking into the country and putting pressure on maternity services – migrants that belonged mostly to the third and fourth categories. The electoral vote at the referendum (which was passed by 79 per cent) and the attendant amendment of the constitution meant that the right to Irish citizenship for children born in Ireland was limited to only those who had Irish parents. Up until then, children who were born in Ireland automatically became Irish citizens irrespective of the nationality of their parents.

Lentin (2007, 7) captures the treatment of the last two categories of non-national migrants succinctly when she writes:

> While limiting the numbers of people allowed to land to present their asylum application, the state seems desperate to bring in economic and labour migrants, seen as economic commodities, vital to Ireland's continued economic growth. Due to shortage of labour in certain sectors, there was a 600 percent rise in the number of work visas granted since 1999.

For those in the third category, workers from non-EU nations who were granted work permits, these were mainly highly skilled workers that were needed for understaffed industries, for example, doctors, nurses and IT professionals. These workers were, in essence, needed by the state. Even though they were granted work permits, these migrants often periodically paid exorbitant fees for their continued stay in Ireland and had no real option when it came to employment mobility (Citizen's Information Board 2023). There was also a demand for low-skilled workers but, with the exception of a few countries that had reciprocal arrangements with Ireland, non-EU migrants were precluded from getting work permits for these jobs. Category three professionals (non-EU migrants) were allowed to bring in their spouses/civil partners to the country on a special purpose visa called *Stamp 3 Join Spouse Visa*. Until very recently, people with 'Stamp 3' visas were not allowed to take up employment and were to be fully financially dependent on their spouses.

I came to Ireland on a Stamp 3 Join Spouse Visa and was unable to access any form of employment. Employers did not want 'the burden' of applying for work permits for people like myself who were legally residents but not allowed into the Irish labour market without special permission. If I wanted to do any kind of work, it had to be voluntary or undocumented work. Such were the stringent conditions of the Stamp 3 residence permit.[1]

---

1 The conditions for holders of Stamp 3 visas have changed considerably in the last 3 years. Holders of the 'Stamp 3 Join Spouse Visas' are now allowed to access the labour market.

Moreover, research (Stamp 3 Association 2018) has shown that this increased the level of domestic violence experienced by this cohort. Something that was compounded by the fact that many racialized women felt distant and, at times, excluded from domestic violence support services which are already greatly under-resourced (Fagan 2008).

Category four migrants, people seeking asylum even before entering the state, were labelled by the state as problematic. In the early 2000s, the government highlighted immigration and asylum as 'serious problems' that needed to be dealt with decisively and urgently (Garner 2004, 438). People seeking asylum flee their countries to seek protection as a result of persecution they face because of their race, religion, nationality, political opinion or membership of a particular group. *The International Protection Act* (2015) protects certain rights for these applicants. Ireland has a very curious history with asylum seekers. In the late 1950s, Ireland took in asylum seekers from Hungary who were fleeing the communist suppression in Budapest. Even though this acceptance of refugees was lauded by many, research shows that the Hungarian refugees were 'quarantined' and housed in centres with abysmal living conditions (Maguire 2004 cited in Meaney-Satori and Nwanze 2021). Today, the conditions under which asylum seekers are kept in Ireland are still a source of contention and agitation by human rights activist groups. Asylum seekers are granted refugee status once their applications for protection are assessed and decided on favourably.

Under the *Refugee Protection Programme* set up in response to the humanitarian crisis in Southern Europe, Ireland pledged to receive 4,000 displaced people through a process of relocation (for asylum seekers) and resettlement (for refugees). Despite this commitment, Ireland has only received about 1,913 people under this arrangement in the last five years. The reception system for asylum seekers, or Direct Provision (DP), is a network of for-profit hotel-style centres that are usually situated away from major towns. Even though applicants are legally expected to have their applications decided within one year, most asylum seekers stay in Direct Provision centres for many years while waiting for a decision on their applications and the conditions reported are often abysmal. After significant criticisms from many commentators, the government Joint Committee on Justice and Equality acknowledged, in a report published in 2019, that Direct Provision was 'not fit for purpose' and joined the many calls for fundamental reform (Joint Committee on Justice and Equality 2019). In the wake of this report, the current Irish coalition government of Fianna Fáil, Fine Gael and The Green Party has pledged to end Direct Provision in 2024.

At the time of writing, and in response to the war in Ukraine, Ireland has also received almost 50,000 Ukrainians fleeing the conflict. The obvious difference and discrepancies in the treatment of Ukrainian refugees from others who have sought asylum in Ireland prior to the war in Ukraine have been spotlighted as evidence of racial discrimination (Kennedy and O'Sullivan 2022). This is most obvious with regard to the allocation of emergency accommodation with some mostly non-EU asylum seekers now immediately finding themselves homeless and sometimes sleeping on the street (McDermott 2023).

Eventually, if they meet certain criteria, and often after many years, people from the third and fourth categories can become naturalized Irish citizens, an occurrence which, on paper, gives them the same rights and privileges as people born in Ireland. Research has, however, shown that this is not the case. Naturalized migrants, especially Blacks and people from other minority ethnic categories are often unable to access employment commensurate to their level of education (Soto and Ruiz Moriana 2020, 15). Consequently, a large number of Blacks and other migrants who are not white, with post-graduate qualifications, are represented disproportionately in the care industry as care assistants (Akinborewa et al. 2020, 129) – again, an understaffed industry where people are 'needed'.

There is also often a disproportionate number of asylum seekers and refugees in FET. About half of this category in Ireland are racialized as 'non-white'.[2] In 2020, of the 1,566 applicants for protection (asylum seekers), 628 (40.1 per cent) were people of African descent or were non-white (Irish Refugee Council 2020, 9), a trend that has been recurring since the 1990s. For the first three years of their stay, they are only allowed access to lower-level Further Education Courses (at QQI Levels 1–4), so they take up this option rather than stay idle in Direct Provision centres that many have described as 'unconducive' and 'depressing' (Meaney-Satori and Nwanze 2021). Others attend further education to acquire English language skills, often through a national network of publicly provided ESOL (English as a Second Language) programmes. With reference to how language is taught in such environments today, Henry Giroux (2021, 76) is critical of its individualistic neo-liberalization that detaches learning from history and is more self-orientated. This, he argues, undermines the creation of collaborative, democratic learning that has the potential to create critically engaged citizens in favour of 'market-based language' that maintains a neoliberal status quo. There is little to suggest this is not the case within FET in Ireland.

---

2 I find the use of the term 'non-white' problematic as it describes people in relation to the dominant group. I have used this term in this article in places where the literature I am citing has used the term in order to maintain the integrity of their writing.

Another major barrier faced by people in categories three and four, especially people from African countries or people who studied abroad in languages other than English, is difficulty in getting their university qualifications recognized. In Meaney-Satori and Nwanze (2021), we found that many people admit that they go into FET to take up courses to prepare them for whatever employment they can get, for example healthcare. Ebun Joseph (2020, 85) describes this situation as problematic and an exercise in 'down-skilling' rather than 'up-skilling' so that people are better able to access low-paid jobs that they are often overqualified for. People also sign up for EFT as a way to progress to Irish universities despite often already having attended university in their country of origin.

Many of the people working in further education settings are also unaware of the preponderance of immigration issues and challenges as well as the impact these have on their students. This lack of awareness of the lived experiences of people had a direct and proportionate effect on student's engagement, performance and general experience in education (Meaney-Satori and Nwanze 2021). I will return to this point in a later section.

(Anti-) Racism and White Supremacy

Now that I have discussed the important histories of people's asynchronous entry into adult, community and further education, and before discussing what anti-racist practice could look like in FET, I believe that a more effective next step will be an understanding of what racism is – get this wrong and it can further perpetuate racism. The first thing to consider is that racism goes beyond individual hostility, insult, or assault on non-white people. If anything at all, these macro-aggressive manifestations of racism (like calling a Black person unacceptable names or other racial slurs) are enactments of much deeper systemic issues that exist (hooks 2010; Eddo-Lodge 2017; Brookfield 2018). I have lived for ten years in Ireland and can count on one hand how many times I have ever been verbally racially attacked. It has happened very few times. Yet, I live with and encounter the real effects of a more structural kind of racism almost every day of my existence. This is through the continual presence of micro-aggressions, which Kehinde Andrews (2018, 220) describes as 'the subtle papercuts that as they accumulate, do enormous damage to the psyche'. Racism is systemic. Brookfield and Hess (2021, 20) describe this succinctly when they write that,

> Racism is a system that is designed to perpetuate the power of one particular racial group over others. This system is maintained by laws and policies and supported by state, judicial, and paramilitary power. When the system works

as it's designed, it has the effect of disproportionately benefiting one racial group who are at the top of the American caste system. In the United States that group is white people.

Even though Brookfield and Hess (2021) write about racism from the perspective of a particular geographic context, I argue that this system of racism is in place in most of the Global North including here in Ireland. Racism is kept in place and perpetuated by an ideology of *white supremacy* which repeatedly portrays whiteness as the norm and that '*others*' people of colour. With white supremacy, people of colour are homogenized as emotional, not to be trusted, easily inflamed and unable to handle positions of authority (Brookfield 2018, 4) while disregarding relevant social–political contexts. The dangerous thing about white supremacy is its pervasiveness and how it has been internalized even by people who are not white and people who detest and fight against racism. bell hooks, a Black feminist educator, began writing about white supremacy many years ago. She narrates in the second edition of her book, *Talking Back: Thinking Feminism, Thinking Black*, 'As I write, I try to remember when the word racism ceased to be the term which best expressed for me exploitation of Black people and other people of color in this society and when I began to understand that the most useful term was white supremacy' (hooks 2015, 292). Race is certainly a necessary term, she argues, however, white supremacy better describes her experiences 'when confronted with the liberal attitudes of white women active in feminist movement who were unlike their racist ancestors – white women in the early woman's rights movement who did not wish to be caught dead in fellowship with Black women'. She continues,

> In fact, these women often requested and longed for the presence of Black women. Yet when present, what we saw was that they wished to exercise control over our bodies and thoughts as their racist ancestors had – that this need to exercise power over us expressed how much they had internalized the values and attitudes of white supremacy. It may have been this contact or contact with fellow white English professors who want very much to have 'a' Black person in 'their' department as long as that person thinks and acts like them, shares their values and beliefs, is in no way different, that first compelled me to use the term white supremacy to identify the ideology that most determines how white people in this society (irrespective of their political leanings to the right or left) perceive and relate to Black people and other people of colour. (hooks 2015, 292)

This white supremacist ideology is so deep-seated and pervasive that it finds expression even in people who are not white (Eddo-Lodge 2017, 85–87).

I often share an experience I once had when I was out in a shopping centre somewhere in Dublin. I saw a group of four or five young Black men walking in my direction. I immediately clutched my bag tighter. I had completed the act before I realized that I had just exhibited white supremacist tendencies. White supremacy socializes society into seeing Black males as dangerous and aggressive and prone to crime. Despite being a Black woman myself, my actions showed a subconscious internalization of this image.

Again, history matters, and I do not think it is possible to understand the enormity and the depth of the problem that white supremacy has become without excavating or tracing, no matter how briefly, its history in economic dimensions which date back to the barbaric Trans-Atlantic Slave Trade era of the seventeenth century. To maintain this inhumane system, slave owners introduced a series of explanations that would justify the forceful abduction of humans from Africa for the purpose of labour. These explanations ranged from Blacks being 'less than human' to biblical justifications for the enslavement of Black people by whites; the raw materials from which modern-day racism was birthed. With the growth of sugar and tobacco plantations in the Caribbean and North America in the early seventeenth century, the demand for (slave) labour exponentially increased and other tactics were used.[3] These included pitting indentured servants, many of whom were Irish, against Black slaves by creating a better social status, or birthright, for people of European ancestry (Dabiri 2021, 55–56).[4] This divide-and-rule strategy had, through a master stroke, deconstructed the mutual interests of indentured servants and Black slaves. Whiteness was used as a ruse – a distraction from the oppression the indentured servants were facing and a tactic that introduced permanent divergence of interests. As indentured servitude was phased out in favour of slaves forcefully stolen from Africa, the proceeds of slavery were invested in industrial productions and new productive techniques (Olende 2018). Eventually, slavery was abolished but, before it was, it had ensured the perpetuity of the capitalist system as well as white supremacy and racism. In its aftermath, every phase of capitalism

---

3 It is important in the context of this narrative to understand that, at this time, the economic gain that was being enjoyed by the Plantation owners, from the work of slaves and indentured servants, was unprecedented in the history of commerce in the world. This alliance between Black slaves and white indentured servants was therefore a threat to the common wealth of what is today America and Britain and could no longer be allowed to continue.
4 In a series of administrative practices which eventually culminated in the codification of laws, the Colonists regulated the relationships between Blacks and hites, giving the latter superior status over Blacks (including Black freemen).

has perpetuated this idea that white people are superior to non-white people (Arruzza et al. 2019, 43). Moreover, the media and popular culture constantly reiterate this ideology as do institutions (hooks 1994). White supremacist thinking is the dominant world order. It is everywhere, including in adult, community and further education spaces, if not actively and intentionally interrupted.

Not all theorists who write about race agree with this link of white supremacy and racism. Neo-Marxist scholar Mike Cole (2009, 2020) has critiqued the white supremacy–racism link on a number of fronts – four of which I will highlight briefly. First, he argues that white supremacy may account for the origins of racism but cannot be used to explain the continued presence of racism in present-day society. Cole also argues that the idea of white supremacy diverts attention from the modes of production and development in capitalism which to him are the real drivers of racism. Another critique of the link between white supremacy and racism is the fact that white supremacy, as a theory, homogenizes whites and does not take cognizance of class inequities among whites. Last, Cole argues that because of the links white supremacy has with fascism and other forms of extremism, it is a demotivating concept and discourages allyship. Some neo-Marxists thus propose, rather than white supremacy, the concept of racialization as the origin of racism. Critical race theorist Sean Walton (2020) has responded to Cole's criticisms and has shown that white supremacy and racialization, rather than oppose, complement each other. I interpret racialization as a process through which a set of traits are erroneously assigned to a homogenized group in a way that disregards sociopolitical contexts. Alana Lentin (2004, 28) describes 'racialization' as 'the relationship of power involved in the assigning of inferiority and its codification using visual signifiers' and 'perceptual codes, beyond those of the skin'.

The Dangers of a Narrow Definition of Racism

One thing is paramount, namely that racism goes beyond individual manifestations and is, rather, a system of operation. To adopt individualist understandings is detrimental to anti-racist work as it forms an erroneous picture that 'racists' are vile, nasty and violent people, some bad apples among an otherwise healthy orchard. Pegging racism at the individual level makes people resistant to engaging in anti-racist discourse because, to their minds, they are already anti-racist anyway. It is important that we correct this narrative. Racism is not something that bad or mean people do. It is not an event. It is a system. It is 'a set of societal, cultural and institutional beliefs and practices **regardless of intention** that subordinate and oppress one race for the benefit of the other' (Western States Resource Center 2003, 6).

I often listen to practitioners' relay to me proudly how they would never condone racial slurs towards students from minority ethnic backgrounds and how they endeavour to treat all their students the same. What such teachers fail to understand is that racism is systematically programmed to be perpetuated, devoid of intention and much more than calling out rude behaviour will need to be done for someone to become an anti-racist practitioner.

Let's imagine a fictitious educator, and call her Claire, who works at one of the biggest FE Colleges in Ireland with over fifty teaching staff. Let's imagine forty-five of these staff are white Irish, four are from other countries in the EU and there is one Black teacher who mostly keeps to herself. Claire says 'hello' to her and helps out anytime they need administrative assistance. In one of Claire's classes, there are fifteen white people and three Blacks. Claire is well meaning and in her own words 'doesn't notice race'. She would never allow the white students in her classroom to pass rude or derogatory remarks to the Black students. In fact, she lists this specifically in her class contract which all students sign at the beginning of the course; a Level 5 QQI pre-law module. This has a 'reading' list with ten books all authored by white men and three YouTube videos of white law professors. Although Claire actively discourages overt negativity and abusive behaviour towards her Black students (which is commendable), she doesn't do much to interrupt the real system of racism that has been programmed to work against and exclude Black students (Brookfield 2018, 6). In fact, some of her seemingly benign actions work to further perpetuate systemic racism, such as her choice of materials that silences the voices and writings of Black and minority ethnic people. Her very existence (and racial silence) in an institution that disadvantages Black people in their hiring practices (McGinnity et al. 2009) makes her complicit in structural racism. I have met many 'Claires' in FET. People who are so adamant that they are anti-racist that they refuse to even engage in a discussion to the contrary. People who hinge their practice on a narrow, incomplete and, I argue, even dangerous definition of what racism is. Practitioners like Claire are likely doing what they think is best and should be supported to understand the structural nature of racism as this will shift their focus from very narrow perspectives of the lives of their racialized students and allow them to understand how factors outside the classroom affect the student both inside and outside the classroom (Blaisdell 2015).

Six Ways to Become an Anti-Racist Practitioner

One of the criticisms levelled against CRT is the perceived hopelessness that it portrays (Andrews 2018, 244). If racism is so deeply ingrained in the fabric of society and is the normal way in which the world is organized, what hope is there for change? What can be done? If racism is political and systemic, what role can a practitioner play in interrupting this system, at least in their classroom? First, I think it is important to reiterate that a classroom is not just a neutral space. Whether teachers realize it or not, the classroom is a political site – its political function being to either liberate or domesticate at every point in time (Freire 1972, 54; Ledwith 2011, 99–100). A teacher by their agenda and choice of methods in the classroom is either feeding into and strengthening the inequitable status quo or they are interrupting it. This is perpetuated by the tendency to think that the work that goes on in the classroom is separate from 'the real world' and that the real world is 'somewhere out there'. Contemporary critical pedagogues disagree with this view of the world and hinge their practice on classrooms being spaces where society can be shaped. I subscribe to Paulo Freire and bell hooks' model of using critical education as a tool to engineering agency in students that will in turn make them experts in recognizing and hopefully dismantling oppression in their lives.

I admit that totally deconstructing the capitalist society as a panacea for racism is a daunting task to present to anyone. I also recognize that many times practitioners can feel powerless and crippled by the seeming enormity of the problem so that they then do nothing at all. So I have proposed some practices that build anti-racist pedagogy. The systems that put racism in place were intentionally put there little by little over many years. The structures that will dismantle it will also have to be intentionally built one block upon another, slowly but consistently for success to be seen.

As racism is more invisible than it is visible, it takes a level of criticality to first uncover it and then proffer workable solutions. My six proposed practices lean on theory, research, my experience and the writings of critical race pedagogues. Some of these tips may seem personal and unconnected to anything that may cause real structural change.

Practice One – Reflect on Your Own Identity

Many times after coming to terms with what racism really is, some practitioners are so enraged with the seeming inequity suffered by the 'othered' that they want to roll up their sleeves and get right into anti-racist work. They usually start by focusing on the needs of their Black (or other minority ethnic) students. As well meaning as this sounds, it is not the right starting point. Rather than starting externally, educators should turn that sequence on its head and start from the self, especially when that 'self'is white. Because much of racism is learnt (Brookfield 2018, 5), the white anti-racist practitioner must do a deep self-search to see how their own internalized racism affects their practice. This self-reflection will not be a one-time event, rather it is continuous because, as we have discussed, white supremacist thinking has been put forward as the dominant and normal way of seeing life for many centuries. If you are a white practitioner reading this, you most likely have racist beliefs as it is impossible to have lived all of your life and not have imbibed these in some form (Kendall 2013; Brookfield and Hess 2021). But those of us who are racialized, in my case as Black, we too should start out with self-reflection and investigate how much of our actions are also backed by white supremacist thinking. A practitioner can bring these beliefs into consciousness through critical reflection, examination of their feelings, dialogues and discussions (Baumgartner 2010; Kendall 2013). A practitioner must continuously interrogate and ask themselves *am I teaching the person in front of me or the ideas that I have about the person in front of me – especially those received from the media and political discourse?*

Usually, when this reflection is carried out properly, it evokes an awakening and practitioners may begin to see (perhaps for the first time) how pervasive white Supremacist thinking is, how much racism goes on around them and how their power and privilege perpetuate this. Some people experience shame, discomfort and guilt at their own complicitness, something Frances Kendall (2013, 119) encourages people not to dwell on as it can impede intentional work towards eliminating racism. Deliberately bringing race and racism to the fore in your mind is a daunting proposal. But it must be done if any effective anti-racism work can be carried out.

The danger of starting anti-racism work from any other starting point other than the self is that the practitioner comes across as being hypocritical and not genuine, and sooner or later their white supremacist actions will surface and negate their anti-racist words. Even after a practitioner has engaged in self-reflection, they may still have white supremacist behaviours; self-reflection and introspection is a journey not a destination. But the lopsidedness of anti-racist work carried out without adequate self-reflection is easily spotted, especially by people who are not white. Power and privilege can be used constructively in furtherance of anti-racist work and an educator can act in such a way that minimizes them when dealing with racialized students and colleagues. However, it must be recognized in the first instance.

Practice Two – Reject a Colour-Blind Ideology

I often meet practitioners (like Claire) who are quick (and proud) to announce how they do not 'see race' and that they treat all their students the same. While this is often a well-intentioned stance, it does not further an anti-racist agenda. On the contrary, it further perpetuates racism (Delgado and Stefanci 2017). You cannot be anti-racist and yet ignore race. You need to see race.

You need to see racism. In fact, a colour-blind stance is a form of silencing and is a pervasive form of avoidance (Flowers 2010) that is in itself a function of white privilege. People of colour do not have the luxury of choosing when they see race and when they don't. They are rather inundated with issues pertaining to race every day. A colour-blind stance further deepens racial inequality by discountenancing and effectively erasing the past and ignoring the inequalities of the present by assuming a meritocratic perspective that puts non-white students on a level playing field with others who have never experienced racial marginalization or 'othering' (Hearn 2009). When an organization operates with a colour-blind ideology, it doesn't collect data on the race or ethnicity of its students, meaning there is no way of researching the possibility of an achievement gap; again, hampering anti-racist efforts.

The irrationality of colour blindness becomes even more glaring when we put it side by side with the treatment of other marginalized groups. It is not likely that to improve the experience of students living with disabilities, an organization will take a 'disability blind' stance. Doing so immediately forecloses any initiatives that may help in ameliorating the hardship that a cohort of people experience. I recently came across a 'Band-Aid' exercise designed by an 8th-grade teacher in America to teach the children in the class about fairness (Chilcoat ND). The teacher asked the children to pretend they had gone out for recess and had gotten hurt. Each child was to assume a particular point on their bodies had been injured and were to get a band-aid for their imaginary injury. Of course, there were all sorts of injury spots – legs, knees, hands, ankles, elbows, faces, everywhere. As the kids came forward for their band-aid, irrespective of where they said their injuries were, the teacher put a band-aid on their wrist. Of course, in a short while, there was a noisy class – why had the teacher ignored the positions of their injuries and put the band-aid on the same spot? She replied, 'because I wanted to treat you all fairly'. The children got the message – fairness does not mean treating everyone the same but about meeting people where they are at and giving everyone what they need to succeed. Adopting a colour-blind stance is putting a band-aid on everyone's wrist irrespective of the real location of the hurt.

Practice Three – Adopt Pedagogic Methodologies that Encourage Dialogue and Inclusion

CRT lists as one of its tenets the fact that the experts in speaking about a minority status and issues of race and racism are those with lived experience and a particular history (Stefancic and Delgado 2017). Consequently, it advocates for spaces to be made available for voices of colour to share their experiences. For anti-racist work to be effective, a practitioner must have some idea of the real lived experiences of people of colour. I recommend any or all of three ways to inquire into people's backgrounds. First, read. Read research done about racialized people, for example Lucy Michael's (2015) report on *Afrophobia in Ireland*, or government policy such as the first *National Action Plan Against Racism* (2005). Read books on the experiences of people of colour in Ireland, for example *What White People Can Do Next* (2021) by Emma Dabiri.

Second, create communal spaces within classrooms and employ pedagogic methods aimed at encouraging the exchange of biographical stories. bell hooks (2009, 53) writes eloquently about the transformative power of stories:

> Stories help us to connect to a world beyond the self. In telling our stories we make connections with other stories. Journeying to countries where we may not speak the native tongue, most of us communicate by creating a story, one we may tell without words. We may show by gesture what we mean. What becomes evident is that, in the global community, life is sustained by stories. A powerful way we connect with a diverse world is by listening to the different stories we are told. These stories are a way of knowing. Therefore, they contain both power and the art of possibility. We need more stories.

Stories are deeply personal and sacred and people are more inclined to share them in spaces where they feel safe and valued. hooks (2010, 20) is also adamant on the need to prioritize building community:

> Knowing all that I know now after more than thirty years in classrooms, I do not begin to teach in any setting without first laying the foundation for building community in the classroom. To do this, it is essential that teacher and students take time to get to know one another.

In another resource (Fitzsimons and Nwanze 2021), I wrote about being a student in two different classrooms. In one, I did not say a word for the whole session but, in the other, I shared biographical stories about my life and my experiences. The difference was the deliberate efforts by the facilitator to create a space where I knew I was valued, and where my story mattered. It was not a space where only I shared my story. Rather, activities and resources were designed for everyone to share their stories – so we all hear about life from various perspectives. Every time I shared my story in that class, I was struck by how differently others experienced the world. My classmates often commented on how they would never have known some of the things I shared if they hadn't had the opportunity to listen. All adult, community and further education practitioners should seek to harness facilitation skills that create spaces where the voices of racialized minorities are valued and heard without putting them on the spot, irrespective of the subject being taught. What would it be like to simply ask people about their lives? Ask questions and honestly 'name' the fact that you do not know much about how life from their perspective looks. This can then be backed up by bringing voices in through diversified reading lists that include literature from outside the Global North.

Practice Four – Embrace Discomfort and Be Ready to Make Mistakes

In my experience, both as a student and as a teacher, I encounter an almost palpable silence every time I try to steer a class discussion in the direction of racism, especially anti-black racism. Yet, research shows that Ireland is showing 'worrying patterns of racism' (O'Halloran 2019). Brookfield (2018, 5–6) suggests reasons for this reluctance to engage, including a fear of saying the wrong thing, concern about opening up uncomfortable discussions, a perceived lack of experience or, for white educators, a reluctance in confronting their own racialized privilege. In Ireland, some educators list a national failure to adequately address the autochthonous anti-Traveller racism as a reason why they shy away from discussions.

The anti-racist practitioner must intentionally choose to move past these fears and engage. Brookfield (2021, 35) writes that

> Part of becoming a white antiracist is recognizing that the work ahead will be raw, bruising and tense, but still being ready to embrace that reality. It won't be conducted in a safe space in which people agree to disagree, everyone's experience is recognized as equally valid, and emotions are kept at a safe distance or controlled by a facilitator who 'doesn't let things get out of hand.' As we move into embracing a white anti-racist identity we must enter brave rather than safe spaces, because 'authentic learning about social justice often requires the very qualities of risk, difficulty, and controversy that are defined as incompatible with safety'. (Arao and Clemens 2013, 139 cited in Brookfield and Hess, 2021, 35).

Practice Five – Commit to Some Form of Activism

Anti-racist practice must culminate in some form of (political) activism which could (or, more appropriately, should) be both personal and collective. Personal activism involves the steps taken within your personal remit that help instigate racial justice. For example, I know a white educator who offers opportunities to minority ethnic people where there is a tie between two candidates – one minority and one not. Her explanation is simple – one of these candidates is more likely to possess the social and cultural capital, or the connections to get through the doors and one doesn't. So, her actions become the capital for the minority person – she uses her privilege to interrupt what would ordinarily have maintained the white supremacist status quo. I also know of practitioners who, irrespective of the module they are teaching, introduce critically the subject of race, racism and inequality and create in their students a critical consciousness of the subject. Personal activism can take any form – from small to big actions. Collectively, educators can join forces with other practitioners or with activist groups to push anti-racist agendas. Larger groups can reach larger numbers and are more likely to gain the attention of leaders who have the power to legislate change.

Practice Six – Embrace an Ethos of Love

> And now abide faith, hope, love, these three; but the greatest of these *is* love.
> (1 Corinthians 13:13, New King James Version of the Bible)

I am of the opinion that at the root of genuine, impactful and transformatory anti-racist work is love. I'm often struck by the silence, surprise and occasional discomfort that follows every time I bring up 'love' in relation to classroom practice. But I am not alone. Like Paulo Freire, I see education itself as 'an act of love' (1972, 62) – this is the glue that will hold all the other five practices together. And so I argue that racial justice work will not be sustainable without it being rooted in love. There is a two-pronged approach to this love ethos – emotional/reparative on the one hand and a political dimension of love on the other. Both dimensions are vital ingredients in anti-racist practice. Emotional or reparative love deals with genuine care for the student as a human being. A compassion, an empathy and a consideration for the trauma that racism has birthed in the life of a student. This branch of love should then lead to a political and transformative dimension of love. Freire (1972, 1994) and hooks (2000, 2009) write about the necessity for love to be connected to some form of liberating politics in order for it to be transformative. In other words, beyond care and empathy, love should compel the activism I wrote about as practice five.

In *Communion, the Female Search for Love*, bell hooks defines love for an educator as 'a combination of care, commitment, knowledge, responsibility, respect, and trust' (hooks 2002, 159), themes she holds firm on throughout much of her writings. True and effective anti-racism work requires this level of selfless interest if we are to end the oppression and exploitation of others. For hooks, love is an intentional choice and something that is central to the practice of a critical educator. Elsewhere she writes, 'When as teachers we teach with love, combining care, commitment, knowledge, responsibility, respect, and trust, we are often able to enter the classroom and go straight to the heart of the matter' (hooks 2009, 161). This, she argues, gives us the clarity to know what to do in a given situation if we are to create conditions for learning. She continues,

> Teachers who are wedded to using the same teaching style every day, who fear any digression from the concrete lesson plan, miss the opportunity for full engagement in the learning process. They are far more likely to have an orderly classroom where students obey authority. They are far more likely to feel satisfied because they have presented all the information that they wanted to cover. And yet they are missing the most powerful experience we can offer students, which is the opportunity to be fully and compassionately engaged with learning.

This ethos of love is the force that will compel an educator to create 'community' where a student can safely share experiences rather than a regimented lecture hall focused solely on meeting learning outcomes. Love will compel a teacher to listen critically and learn from the stories shared by the marginalized student. It will refuse to reduce anti-racism initiatives to a tick-box exercise and will cause a practitioner who ordinarily is a beneficiary of (white) privilege to use that privilege to open doors for others – doors that can only be opened by whiteness. An ethos of love will cause a practitioner to recognize that a racialized student walks into the classroom with an extra layer of baggage put upon them by a white supremacist society. They will resist a one-size-fits-all educational experience and will be committed to evangelizing, at some point in every module, the anti-racism sermon, whatever subject is being taught. An ethos of love will pause and reflect on how their decisions impact others. Working from a standpoint of love is not easy but inherent in this ethos is a transformative power that can break down these walls of division, segregation, prejudice, distrust and hate that have been built up for centuries.

Final Thoughts

Structures come into place when actions taken by individuals endure for a long period of time. If new counteractions spring up from individuals and these actions gather momentum and become societal common sense or the norm in society, we will be moving in the right direction. With Ireland's change in racial demographics and the role of adult, community and further education in the lives of many migrants, practitioners can no longer shy away from engaging in anti-racist practice. We must unlearn white supremacist practices and (re)learn ways of deconstructing racism within the system. If the system is not neutral, then neither are we as practitioners (Freire 1972). So we must take a stand.

Chapter 4

NEURODIVERSITY AND INCLUSION IN FURTHER EDUCATION AND TRAINING

Jane O'Kelly

This chapter is a reflexive journey through the literature on Autism and the issues impacting societal and educational learning contexts for neurodivergent adult learners. The following sections explore some aspects of Autism and the autistic experience in society and in educational settings, particularly higher education and Further Education and Training (FET). The voices of autistic people and their allies are growing louder in influencing policy and strategies traditionally oriented to a neurotypical majority. The increasing awareness of neurodiversity, its complexity and its prevalence in society is welcomed as part of the need to make inclusion an action and a reality rather than an aspirational concept. The discussion acknowledges the ambition of Universal Design for Learning and the aim to embed its inclusive approach in all aspects of teaching and learning across education settings. The acknowledgement of the importance of the continuum of lifelong learning for autistic people is underpinned by the need for recognition of a continuum of awareness, understanding and accommodations for autistic people as they navigate society and educational provision. Autism is one of a number of neurodevelopmental differences or neurotypes, which are relevant to the concept of neurodiversity which has had a major impact on social inclusion and participation in recent years.

Autism

Horgan et al. (2023, 526) describe Autism as a 'neurodevelopmental condition or difference formally characterized by a shared dyad of challenges in social communication and repetitive behaviours which may also include difficulties in social interaction and sensory processing.' In a study of terms used by the autistic community in the UK researchers found that there was no universally accepted way to describe autism and that the context of the person and the heterogeneity of the autistic community needs to be acknowledged (Kenny et al . 2016). Although Autism is often referred to as a 'spectrum', it is emphasized that this term may be too linear and an oversimplistic representation of the 'diverse, changing nature and experiences of autistic people' (Goodall, 2020, p. 2). AsIAm (2023) refers to the recent publication of the diagnostic framework DSM-5,[1] which presents Autism as an umbrella term in order to capture the 'spectrum' or different ways that Autism can present in individuals. They note that the language in the DSM-5 is perceived as negative and disabling by the autism community and does not represent modern views of autism. Goodall explains that, in his view, the 'concept of a "spectrum" is too linear and an over-simplistic representation of the diverse, changing nature and the experiences of autistic people' (Goodall 2020, 2). Autistic people explain in their own words that 'one could either be autistic, or non-autistic and that although Autism itself was a spectrum, humanity is not a spectrum between non-autistic and autistic (i.e. not everyone is a "little autistic")' (Botha et al. 2022, 435).

Neurodiversity

The term 'neurodiversity' was originally coined in relation to Autism and several conditions traditionally pathologized and associated with a deficit including dyspraxia, dyslexia, attention deficit hyperactivity disorder (ADHD), dyscalculia, autistic spectrum (AS) and Tourette's syndrome (Singer 1999). A neurodivergent person is someone with one or more of these conditions and a neurotypical person is someone without these conditions.

Neurodiversity is a concept that views Autism and other conditions such as ADHD as a natural neurological variation contributing to the complexity of humanity in a similar way to the diversity of ethnicity, gender and sexual orientation (Walker 2012). The concept of neurodivergent people as a minority population within a majority of neurotypical people is analogous to the challenges faced by other minorities such as LBGTQIA+ people. The neurodiversity movement is a social justice movement that seeks equality, respect and societal inclusion (Silberman 2015). Davies (2022, 18), an autistic music therapist, writes of the positive traits of Autism such as honesty, attention to detail, good memory and the ability to hyper-focus (traits also recognized by Russell et al. 2019) and acknowledges the challenges of sensory processing or executive functioning difficulties that increase 'minority stress'. The minority

---

[1] DSM-5 refers to the *Diagnostic and Statistical Manual of Mental Disorders* and is the handbook frequently used by healthcare professionals across the world as a diagnostic tool.

stress model explains the impact on the health of stigmatized minority groups living in a majority population. The model can illustrate the stress and resulting health implications for neurodivergent people who are often ostracized and experience discrimination in a society that is designed for a neurotypical majority (Botha and Frost 2020).

Kapp et al. (2013) contend that the neurodiversity movement celebrates Autism as an inseparable aspect of identity rather than a disorder that requires a medical approach to causation and cure. Autistic people are speaking about difference rather than disorder and disability although it is acknowledged that sometimes disability will accompany difference in the intersectional nature of a lived experience. Griffin and Pollack (2008) assert that the concept of neurodiversity argues that an atypical neurological wiring is a normal human difference that should be tolerated and respected like any other human difference. Robison (2015), an autistic adult and blogger, contends that 'Neurodiversity is reality and integrating the population into schools and workplaces is wise whenever you want the maximum benefit of human intellect. It's also more common than most people know, so efforts at accommodation make good sense'.

Across the world, the number of people being diagnosed with autism spectrum disorder (ASD) is rising.[2] The factors contributing to the rise include an 'increase in community awareness and public health response globally, changes in case definition that have broadened diagnostic boundaries over time, increased diagnosis of milder forms, and an increase in the identification of autism in previously under-diagnosed populations defined by sex, geography, race/ethnicity, or Socio Economic Status (SES)' (Zeidan et al. 2022, 786). The prevalence rate in adults is difficult to estimate due to assessment practices and societal awareness changing from when adults were children and systemic barriers to diagnosis for adults. The Department of Health Report, 'Estimating Prevalence of Autism Spectrum Disorders (ASD) in the Irish Population: A review of data sources and epidemiological studies' (2018) suggests that there is a robust case for adopting a prevalence rate of 1–1.5% of Autism in Ireland (Department of Health 2018).

The concept of neurodiversity is an inclusive understanding of Autism that removes the medicalized, deficit understanding of autistic characteristics and refuses to accept the dehumanizing and demeaning stereotypes of media and anecdotes. Autistic participants in Monique Botha, Bridget Dibb and David Frost's 2022 study of Autism and stigma 'rejected person-first

---

2 Zeidan et al. (2022), in a systematic review of prevalence worldwide, have found a median prevalence of 65/10,000 as opposed to 62/10,000 in a previous review in 2012.

language with the argument that they should not be required to remind people of their humanness and to increase the salience of their autistic identity' (Botha et al. 2022, 445). They contend that they are not people with autism but 'autistic people' coexisting with non-autistic people.

The experience of *othering* in society for autistic people is common. Milton et al. (2012) suggest a 'double empathy problem', where the complexities of social interaction between autistic and non-autistic people are a result of both sets of people being unable to read each other's minds. Similarly, Alkhaldi et al. (2019) acknowledge that autistic people may be perceived as lacking empathy or understanding of non-autistic perceptions but equally the same can be said for non-autistic people and their understanding of the autistic experience. The perception that autistic people lack empathy is perpetuated by media depictions of autistic 'savants' or fictional stereotypes such as the comedy-drama film Rain Man and the fictional television character Sheldon Cooper.

Autistic people have described Autism as 'value-neutral, akin to height, skin colour, and handedness, asserting that any value attributed is that of society rather than of autism itself. It is not a disease or a disorder' (Botha et al. 2022, 436). Nonetheless, Hebron and Humphrey (2014) found that bullying is a major issue for young people on the autistic spectrum in mainstream schools as they are vulnerable individuals prone to peer rejection. They emphasize that the 'toxic combination of social difficulties, anxiety and bullying is likely to lead to poor educational outcomes' (Hebron and Humphrey 2014, 30). Research by Hoover and Kaufman (2018) also found that children with ASD are three to four times more likely to be bullied by their peers than children without disabilities or 'typically developing children' (Maïano et al. 2016).

Sterzing et al. (2012) in their study of bullying and ASD suggest that schools need to educate students about ASD, review their inclusion strategies and practices and 'target inclusion of students with ASD into protective peer groups' (1063). They emphasize the need for schools to teach social skills and empathy to students towards their peers with ASD and developmental disabilities. Schools can be difficult places for neurodivergent people. Orsmond et al. (2013), in a US study of social participation among young autistic adults, found that almost one-third of young adults with ASD in a representative national sample were socially isolated. They further found that there was no drastic change to low or very low rates of social participation from high school to early post–high school years even though the context had changed with the transition to adulthood. They recommend a focused intervention on supporting social participation for young adults with ASD from community stakeholders and support groups.

Stigma – External and Internal

Autistic people frequently report 'masking' or camouflaging, using strategies to camouflage the fact that they are on the Autistic spectrum to 'fit in' to the non-autistic world (Dean et al. 2016; Hull et al. 2017). In a study on stigma, Botha et al. (2020) present findings from discussions of autistic people who explain how the negative framing and perceptions of autism can make autistic individuals feel pressure to conceal their status and camouflage as non-autistic. This is despite the impact on their mental health (Cage et al. 2018a).

Moreover, Cooper et al. (2017) indicate that identifying positively with an autistic identity 'mediates the relationship between self-esteem and mental health difficulties'. This identification can be difficult considering Wood and Freeth (2016) have shown that non-autistic people hold multiple stereotypes towards autistic people with only two positive aspects of 'high intelligence' and 'special abilities'. Autistic adults have stated that they are 'caught in a double bind, recognizing that both disclosure and failure to disclose result in negative consequences' (Botha et al. 2022, 435).

The classification of autism as a disability or a deficit is debated by advocates of neurodiversity while acknowledging the wide variation of individual support needs across the autistic spectrum. Michael Oliver, a disabled activist and lecturer, coined the phrase 'social model of disability' in 1981. He stated that 'this new paradigm involves nothing more or less fundamental than a switch away from focusing on the physical limitations of particular individuals to the way the physical and social environment impose limitations upon certain categories of people' (Oliver 1981, 28). Watson (1998, 60) suggests that the social model of disability argues for disability to be seen as a collective experience where the collective results in a political, social and cultural identity. Giri et al. (2021, 104) conclude from their study of people with learning difficulties and/or autism and their carers that disability theories like the 'social model of disability' need to go back to looking at inclusion, citizenship and independence, based on the real-life experience of people with a learning disability.

Autistic Adults

Autism in adults can be more difficult to understand than Autism in children. As Lord et al. (2020, 1692) states,

> Persons with Autism Spectrum Disorders (ASDs), or autistic people, reflecting the preference of many self-advocates will be adults for far longer than they are children, yet we know much less about the behaviour and the trajectories of development into and during adult life than we do about those during childhood.

Bullying in compulsory education, as discussed earlier, has implications for autistic adults and their navigation of adult life. Howlin and Magiati (2017) found, in their study of outcomes for autistic adults, that experiences such as the frequency of bullying in childhood and current levels of perceived stress were the two factors that autistic adults self-reported as contributing to poor quality of life. They also self-reported that better-developed daily living skills and good physical health contributed to a good quality of life (Hong et al. 2016). Milton et al.'s (2022, 1902) revisiting of the double empathy problem ten years on reiterates the need in society for understanding and rapport-building without the assumption that autistic people and their social deficits need normative remediation.

Further Education and Training and Tertiary Education in Ireland

The FET sector provides a continuum of learning opportunities from Level 1 to Level 6 of the National Framework of Qualifications (NFQ) 'focused on both core and specific skills development, accompanied by a range of learner supports to facilitate the active inclusion of all citizens' (SOLAS 2020, 21). At the time of writing in 2023, the Irish government is currently developing a vision for a unified tertiary education and research system to develop Ireland's higher and further education and research and innovation systems. The aim is to provide more 'diverse and aligned learning and development opportunities across a broad spectrum with clear and extensive pathways for learners and researchers and a more seamless system overall'. According to the government department responsible for this realignment, these opportunities will focus on a 'consolidated approach to inclusion across the whole of the tertiary system to enhance strategies to address socio-economic disadvantage and the underrepresentation of groups' (Department of Further and Higher Education, Research, Innovation and Science (DFHERIS) 2022).

Active Inclusion in FET

The SOLAS *Further Education and Training Strategy 2014–2019* states that 'active inclusion means enabling every citizen, notably the most disadvantaged, to fully participate in society including having a job' (SOLAS 2014, 91). The more recent *Future FET: Transforming Learning – The National Further Education and Training Strategy 2020–2024* (SOLAS 2020) has three core pillars of building skills, fostering inclusion and facilitating pathways. These pillars are supported by an inclusive ethos through four key actions: consistent learner support, rooting FET in the community, targeting priority cohorts, and literacy and numeracy supports.

The sixteen Education and Training Boards (ETBs, described in more detail in Chapter 1) have responsibility for education and training programmes through FET, aspects of youth work and formal education provision. FET programmes delivered through the ETB national network offer certification for programmes at levels 1–6 on the National Framework of Qualifications. Their representative body, Education and Training Boards Ireland (ETBI), acknowledges that learners on these programmes come from a,

> spectrum of socially, economically and educationally disadvantaged groups, including those facing literacy, numeracy and digital skills challenges, early school leavers, low skills workers, people who are unemployed, people in employment, Travellers, lone parents, migrants, people suffering from rural isolation and people with disabilities. (ETBI 2021, 12)

A recent study by ETBI of the role, contribution and impact of FET services on Active Inclusion in Ireland found that 'the most commonly identified benefits and outcomes for ETB learners were increased self-confidence and self-esteem (97%), social benefits and outcomes (84.3%), education benefits and outcomes (83.8%), employment benefits and outcomes (76.3%) and community benefits and outcomes (63.6%)' (ETBI 2021, 9). The report acknowledges that adult learners are not a homogenous group but a diverse range of learners with different dimensions including 'previous education, personal disposition, current circumstances and cultural heritage' (2021, 12). Amidst the same report, areas of active inclusion most commonly identified to be prioritized in the future in the ETB FET sector were learner supports, additional resources and funding, and training and CPD for staff. Requests from learners and staff included acknowledging the sensory impact of the learning environment for autistic learners and the need for training for educators and trainers in disabilities such as Autism and ADHD (ETBI 2021, 50).

Although research shows that many autistic adults depend on family and may live at home for longer, Howlin and Magiati (2017, 70) suggest that there is a dearth of research on factors associated with good or poor social and psychological outcomes as few studies consider 'family, school or wider social influences'. They are not alone in their concerns. McGuckin et al. (2014) cite Trant (2011) who outlines the following challenges for further education in ensuring access for students with special education needs (SEN): relatively low numbers accessing the Disability Fund; low participation rates of students with sensory impairments, physical disabilities and multiple disabilities; lack of participation targets; and the fact that only full-time students are eligible (30).

There are some supports. The Fund for Students with Disabilities (which is not means tested) is available to undergraduates with disabilities studying in full-time publicly funded courses that rank at Level 5 or higher on the national qualifications framework. However, FET-run VTOS (Vocational Training Opportunities Scheme), Teagasc (the agriculture and food authority) and part-time and private courses are not eligible. The non-profit organization AHEAD (2023) describes this fund as 'designed to cover many of the educational support requirements which students with disabilities may require to compete on a level playing field with their peers'. The fund does not go directly to the student but to the disability/access officer of the institution who then puts supports in place. To enable this, relevant documentation such as assessment or diagnostic reports to support an application must be supplied by a person with a disability to access services.

On paper, this looks like a useful support structure. However, the support of a disability officer may not be available in all ETB settings. One project between the City of Dublin ETB and the National Learning Network provides a disability officer across eight colleges of further education in Dublin (Rehab Group 2023). Younger students can avail of alternative support as some Youthreach Centres provide individualized support for learners through the Special Educational Needs Initiative (SENI, est. 2007). SENI continues to provide specific forms of support to learners and to build staff capacity in twenty Youthreach centres nationwide (ETBI2021).

Where supports are not in place or are inadequate, autistic adults entering FET may find it challenging to engage in a setting that is less structured than formal education and generally not connected or required to engage with family or other support systems that may have advocated for them in the past. In support of this assertion, Cai and Richdale (2016) found that autistic adults without a formal diagnosis may struggle with an unstructured setting without the previous scaffolding support of teachers and family. Issues regarding diagnosis, disclosure, privacy and GDPR stipulations may inhibit the ability of post-secondary settings to communicate with the autistic student and their support network. While it is acknowledged that 'active inclusion and community development have always been a central tenet of the work of ETBs and FET providers', there is a recognition that more needs to be done with a need for 'consistent and integrated support offered to all learners in all FET settings' (SOLAS 2020, 45).

FET settings do provide learner supports including adult guidance services, learner forums, needs assessment, vocational mentoring and coaching although it has been recognized by ETBI that these vary depending on the region and the setting. In addition, 'small classes allow students to benefit from one-to-one interaction' in Post Leaving Certificate courses (Sneddon 2021, 232).

Current Shortfalls in Support

The number of people with disabilities accessing post-compulsory education is rising. Taking higher education first, a recent report from AHEAD indicates that relative to 2019/20, there have been significant increases in the registration of individuals with higher education disability services including Asperger's/Autism (up 23 per cent), ADD/ADHD (up 24 per cent), and Neurological/Speech and Language (up 18 per cent). Asperger's/Autism was registered for just over eight per cent of all students[3] registered with disability support services (Healy, Ryder and McGuckin 2022).

In terms of FET, the latest figures count 13,098 people with disabilities enrolled in FET courses. This figure constitutes '7.3% of all learners enrolled in the same year. Of the learner enrolments that reported a disability, 45.5% were men and 54.5% were women' (SOLAS 2019). Sixty-six per cent of these adults were older than twenty-five years of age and these enrolments are concentrated among Adult Literacy, Community Education, and Back to Education Initiative (BTEI) programmes (Dulee-Kinsolving and Guerin 2020). It is not possible to identify the prevalence of autistic learners in the data as this information is not collated. Transitioning from school to FET has been identified as a challenging process. One report commented that 'in contrast to higher education, there were few, if any, targeted initiatives to support access, transfer and progression for students with SEN and initiatives and when they occurred, tended to be localised' (McGuckin et al. 2014, 26).

The National Disability Authority and National Council for Special Education (2017) recommend that a mapping exercise be carried out to understand and identify the areas of need to prepare young people with disabilities for life after school. This would consider 'responsibilities for delivering the supports, identification of individuals/organizations who are suitably equipped to deliver the supports and resource implications (funding, staff, training, etc.)' (National Disability Authority 2017, 20). Their findings reflect the recommendations of Doyle, McGuckin and Shevlin (2017) and their study of parent perspectives of supported transition planning for young people with special educational needs and disabilities (SEND) in Ireland. They found that transition partnerships require the 'active involvement of young people with SEND, their families, schools and providers of post-secondary education' (Doyle et al. 2017, 279). The researchers suggest that there are opportunities to develop action plans, interactive online tools of accessible and portable e-portfolios and the 'acquisition of hard and soft skills'. These tools, developed

---

3 8.3 per cent ($n = 1,484$) of the total number of students of 17,866 registering with disability support services in 2020/2021.

collectively and continuously adaptable, can potentially be transferred for use in post-secondary settings. Similar recommendations were made by McGuckin et al. (2014) who suggest a national policy on the transition of people with Special Educational Needs (SEN) to further and higher education and that the state consider,

> the development of targeted access initiatives for further education provision (as happened for higher education) to increase the capacity of further education to support the academic and social needs of students with SEN making the transition to, and progressing through, further education. (McGuckin et al. 2014, 100)

Much more recently, the UN Initial Report of Ireland under the Convention on the Rights of Persons with Disabilities (2021) found that, in FET,

> Specialist Training Providers (STP) deliver flexible training programmes for people with disabilities including ICT and vocational multi-skills. Specialist vocational training can feature additional training duration, adapted equipment, transport arrangements, and enhanced programme content as required. An enhanced trainer-learner ratio is available on these programmes. In 2019, 3,705 students participated in Specialist Training Provision. (Committee on the Rights of Persons with Disabilities 2021, 47)

The same report informs us that SOLAS is currently conducting an independent evaluation of STP.

The decision to disclose also influences the ability of the autistic learner to access services in education and training settings. The limitations of health services including mental health and the cost of assessments and supports through private providers make the production of documentation a challenge for many. Recent changes in SEN provision in formal education recognize the deficit of key services such as the assessment of ASD in the health system by relaxing the criteria of proof of assessment while also acknowledging the need for the provision of specific educational and behavioural supports in formal education. The United Nations Convention on the Rights of Persons with Disabilities (UNCRPD) (United Nations 2007) states parties shall 'ensure that persons with disabilities are able to access general tertiary education, vocational training, adult education and lifelong learning without discrimination and on an equal basis with others' (cited in McGuckin et al. 2014, 16). Ireland ratified the Convention on the Rights of Persons with Disabilities (CRPD) on 20 March 2018 (Department of Children, Equality, Disability, Integration and Youth 2021).

Widening Access to Higher Education

There is an increasing body of research evidence that reflects the challenges facing autistic people in universities including challenges in social participation (Anderson et al. 2019), limited student engagement (Elias and White 2017) and not receiving the university supports they need (Personela et al. 2020). Although the autistic students regarded 'caring relationships as the most favourable supporting factors', Pesonen et al. (2020, 18) point out that 'participants had expectations of individualized support which was also related to perceived supporting factors and shortcomings in those'. Cage and Howes (2020) identified two sub-themes relating to a lack of proactive support in college, namely not knowing *who* could have helped and *what* could have helped. The autistic people they engaged with described needing one centralized contact 'as expressing their difficulties to many different people was exhausting' (Cage and Howes 2020, 1673). We know that environmental interventions such as peer mentoring, in particular, have shown effectiveness in higher education settings (Siew et al. 2017). In support of this, MacLeod (2010) suggests that 'autistic students supporting each other can be an important and valued form of peer support', that there is a place for 'tailored, context-specific online networks', and that these approaches provide 'space for developing collective consciousness and personal self-confidence to develop strong leadership from autistic voices to represent the autistic population' (MacLeod 2010, 23).

In their study of what autistic students want, Beardon et al. (2009, 42) contend that 'valuing diversity necessarily involves a degree of sensitivity from individuals and a cultural shift from the top away from tolerating, to facilitating, towards valuing'. This 'cultural shift' in the recognition of autism may be changing the approach of tertiary education towards 'valuing' and is only possible because of increased representation of autistic people through representative groups and charities. In my view, there is also more understanding from academics and educators that inclusion necessitates action.

In 2018, Dublin City University (DCU) collaborated with AsIAm and Specialisterne Ireland to become the world's first 'Autism Friendly University', a designation informed by the conclusion of a research project with students and staff (Sweeney 2018).[4] This led to the development of eight principles of an

---

[4] The Neurodivergent Society, the first of its kind in Europe, was established in September 2019 by Laoćín Brennan and has grown to be an inspiring and exciting model for recognition and inclusion of neurodiversity in education. The society, with some support from DCU, aims to provide a community where like-minded students are accepted and supported, and the promotion of awareness and acceptance of neurodiversity is accepted as a benefit to society (DCU Neurodivergent Society Constitution 2019).

autism-friendly university including encouraging and enabling autistic students to participate in university life, building capacity to equip autistic students for academic and social life in university and combatting stigma associated with autism. The aforementioned accompanying report by Sweeney et al. (2018, 5) found that, although most autistic students felt they had the academic skills to attend DCU, only half felt that they had the social skills needed to succeed at university. As indicated at the beginning of this chapter, experiences of social exclusion, including being bullied and left out by their peers, especially during the teenage years, could at least partially explain why socializing may be particularly emotionally charged for someone with multiple, negative peer-group interactions (Beardon and Edmonds 2007). In 2023, a further phase of the DCU project was launched with an expanded remit to address the need to support autistic employees.

While further details on the landscape within higher education are beyond the scope of this chapter, readers may be interested in studies on a tendency for staff to act in response to situations rather than proactively (Wray and Houghton) and the importance of a Universal Design Approach (Clouder et al. 2020) which will be discussed in more detail shortly.

Teaching Neurodivergent Learners in FET

There is a paucity of specific research available on the experience of neurodivergent learners in FET in Ireland. Elias et al. (2019, 263), in their study of educators' perspectives of transitions for students with Autism in post-secondary education in the United States (US), observed challenges in the areas of competence, autonomy and independence, and the development and sustainment of interpersonal relationships. In a separate study, findings from interviews with parents and young autistic adults in the US found that all participants made it clear that 'supports and services [in post-secondary education settings] needed to be flexible enough to meet individual needs and be more comprehensive, continuous, and integrated in order to be most useful' (Sosnowy et al. 2018, 37). Neurodivergent people seek diversity, equity and inclusion (DEI), appropriate disability accommodations and supports acknowledging sensory issues and challenges, and accessibility of communication. This accessibility facilitates the need of neurodivergent learners to include others in their support network and use accessible modalities of communication with stakeholders when in post-secondary education (Dwyer et al. 2022).

In my view, much of what the National Council for Special Education (NCSE) and the Department of Education has provided as guidelines for schools and teachers working with autistic students in formal education setting has relevance for educators and autistic adults in FET or university settings. Some 13,703 students (1.55 per cent of all students) in Irish schools have been diagnosed with ASD, which is one in every sixty-five students in school (NCSE 20165;). The Department of Education has highlighted that teachers require specific expertise in areas such as understanding the 'characteristics of autistic learners; implications for teaching and learning; individualised planning and assessment; incorporating the particular interests and motivations of autistic learners; teaching and learning of social and communication skills; and the generalisation of skills' (cited in Government of Ireland 2022, 2). Inspectors in post-primary schools in Ireland noted that where teaching was effective for autistic students, it included 'highly differentiated approaches, good overall teaching skills, very good use of visual materials, support for self-regulation and targeted work on the development of social skills' (Department of Education and Skills 2020, 44). Practitioners in FET also need to develop pedagogical skills and awareness of neurodiversity and the characteristics of neurodivergent learners. The following two approaches are relevant:

– Universal Design for Learning for an inclusive understanding and design of learning environments.
– Co-participative research approaches supporting communities of research practice of autistic and non-autistic people.

Each approach will now be discussed.

Universal Design for Learning

Universal Design for Learning is a set of principles and guidelines that aim to develop expert learners by using a variety of teaching methods in order to lower barriers to learning and give all learners equal opportunities to succeed (AHEAD 2021). This can be done through multiple means of engagement, multiple means of representation and multiple means of action and expression (CAST 2018). The UDL framework recognizes that 'every learner is different, that learning or training needs to be adaptable and responsive and that, in fact, there is no such thing as the average learner' (Burgstahler 2009).

SOLAS (2020) has embedded the use of UDL in its FET national strategy by stating that all FET programmes should provide 'consistent and integrated support offered to all learners in all FET settings' and by 'applying good practice guides and toolkits on inclusive practice across the system, adopting a universal design for learning (UDL) approach in shaping its future provision' (SOLAS 2020, 45). *A Conceptual Framework of Universal Design for Learning (UDL) for the Irish Further Education and Training Sector* has been designed by Quirke and McCarthy (2020) for SOLAS with training and resources available to FET practitioners nationwide. While some educators believe that they already adopted a universal design approach to teaching, the emphasis on UDL in FET and higher education focuses on a shared philosophy and approach that 'can be applied and adopted by all practitioners' (Quirke and McCarthy 2020, 42).

The framework emphasizes that the 'practitioner that leads the learning process is central to the experience of the learner'. They acknowledge that the practitioner can be a teacher or a trainer, a vocational expert or working in learner support. The focus is not on the professional but on the learning experience that is provided to all in an inclusive learning environment. UDL is 'very much about teamwork and taking a multidisciplinary approach' (42). The new framework for UDL in FET puts the learner at the centre of the 'UDL wheel for FET' with the inclusive engagement of practitioners supporting and facilitating the inclusive learning experience. The UDL Wheel for FET is underpinned by four values that are central to UDL: 'Inclusion – recognising that the core philosophy is one of inclusion; Intentionality – intending to adopt and practice inclusion and UDL; Appreciation – recognising the value of being interdisciplinary and multidisciplinary on a shared inclusive agenda; and Acceptance – that the philosophy and practice needs to be instinctive, thus believing that it is ever changing and reactive to the audience it seeks to engage with' (58).

Grummell and Murray (2015, 437) point out that students in FET are not the same as students in second and higher levels as they are typically 'non-traditional, interested in vocational education and accessing education in alternative ways'. In particular, learners in community and adult education can experience a setting 'closer to social movements, community development on the one hand, and to personal, remedial or human resource development on the other hand' (Connolly 2006, 4). Consequently, the UDL approach is particularly appropriate for FET learners as FET 'is both learner-centred and participative in its pedagogical approach' (SOLAS 2014, 56). Moreover, David Rose, a key proponent of Universal Design for Learning points out that UDL puts the label 'disabled' on the curriculum rather than the learner (cited in Quirke and McCarthy 2020, 41).

Davies et al. (2013, 210) concluded that as little as five hours of group instruction for education instructors on the use of UDL principles and teaching strategies effectively increases the implementation of those strategies and that students reported a positive change in engagement. In principle, there is scope to ensure this happens. The FET *Professional Learning and Development Statement of Strategy 2020–2024* aims to 'create a more powerful culture of learning among FET practitioners; facilitate easier access to professional learning and development and build confidence and capability of FET practitioners to assure a quality learner experience' (SOLAS n.d., 9).

Co-participative Research

The greater use of co-participative research approaches at all levels of the research process – prioritization of research topics, funding, research design, data collection, analysis and write-up – can contribute to the promotion of the voices of autistic people in research that can be used as evidence for improvements in social policy and societal change. Fletcher-Watson et al. (2019, 944) suggest that participatory research includes 'leadership by autistic researchers, partnership with autistic people or allies in research, engagement with the community (e.g. via social media) and consultation with relevant individuals or community organisations'. In practice, Fanjoy and Bragg (2019, 5) acknowledge that 'despite the ideals of democratic participation and shared knowledge production, research projects take place within a real-world context of limited resources, short timelines and unequal power relations, all of which come to play a role in how knowledge is produced, shared and experienced' (2019, 5). Fletcher-Watson et al. conclude that there is an opportunity to 'create a burgeoning, merged community of research practice, including autistic and non-autistic people and other partners who work collaboratively to create facilitative environments and resolve important, relevant questions' (Fletcher-Watson et al. 2019, 951). The use of co-participative research approaches is growing with the voices of autistic adults as researchers and participants contributing to an important evidence base. In my view, this evidence base has the potential to inform and transform educational and societal environments and practices for autistic and non-autistic people.

Conclusion

This chapter explored the complex experience of autistic adults negotiating neurotypical education and training environments and the potential ways that FET can accommodate neurodiversity in the learning environment. Autistic adults and their families, as the primary caregivers in childhood and allies in adulthood, are navigating a complex societal landscape where awareness of autism and neurodiversity is slowly growing. The change in approach can be seen by social movements and calls for the assessment and presentation of autism to change from a solely medicalized model to a social model that acknowledges the complexity of individuals, their needs and their personal journey through society.

The challenge of teaching and supporting autistic adults in tertiary settings is also explored in light of ongoing change in the FET and tertiary education space. There have been welcome and positive moves to inclusive approaches such as Universal Design for Learning that can bring real change and action towards implementing intentional humanist approaches of dialogue, equity and co-construction and co-participative research approaches that align with Critical Disability Studies and Critical Autism Studies that 'aim to address the lived experience of autism and actively engages stakeholders, including autistic individuals' (MacLeod 2019).

It is clear that there are initiatives and programmes being implemented to address inclusive practice in FET and to underpin the State's commitment to active inclusion. The commitment to the consolidation of approaches to inclusion across the tertiary education system (DFHERIS 2022) and a recognition of the need for a consistent and integrated support offered to all learners (SOLAS 2020) is welcomed. It is important that the needs of autistic people are identified, acknowledged and met as part of this integrated support. This can be done through a range of methods including an examination of existing research on and from the autistic experience of post-secondary education, an exploration of teaching practices and pedagogies from formal education to inform continuing professional development for FET practitioners and, as a priority, through seeking out and listening to the voices of neurodivergent people.

Chapter 5

ADULT LEARNING IN GROUPS: 'A PRACTICE OF FREEDOM'

Bríd Connolly

Now, after a few years of lockdowns, it's the ideal opportunity to unpack what happens when adults learn in groups, in face-to-face environments. These lockdown years revealed – at least to me – a dark underbelly of civil society (Gallagher 2022), with a proliferation of attacks on emancipation (Evaristo 2022) that has accorded with the rise of right-wing politics and the elections of Trump, Modi, Orban, Erdoğan and, the more recent, Meloni.

Meeting face-to-face in groups contrasts meaningfully with virtual meetings, with regard to the social aspects of learning, and the practice of equality, emancipation and critical reflection. A central principle of adult learning in groups is consciousness-raising or, as Freire names it, conscientization (1972), to alert learners to the complex and nuanced causes of oppression and inequality, with emancipatory intentions. Despite the advances in technology, especially with Zoom and MS Teams, which responded in solidarity to the critical situation of the pandemic, the social aspect of learning was, and still is, extremely difficult in the virtual world. In group work terms, practice was focused on *task*, that is, doing the job of imparting information, communication, and making decisions, but hardly any space for *maintenance*, that is, the care, repair and upkeep of interpersonal relationships, what Klaus calls soft skills (2007). I draw on the integration of process and goal in another publication – *Adult Learning in Groups* (Connolly 2008) – to illustrate. We can see that technology works very well on TV news and current affairs, but not so well for TV comedy and panels, where an audience is needed to make it experiential, emotional and interactive.

Further, while pennies might no longer be legal tender, they remain useful in illustrating the insights we have developed because of social changes in the recent past. For me, a penny conclusively dropped when education moved online during the pandemic. Again, this was enacted in solidarity, with people going to great lengths to learn how to use the technology and to extend its capacity to facilitate learning. It was the best that could be done in such a critical time. But with time to reflect, it has become clear that education is in danger of being perceived, not as an essential element of becoming more fully human in community with one another but, rather, as a narrow, instrumentalized process of *teaching and testing*. That is, teaching by one-way lectures because it was impractical, if not impossible, to engage in dialogue and discussion. And testing with assignments based on the memory of the content of the lectures. Freire formulated this approach as the *banking concept* of education (1972, 45–47), with the students framed as empty vessels to be filled by the teachers' inputs. During the pandemic, the scramble to employ online platforms, like MS Teams and Zoom as the conduit for teaching, was quickly followed by an acute focus on examinations, culminating in the conclusion that testing was the only way to assess learners. Sarah Coss discusses assessment in great critical depth in her chapter but my point here is to highlight that the omission of all of the other dimensions of group work in education, such as dialogue, discussion, groups, project work, connection, care, relationship and so on, projects a clear message that these are seen as secondary elements of education, rather than essential. An approach without these core aspects of group work discourages critical consciousness and, ultimately, amounts to education that funnels students into professional, skilled and unskilled work and the associated social benefits (or not).

In this chapter, I focus on adult learning in groups but, as an aside, I think it is important to acknowledge that testing, particularly the Leaving Certificate (Ireland's school-based terminal exam), as highlighted by the Department of Education,[1] reduces education to a series of measurable results which determines unequal outcomes for the population. Further, the harder the learners work in providing answers within the matrix of acceptable measurable responses, the better their results. The ultimate outcome of teaching and testing is that people who follow the set curriculum are rewarded for it. This is the opposite of critical thinking, citizenship, democracy and social participation and is closer to the marketization of education in a neoliberal economy (Fitzsimons 2017a). It establishes inequality and unfairness, rather than ensuring that everyone has a basic level of education, at the very least. And it perpetuates the homogeneity of

---

1 There have been a number of name changes to government departments. The Department of Education (1924–1997), then Department of Education and Science (1997–2010), then Department of Education and Skills (2010–2020) and then a return to Department of Education 2020–date).

the teaching profession, those who achieve high Leaving Certificate results at the traditional age, benefiting from these inequalities and reproducing them in the *teaching and testing* deficit model of education.

However, the outcomes of this deficit model may not be altogether clear, ultimately. As mentioned above, we have also witnessed the rise of conservative politics, locally and globally, from the emergence of nationalistic political parties, like The National Party in Ireland and their role in the current anti-immigration campaigning, to Trumpism in the USA and nationalist Hinduism in India. Language has emerged to disparage progressive social movements, with the derisory use of terms such as 'woke', 'cancel culture', 'identity politics', 'social justice warriors' (SJW) and 'all lives matter' (ALM), undermining social movements, particularly in the western world, since the 1970s. That is the backlash to the social progress of minorities and subordinate groups, including women, people in poverty, Black and Brown people, LGBTQI+ and people with disabilities. What we have witnessed in recent years is resistance to the quest for equality by the conservative right resulting in what Evaristo (2022) calls 'the war on emancipation'.

I know that other contributors to this collection will likely explore the rise of the right in the context of adult and community education, but I want to focus on the framing of the term *woke*, what it means, what are the implications and where all these elements fit in group work in adult learning.

And so, I reflect on the social changes, particularly in Ireland but linked to global trends, that we have witnessed since I wrote *Adult Learning in Groups* (Connolly 2008), which was written in the exhilaration after the publication of the *White Paper on Adult Education: Learning for Life* (Department of Education and Science). As adult and community educators, we expected a new era in plain sight for the field, combined with advanced theories in discipline. However, this did not come to pass.

All the same, I continue the argument made in *Adult Learning in Groups* (Connolly 2008) that learning in groups is a paradigm for the social progress of equity and equality. Equality has been discussed in philosophy since the Greek philosophers but this discussion has moved into a more complex and nuanced interrogation with the advent of human, civil and cultural rights (Gosepath 2021). It is inextricably linked to justice, as framed by the work of John Rawls (1971) on justice as fairness (Wener 2021). Lynch and Baker (Lynch and Baker 2005) have taken up this baton, particularly in relation to equality in education and the foundation of the Equality Studies Centre, at University College Dublin (UCD).

The history of adult and community education shows that, in the wider Irish society, it has always addressed social inequality, drawing on social justice, particularly from Catholic social teaching with which Freire identified, but framed for the more recent conditions by Khechen (2013) which again draws on Rawls (1971). Adult, community and further education, now awkwardly renamed as FET, has been intimately involved in social justice, from literacy issues and the failures of formal education to the evolution of praxis and non-traditional doctorates. As the discipline has developed its distinct ontology and epistemology, learning in groups has revealed the social aspect of human development, the profound shift from cognitive individualism, more typical in mainstream education. Simultaneously, on the personal level, people's lives have been transformed, as consciousness-raising exposed the social aspects of personal experience. Further, critical reflection on our own strengths and limitations disrupts the conservative framing of binary oppositions, such as learning or teaching, theory or practice, strong or weak, thinking or doing, leaders or followers and so on. The major flaw in binary thinking is that one of the two is always, or nearly always, subordinate to the other, so followers are subordinate to leaders, and so on. Yet, leaders in a democratic society do not require unquestioning followers who will do as they are told, without protest. What democratic leaders need is co-operation, interrogation and solidarity, with input on the decisions of the leadership, in contrast to authoritarian leadership.

In terms of education, teachers, lecturers, tutors, educators, etc. are not the opposite of learners, with that implication of active practitioners and passive learners. Adult educators do draw on their own prior learning, but they also learn with students. And further, learners do not fall neatly into the traditional binary divisions of those who are 'brainy', that is, academically intelligent, versus 'thick', that is, those who do not adhere to the markers of academic success. In these traditional divisions, this is mirrored in schooling with a vocational emphasis in contrast to schooling with a scholarly emphasis. However, adult education focuses instead on what it is to be fully human in a society that values everyone.

Further, group work in adult learning disrupts traditional hierarchies, especially with regard to class, gender, race and ethnicity. For many people, even the architecture of a traditional classroom and lecture theatre re-enforces the hierarchy of teachers over students, while group work must take place in circles or clusters, all on the same level. And, in adult learning group work, we have access to, what Thompson calls, 'really useful knowledge' (1996) when she draws on Johnson's history of the term (1988). The facilitated group space allows us the opportunity to discuss the meanings and implications of our knowledge, experience and thoughts. In the next section, I will discuss what I mean by group work, in the light of developments within the discipline of adult and community education.

Working in Groups

Group work in adult and community education is how we collaborate in order to pool resources. In groups, collaboration is facilitated through discussion and dialogue; input, particularly on wider social structures and trends; thinking out loud, reflecting, arguing, challenging our assumptions, learning new knowledge and creating new knowledge. Group work starts where people are at (Freire 1972). However, group work facilitates the transformation from that starting point to deeper social, cultural and personal analysis. Interdependence within groups is central (Smith 2008). This is contrasted with individualized independence, which is probably more typical in formal education, or task orientated, which is more typical in teamwork.

However, group work is not confined to education. When group work is applied to contexts other than adult education, it is framed within the original theory of those contexts. Thus, in the business world, where skills predominate, the term *soft skills* is often applied to working in teams, where communication, interpersonal relationships and self-direction are needed. And the binary opposite is hard skills, which are seen as expertise in technical and practical terms. Thus, hard skills are considered the primary skills and soft skills are secondary. Interestingly, sports teams seem to be more aware of these so-called soft skills and managers and coaches like Jim Gavin of Dublin GAA football, or Jürgen Klopp of Liverpool FC, clearly understand the role of soft skills, and make the most of them. Obviously, hard skills are primary in winning matches but in this framing, soft skills gain a status that was traditionally seen as irrelevant or substantially subordinate. Work and sports teams have raised the status of soft skills, but in quite a utilitarian way.

This can be referred to as purpose, task or goal-centred, with due attention to the well-being of the people involved. All the same, group work in adult learning can borrow from teamwork, especially with regard to finding a role for every member of the group and helpful or unhelpful behaviour, for example, dealing with difficult people in a constructive way, as Klaus maintains (2007). Group work is thus a model for inclusivity, participation, democracy and equality.

Alternatively, another context for group work that prevails is that of therapy or therapeutic settings, that of enabling and facilitating clients to heal their trauma and hurt. Obviously, our prior experience of family, community, education, health and so on, both conscious and unconscious, is helpful in sorting out our personal issues and trauma in therapy. But it is vital to remember that our earlier lives are also shaped by wider power structures, class, race and gender. Adult and community education has the wider purpose of analysing those structures and experiences. And these wider hierarchies of power and influence are central in connecting the personal and the social, viewing and analysing an individual experience through the lens of broader social phenomena. For example, if adult learners have difficult experiences in school, they can bring those experiences into the adult learning group, mistaking adult educators for strict, hurtful teachers. Thus, adult educators can understand it when students express hostility, fear, uncertainty or other negativities. This is often described as client-centred, and when applied to education, it is centred on the needs of students and pupils – namely, learner-centred. Again, group work in adult learning can mirror this approach by starting with the learners and their needs and desires. This comes in particular from Carl Rogers and his work based on a humanistic philosophy (1995).

A further model of group work stems from adult learning in groups in the USA, particularly in the work of Myles and Zilphia Horton on civil and labour rights in Highlander Folk School. Highlander was modelled on the Folk High Schools of Europe, inspired by Grundtvig's vision in the 1830s of education for the people (Danish Folk High Schools 2022). Highlander started in the 1930s, in response to these wider hierarchies of power and the oppression of workers, both industrial and agricultural. The Hortons were impressed by the informality of the Danish model, the close relationship between teachers and participants, and the use of culture (Highlander Research and Education Centre 2022). Highlander quickly became associated with human and civil rights movements, with special connections with Rosa Parks, Dr Martin Luther King, Jr, and Pete Seeger (Horton 1998). And, interestingly, Zilphia Horton, a musician, composed the anthem of these movements, *We Shall Overcome* (Hodge 2017).

Horton worked with small groups, in order to understand fully how adult education worked in practice. This became the template for transformative adult education. But what Brian and Elbert (2005) discovered in their research was that the characteristics of transformative education show that small groups in themselves are the essential ingredient rather than simply a practical vehicle to get to transformation. These characteristics include the following:

1. Providing a safe place to encourage discourse and reflection.
2. Assuming adults bring with them a wealth of prior knowledge and experience.
3. Helping people discover they are not alone; others share similar problems.
4. Facilitating independent, critical thinking and planning for the future.
5. Helping people (especially the disempowered) to develop their voice and confidence to act.
6. Solving problems and answering questions through synergy.
7. Encouraging lifelong and diverse learning as means for a change.

8. Promoting the idea that everyone is an important member of a community and can work within it to make changes.
9. Implementing continuous improvement and effective organizational principles.

(Brian and Elbert 2005, 5)

These characteristics resonate in the discussion in Chapter 5 of the government *White Paper Learning for Life* (Department of Education and Science 2000, 113) which focuses on 'Community Education' as it developed in Ireland, which includes the following:

1. Its rootedness in the community, not just in terms of physical location but also in that its activists have lived and worked for many years within the community and have deep knowledge and respect for its values, culture and circumstances, and an understanding of community needs and capacity.
2. Its problem solving, flexible focus, based on trust.
3. Its focus on process rather than syllabus – participants are engaged from the outset as equal partners in identifying needs, designing and implementing programmes and adapting them on an ongoing basis.
4. Its respect for participants and its reflection on their lived experience.

Collective synergy is essential in these characteristics, fostered by interdependence within groups and, most importantly, the recognition and acknowledgment of this interdependence.

Nevertheless, when people participate in group work in adult learning, regardless of the prior sources and expectations, they may have a transformative experience as they begin to look at themselves and their worlds in profoundly different ways.

Of course, it is not just a case of creating a circle with a group. Everything depends on the *intention*. So even if it is learner-centred, we need to be critical and curious: Is the intent to create a learning environment that fosters personal and social development, or is the intent to maintain individualized success?

That is, what takes place in adult and community education is more than learner-centred, including interdependence, collaboration, dialogue and so on. As the White Paper says, a key priority area is Consciousness-Raising, allied to Citizenship, Cultural Development and Community Development (Department of Education and Science 2000, 12). This echoes Freire's conscientization which he locates as being central to critical pedagogy (1972). But Freire's conscientization is not identical to feminist consciousness-raising as framed in the White Paper. It took bell hooks to extend Freire's work into a 'really useful' analysis of gender relations with her take on feminism, community and, centrally, transgression (hooks 1984, 1994, 2000, 2003). She asserts that

> without the capacity to think critically about our selves and our lives, none of us would be able to move forward, to change, to grow. In our society, which is so fundamentally anti-intellectual, critical thinking is not encouraged. (hooks 1994, 202)

In other words, consciousness-raising is the process that enables us to think critically about our own lived experience and how it is shaped by wider social forces. She focuses on the practice of thinking critically in an anti-intellectual context but, further, that intellectual interrogation investigates the causes and sources of the wider social forces. Freire recognizes the impact of wider social forces on lived experiences, but he doesn't recognize that gender is one of those wider social forces. And hooks asserts that it is (and I heartily agree, of course). Drawing on her own scholarship and experience, she argues convincingly that feminist thought is a crucial dimension in conscientization. This is the main purpose of the consciousness-raising process.

Consciousness-raising Groups

While I recognize that there is still a significant way to go, the women's movement was probably the most important social movement of the twentieth century. The status of 51 per cent of the population as 'the second sex', as Beauvoir (1953) put it, was a key turning point in challenging the essentialist perspective, that human society was organized on the basis of essential qualities, that were unchanging and unchangeable in time. That is, having a universal validity, rather than a social, ideological and intellectual one (Miriam Webster Dictionary 2022). Beauvoir's phrase, *One is not born a woman, but rather becomes one* (1953), encapsulated the concept of social construction, and thus laid the foundations not only for women but also for the social construction of all categories, including race, class, sexuality, ethnicity, ability and all the other groupings which were considered *The Other*, that is, subordinate to the superordinate elites, especially the hierarchy, patriarchy, royalty, aristocracy and rulers of all hues.

Further, the Women's Movement is a grassroots movement, driven by the people who participated rather than a self-appointed leadership from outside the membership. According to McCammon, there were thousands of grassroots meetings and groups in the 1970s in the USA (McCammon et al. 2017). And this was beginning in Ireland too, at that time. For example, women met in a restaurant in Dublin, Gaj's, in the form of a consciousness-raising group. They planned direct action, with the Contraceptives Train protest in 1971, organized by the Irish Women's Liberation Movement, as it was at that time (Stopper 2006; Sweetman 2020), to protest the ban on contraception in the Irish constitution. This ban was based on the Catholic ethos that prevailed as a national ethos in 1937 when the second constitution of Ireland was put to a referendum. Incidentally, the result of that referendum was tight, 56 per cent in favour, 44 per cent against, approximately (Government of Ireland 2020). Consciousness-raising transformed the traditional – albeit relatively recent – politics of left and right, with the potential of social movements. This consciousness-raising amounts to an awakening of the mind and body to what is often referred to, for the lack of a better term, as social reality (Yu 2018).

In terms of adult and community education, consciousness-raising has proved very influential in metamorphoses from traditional pedagogy to critical pedagogy as a cornerstone in education for equality and emancipation. In a recent conversation with Ira Shor and Ted Fleming, Ira Shor confirmed that Paulo Freire's wife was his foremost mentor (Shor 2021). I was lucky enough to be part of that dialogue on the legacy of Freire to adult education both in Ireland and internationally, organized by the Department of Adult and Community Education at Maynooth University in November 2021. Ira Shor confirmed that Nita Araujo Freire, Freire's wife, participated in feminist consciousness-raising groups and this participation was crucial to her influence on Freire's framing of critical pedagogy (Kirylo and Kirylo 2011). And this is further confirmed by Freire's own assertion that her notes were vital to *Pedagogy of Hope: Reliving the Pedagogy of the Oppressed* (Freire 1994). So again, it's important to stress that Freire's concept of conscientization is close, but not identical in meaning and timing to consciousness-raising. Rosenthal (1984) asserts that consciousness-raising emerged from the women's movement in the USA, as I said above. A piece of research carried out in the 1970s presents an insightful overview of the experience of the participants (Kravetz 1978), with a focus on the outcomes of participation. However, while Rosenthal argues that consciousness-raising groups influenced psychotherapy, each of these groupings has different intentions and outcomes, as well as structures, with consciousness-raising groups self-organized and members taking facilitative and participative roles as appropriate, while qualified therapists are essential in the psychotherapeutic groups.

In contrast, as learning in groups emerged as an appropriate practice in adult and community education, and continued to be encouraged within this newly aligned FET sector, the discipline ring-fenced the original intention, that is, the quest for equality and fairness through education and deprioritized outcomes, personal and social development in the context of relationships, critical thinking, citizenship and democracy.

However, there is a vital difference between the consciousness-raising groups I spoke about earlier and group work in education. In consciousness-raising groups, there was no facilitator, but there was a rule that everyone had the opportunity to speak and that everyone else listened. In education, there is an additional member, that is, 'the adult educator' (or 'teacher' if this expression sits more comfortably with you). The role of critical educators includes their knowledge base, both experiential and scholarly; their approaches to facilitation; their commitment to emancipatory social change and their commitment to both speaking and, very importantly, listening to discussion and linking it to social analysis. Thus, their role in learning groups is to move discussion, experience and inputs from the individual to the social, from the personal to the political, as the women's movement says.

The Politics of Education: Overt and Covert Purposes

Rubenson (2011) explores the breadth of adult learning and education, drawing on thinking around the world, from the USA to Bangladesh, from Australia to South Africa, and highlights topics from women's community education and adult learning for seniors to HIV and nation-building adult education. Both the participants and the adult educators are drawn from a wide range of backgrounds and experience, for example, labour, disability, poverty, gender and many others immersed in social activism.

On the other hand, education as a social institution rarely embraces this scope, focusing instead on outcomes related to the economy, social capital and higher incomes, for example, in Roser and Ortiz-Opina (2016). That is, education, including schooling, training and university, is primarily seen as the route to the world of work and the economy of the state. However, this is both an overt and a covert agenda, and it diverts attention away from the wider purposes, that is, building a better society, which should be central to adult education. Moreover, the binary set-up of mainstream education, as explored above, reinforces the diversion. Even the focus on meritocracy takes away from the overall purpose, with the individualization of merit and the associated rewards prioritized over everything else. As mainstream education shifts slowly towards learner-centredness, group projects and some elements of working in groups, it still misses the crucial aspect of consciousness (Seth 2021). Seth's research shows that consciousness occurs in the body, specifically in the brain, with the implication that it remains individualized. However, uniquely focusing on the brain fails to disrupt the status quo which can only be achieved by collective consciousness raising,

Adult learning in groups is essential to this perspective. First, it disrupts the teaching and testing dyad. Further, it shifts the focus of education from the individual in the classroom to a learning environment in the wider society. Finally, it casts a critical prism on the education system as it has developed in response to economic, social and political forces.

Group Work and Care

Noddings positions care at the heart of education, which ought to create loving and lovable human beings and not simply academic results (1992). However, we know that in the intervening years since 1992, in the USA at least, schools have become a site of struggle with regard to what's on the curriculum, not to mention the appalling shootings targeted at children and teachers. Thus, in spite of care, critical thinking and the innovative pedagogy of hope, that have been proposed over the years, education is still a social institution where the overt and covert curricula compete with one another to have a major impact on society. Bernadine Evaristo, in her essay on BBC Radio 4, tells of the campaign by a school authority in South Dakota to ban her novel, *Girl, Woman, Other*, on the grounds that it is unsuitable for 17- and 18-year-old students. Her book is about women's struggle, but also about love, care and hope, yet the school authorities deem it unsuitable for school children. This type of campaign is waged on many fronts but, in this case, Evaristo argues that the aforementioned war on emancipatory ideas challenges the status quo. In other words, she argues that it is a war on *woke*, a war on consciousness-raising, and resistance to the potential for equality and fairness.

In Ireland, thankfully, we are not at that point, though we have had a very long history of book banning, with the explicit intention of keeping Ireland free from 'corruption', as defined by state-appointed censors. While book banning may be in the past, the struggle for equality is not over. Kathleen Lynch has long been a critic of mainstream education in reproducing the status quo, especially in her work with colleagues on equality in education, with a critique of the approach based on equality of access for groups who would otherwise be excluded (Lynch and Baker 2005). Further, she agrees with hooks (2000) on the issue that human society cannot survive without love and care, but hooks – and Lynch – argues that it is primarily perceived as a private matter rather than a political, economic or even a public matter. If we look at the elements identified in Highlander and the White Paper, that is, safety, trust and community, it is clear that these could not happen without care and love.

When we examine group work in adult learning, that is, the way we collaborate in order to pool resources, we acknowledge that adult educators are vital in order to bring new knowledge into the group but also to ensure fairness and equality in dialogue and discussion, drawing on their own continuous learning (O'Neill 2015). Members of the learning group embody social factors, from status to class, from experience to prior knowledge. Adult educators must ensure that these social factors do not weigh in favour or against other members, with a particular focus on their own embodied factors. Equality and fairness underpinnings come from thinking on justice, equality and fairness, explored above, but there is also a radical or critical humanistic dimension to it (Plummer 2022).

Critical humanism extends Rogers' client-centred approach, by embracing wider social progression, including the liberation movements of the late twentieth century and into the present, including feminism, LGBTQI+, race, ethnicity, disability and so on, such that every adult learning group not only 'includes' as the terminology goes but changes its nature fundamentally. That is, the critical humanistic dimension of adult learning groups reflects unconditional acceptance of the broad diversity within human society and does not simply subsume these social categories into existing norms and values.

And this is where the conservative traditionalists have a problem: The nature of society is changing towards equality and fairness, and they are mounting a backlash against their loss of prime position in the social hierarchies. And they wage the war on emancipation, as Bernadine Evaristo says so eloquently.

Conclusion

Education is primarily social and can be a key dimension for human development. Yet, the focus on teaching and testing means that learners are relegated to being consumers of teaching where their role is to reiterate what is taught in tests, in order to be considered *educated*.

However, adult and community education has long offered a key critique of the limitations of schooling, and it is heartening to work with colleagues who are working to change the nature of the traditional provision, particularly as the field has become feminized without being feminist. Further, as Lynch and Baker say, addressing educational disadvantage has focused on providing so-called equality of opportunity, while ignoring equality of outcome (2004). Adult and community education emerged in the first instance to provide education for people deprived of it, internationally through, for example, the Folk High Schools (Danish Folk High Schools 2022). When more universal education became the norm, at least in the Western world, adult education responded to the failures of formal provision. NALA's website explains the reasons behind the failures of the education system in Ireland (NALA 2022) and this remains stubbornly static, in spite of nearly fifty years of interventions and the growth of equality of opportunity approaches in schooling.

Policymakers may be reshaping the positioning of adult and community education, but perhaps its most important aspect is the clear demonstration that learning in groups benefits participants not only personally but also socially and culturally, with the attendant analysis of power, influence and repression. And educators and learners embody these analyses and bring them into the learning environments and out again.

And that's why there is a backlash against it. Critical adult and community education aims to bring about equality and fairness through the practice of freedom. And adults learning in groups are on the front line of the defence.

Chapter 6

TOWARDS CRITICAL AND POSTCRITICAL GLOBAL EDUCATION

Eilish Dillon

We live in an increasingly complex, interconnected and challenging world. When all aspects of our lives are changing faster than many of us can handle, and our very existence is threatened by pandemic after climate emergency after violent conflict or racist attack, the role of education in supporting us to live well in this world seems ever more important, yet ever more challenging. But what kinds of education can help us to address immense challenges such as inequality, the climate crisis, exploitation and violence? How can we better learn to live respectful, creative lives that enable us to deal with the implications of current systems while building communities of resistance and hope? These are some of the challenging realities and questions that underpin a growing interest, in recent years, in the potential of global education (GE). But what does that global education mean for Further Education and Training (FET) and adult education more broadly? How can it be integrated into different education practices?

Existing research and attempts to map GE activity in adult, community and further education in Ireland since the mid-2000s (Bailey 2009; GENE 2015; Bracken 2020; Oberdofer et al. 2022), all highlight some really creative and innovative global citizenship education (GCE) projects and activities taking place in different settings across the island of Ireland. The submission of the IDEA (Irish Development Education Association) Community Sector Working Group to the Global Education Network Europe (GENE) review of GE in Ireland, in 2015, for example, highlights that it is taking place across a wide range of adult community education (ACE) settings, such as community development projects, community education centres, further education centres, NGOs, women's groups, family resource centres and community gardens. Development education (DE) is reaching many target groups, including second-chance learners, unemployed people, disadvantaged young people, adult basic education learners, older people, migrants, travellers and trade unionists. DE is being integrated into existing ACE programmes, including literacy, horticulture, cookery, IT, social studies, creative arts, youth and community work training, Back to Education and work-related learning. DE provides practical support for the adult and community sector, including accredited (QQI) training, resources, good practice guidelines and on-request workshops (Bracken 2020, 67).

A more recent survey of activity in the area identifies considerable disparities in the extent of GE activity in the different sub-sectors of FET in Ireland and the need for 'more "fine grained" research to capture the various creative efforts on the part of providers currently active in this sector' (Oberdofer et al. 2022, 44).

In this chapter, I address the importance of critical and postcritical GE across FET settings. Exploring different types of GE, I highlight important considerations for practice. I emphasize the need to move beyond comfortable, individualized or simplistic notions of what GE should be. In the context of an interdependent, fast-changing, unequal and existentially threatened world, focusing on personal growth, individual action or technical solutions alone is not enough. Nor is offering easy prescriptions. More focus is needed on addressing structural problems, as well as on alternatives, while linking the local and the global. Difficult as it may be, it's time for global education to help us face our complex, interrelated and often overwhelming realities head on (Todd 2009), with 'global skills' (Bourn 2020). And we must become deeply aware of the ambiguous (often negative) roles we, as educators and learners, play in the systems that privilege the few through the exploitation of the many (and of the environment).

What Is Global Education?

As the enormity and interconnection of the challenges that face humanity and the planet become increasingly unavoidable, the need for some form of global education that enables us to understand and deal with multiple forms of inequality and injustice, as well as with environmental collapse, has come to the fore. This is reflected in the rise in popularity of different educations, often called adjectival educations, which are associated with the global, especially since the 1990s. These include GCE, development education (DE), human rights education, anti-racism and intercultural education, social justice education and education for sustainable development. For this chapter, I am using the term global education (GE) as an umbrella term for these different educations, which were developed to address value-based and political priorities for a better world.

Though there are national and regional differences in understandings and influences on GE, Bourn (2014) has traced a general historical trajectory in international policy from development and human rights education to education for sustainable development and global citizenship education. As such, over time, a recognition of the need for education which is critical, transformative and global and the trends in how this is framed have become central to international education and development policy frameworks such as the Sustainable Development Goals (SDGs). SDG Goal 4, for example, advocates for access to quality education for all, with Target 4.7 calling on countries to

> ensure that all learners acquire the knowledge and skills needed to promote sustainable development, including, among others, through education for sustainable development and sustainable lifestyles, human rights, gender equality, promotion of a culture of peace and nonviolence, global citizenship and appreciation of cultural diversity and of culture's contribution to sustainable development. (United Nations 2023)

Recognizing that education is not just for children or for formal settings, Mark Kearns highlights that 'the Framework for implementing the SDGs or Incheon Declaration further emphasizes the need to reach all learners, with progress being measured according to the extent to which this is mainstreamed at all levels in national education policies' (Kearns 2021, 6). Despite this, Melíosa Bracken (2020) shows that the policy space for GE in adult, community and further education in Ireland is challenging. She argues that, since national policy has changed since 2013, the critical pedagogical principles underpinning a lot of adult and community education in Ireland have been undermined, with a shift in discourse towards FET based on market and employment imperatives. In this context, Bracken (2020, 55) suggests, 'opportunities for DE [or GE] with adult learners are severely limited when adult education is viewed primarily through an employability lens, and that a more enabling policy environment is needed to ensure effective and high-quality development education opportunities are readily available for adult learners'. Offering an analysis of GE policy in Ireland through a discourse analysis of DE, GE and ESD government strategies, she highlights that GE policy is very weak in adult, community and further education as it reinforces the technical skills and market-driven emphasis of FET policy.

In this context, five key lessons about integrating GE into these settings have been learned: First, governments often need to be reminded that GE is not just for children. All learners need opportunities to engage with the complexities of the realities that shape their lives and which they are part of, and which address local–global connections and divides and people's lived realities. Second, FET is a heterogeneous space. This leads to specific challenges when it comes to integrating GE. Oberdofer et al. (2022) explain some of these:

> [U]nlike the formal school system, the ACE [adult community education] sector comprises a vast array of accredited and non-accredited provision incorporating vocational and non-vocational courses, skills-based training, personal development as well as GCE related learning activity. Moreover, this demands a particular educational approach and pedagogy that is more suited to adults and adult learning contexts. In short, there are significant and complex challenges for those working in the GCE-ACE space that remain different to, say, embedding GCE in the primary, secondary or third-level contexts. Further challenges relate to reaching out to marginalised, hard-to-reach groups such as members of the travelling [sic] community and refugee groups. (Oberdofer et al. 2022, 28)

Third, in Ireland, and likely elsewhere, there is a need for more capacity building of practitioners, and 'the development of a long-term, sustainable approach for embedding GCE in the ACE sector and that this is adequately funded and resourced' (Oberdofer et al. 2022, 13). Fourth, GE is not just a subject to be added to other subjects and specialisms. Specific learning contexts, subjects or modules that focus in particular on GE are useful, but it has most impact when it is integrated into all aspects of facilitation, learning, culture and curriculum. Finally, GE is not just about learning about global issues or global cultures but it is an approach to learning, curriculum, culture and education practice. As such, it is underpinned by (and associated with) different philosophies or ideas about education, different understandings of its role in addressing contemporary global challenges and different pedagogies. For adult, community and further educators, it is important to understand how different approaches to, or types of, GE affect the quality, relevance and criticality of how they integrate GE into their education practice.

Different Types of Global Education

There have been many attempts to explain different types of, or approaches to, GE, GCE and DE (see, e.g., the work of Karen Pashby et al. 2020). These are general types that simplify more complex realities in order to help our understanding of them. Andreotti (2006), for example, differentiated between 'soft' and 'critical' GCE. She later developed a more comprehensive framework of narrative types – technicist instrumental, liberal humanist, critical and postcritical, and other (Andreotti 2014). In my research with development educators in Ireland, while identifying overlaps between them, I drew on Andreotti's work to understand different 'discourses' (e.g. ways of talking based on different assumptions) of DE or GE that facilitators tend to draw on – technical, liberal, North/South, critical and postcritical discourses (Dillon 2017). Bearing in mind that descriptions of different discourses or types of GE tend to hide the nuances, overlaps and contradictions often involved and that it is important to differentiate between what is said about what GE is and its practice, I discuss three types (approaches to GE which are associated with different assumptions and practices) here. These are a (1) a technical/liberal approach, (2) a critical approach and (3) a postcritical/alternative approach. I outline each of these in Table 6.1.

Liberal/Technical Global Education

As summarized above, a technical/liberal approach to GE tends to be focused on an understanding of global challenges as problems to be solved by including more people (and countries) in a better, fairer and more sustainable global system. Learners are viewed as individuals who influence (in their personal and local contexts) what's happening in the wider world, which can be viewed as somewhat disconnected from, and otherwise largely irrelevant to, them. Within this broader approach, emphases on the technical draw on instrumentalist thinking (Andreotti 2014), which are based on 'cryptopositivism' (Kincheloe and Tobin 2009) or evidence-based, scientific, objective, problem-solving knowledge. These are the types of knowledge, associated with traditional forms of learning and a policy-led FET approach, which promote instructional and transmission-type pedagogies or sharing knowledge about issues. At its weakest, this approach is overly individualistic and focused on personal growth rather than structural change. These translate into GE which focuses on mindset change, developing attitudes or individual acts of kindness, for example.

Though arguably not problematic in themselves, the limitations of the assumptions about the world and learning in technical/liberal GE become clear when viewed in the context of other, more critical understandings of education, change and action. The implication of a technical/liberal construction of action, as indicated by Khoo (2006) and Gaynor (2016), is that it can lead to the type of superficial, individualized and apolitical action that many educators themselves are critical of. Bryan and Bracken (2011), for example, argue that there is a danger of GE promoting an understanding of action as being about the three Fs of fundraising, fasting and having fun and this is especially the case as there is often vague talk about encouraging learner engagement with global issues. At its best, liberal/technical GE can translate

Table 6.1 Three types of global education.

Assumptions	Liberal/Technical GE	Critical GE	Postcritical/Alternative GE
Challenges Facing the World	Inequality, human rights abuses, environmental destruction, violence and poverty which are in the world. These can be reduced through integrating more people into a fairer, more sustainable global system.	The world is divided and interdependent. Socially constructed political, economic and social structures underpin rising exploitation, inequality, human rights violations, environmental destruction, violence and poverty. These have led to a world in crisis – global systems need to be transformed.	We live in a 'VUCA' world – volatile, unpredictable, complex and ambiguous (Stein 2021) – where realities, relationships, challenges and responsibilities are multiple, multi-layered, interdependent and interconnected.
Knowledge for a Better World	Technical, scientific, 'evidence-based' and shared knowledge for innovation, new technologies, problem-solving and results-focused solutions.	Critical understanding (conscientization), reflection (critical literacy) and action (praxis – Freire 1970) for economic, social and political structural transformation at local and global levels.	Self-reflexivity (Andreotti 2014) – deep knowledge which questions assumptions, practices and relationships including those reinforced in GE. Valuing of multiple and subjected knowledges, alternative practices and respectful ways of living.
What GE Is Trying to Achieve (Learners and Skills)	Emphasis on education for a better world – learning for individual skills development, attitudes and values that support action for change.	Emphasis on education for transformation – learning to empower collective action for structural change. Learners as subjects and agents of change, and importance of values and analytical, diagnostic and action-based skills.	Emphasis on education for alternatives – Learning to deal with the complexities, unpredictabilities and ambiguities of our world today 'head on' (Todd 2009).
Pedagogies (The Role of Educators and Good Practice)	Pedagogies of transmission – facilitator as knowledge sharer who creates opportunities to learn about different issues and spaces to explore learner experiences, options and solutions to the challenges facing our world.	Pedagogies of praxis – facilitator and mentor who creates 'safe spaces' for critical reflection, analysis and dialogue which supports individual and collective transformative action and radical hope as part of the praxis cycle.	Pedagogies of connection – emphasis on unlearning taken-for-granted and damaging assumptions and practices; on engaging learners emotionally with 'difficult knowledge', to engage with the 'messiness' of the world and to support learners to make connections at all levels.

a limited skills agenda into something more critical, but this is particularly challenging in the context of neoliberalism and the growing commodification of education (Giroux 2004; Lynch et al. 2012; Fitzsimons 2017a).

Reflections on the individualism at the heart of technical/liberal approaches to GE also highlight tensions regarding the politics of education. For some, education is at its most political (and potentially transformative) when it is nonprescriptive and focused on individual learning. But an overfocus on the individual leads to a lack of consideration of broader economic and political structures, or of complex interrelationships. For others, education is at its most political when it is driven by a particular vision of society and a clear politics of transformation. But fixed outcomes can undermine participatory and experiential learning processes. Are these positions incompatible? Can GE meaningfully engage learners as individuals without reducing complex global issues to individual experiences and technical responses? Can broader structural approaches embrace the value of acknowledging people's lived experience, linking the personal and the political, so to speak (Dillon 2019)? In the next section, I introduce critical GE which tries to address these tensions.

Critical Global Education

Many highlight the important influence of critical pedagogy on critical GE and ACE. Associated with the work of people like Paulo Freire (1972), bell hooks (1994), Patti Lather (1998) and Henri Giroux (2004, 2020), critical pedagogy emphasizes participatory and non-hierarchical learning processes, critical conscientization and praxis (the interplay between understanding and action) and the value of grassroots (and subjugated) knowledges and activism. Contemporary critical pedagogy embraces feminist concerns about the position and role of women and gender politics, feminist research and engaged pedagogy (following bell hooks 1994), concerns about ecology and sustainability (McLaren and Houston 2004) and critiques of neoliberal individualization and the commodification and securitization of many education systems (Giroux 2020).

While critical GE reflects different philosophical influences and assumptions about the role of education, at the heart of critical GE is an assumption that education is not neutral and that it plays a political role in society. Whether in support of the status quo or transformation, education (and the processes, relationships, institutions and pedagogies associated with it) actively influences how we live, what and who are valued, and what is included, excluded, exploited or celebrated. Critical pedagogy resonates with a lot of adult, community and further education practitioners.

The influence of critical pedagogy on GE is evident in a range of definitions and descriptions of GE in policy and academic literature over time. In the Irish context, GE was mostly framed as 'development education' up until the recent shift to the language of GCE and GE. Whether framed in development, human rights, global citizenship or sustainability terms, these reflect different understandings of global challenges. These, in turn, influence different understandings of what constitutes meaningful critical and transformative global education when it comes to knowledge, values, politics, learning and facilitation processes, relationships, and outcomes or actions associated with it. Global education that focuses on divides, for example, tends to emphasize its role in addressing global economic, political and cultural systems and structures of inequality, injustice and exploitation. Influenced by Marxist, neo-Marxist and other structural critiques of capitalist dominance and neoliberal power, critical GE emphasizes adult education's role in enabling learners to understand what's going wrong in the world, the 'root' causes of it and how unjust and exploitative economic, social or political systems can be overcome through collective action, social movements and global solidarity. It engages learners with questions around wealth and privilege, structural power, complicity, coloniality and responsibility. This type of global education is extremely important in supporting the understanding and critique of big systems and structures in the struggle for justice, as well as local–global relations.

There is also a growing emphasis on global interrelationships and interdependencies. By the 1990s, for example, understandings of DE had shifted, according to Michael Kenny and Siobhán O'Malley, to 'a learning process which proceeds from knowledge to action. It has evolved from being education about developing countries to a broader concept of education for global citizenship' (UNICEF's 1992 definition cited in Kenny and O'Malley 2002, 11). Equally, Kearns argues that a more socially constructivist approach to GE, influenced by critical pedagogy, and which echoes a lifelong learning or adult education approach developed which presented a learner as 'an active, globally minded citizen who is an advocate for positive change in their own locale and this change is in some way connected to global issues or problems or "glocality"' (Kearns 2021, 10).

As understandings of DE developed, there was a growing emphasis on global interdependence, on the intersectionality of different issues and challenges and their relevance to people's lives, on the complementarity and congruence between different adjectival educations and on shared participatory and critical methodologies (IDEA 2013). This more complex and integrated understanding of the world and of what's involved in GE, which sees the learner as the focus (as a subject rather than object of learning) is evident in The European Declaration on Global Education to 2050, adopted in November 2022. It defines GE as

> education that enables people to reflect critically on the world and their place in it; to open their eyes, hearts and minds to the reality of the world at local and global level. It empowers people to understand, imagine, hope and act to bring about a world of social and climate justice, peace, solidarity, equity and equality, planetary sustainability, and international understanding. It involves respect for human rights and diversity, inclusion, and a decent life for all, now and into the future. Global Education encompasses a broad range of educational provision: formal, nonformal and informal; life long and life wide. We consider it essential to the transformative power of, and the transformation of, education. (GENE 2022, 2)

This critical and transformative version of GE sounds great. At the same time, however, the extent to which such critical aspirations are matched by GE practice in FET settings remains unclear. Broader research in Ireland shows that GE practice is patchy in relation to realizing these critical aspirations and that it is constrained by a number of factors including institutional cultures, funding arrangements and a lack of debate around GCE (Dillon 2017). Some also argue that this version of GE does not go far enough. In the next section, I discuss these issues with reference to postcritical/alternative GE.

Postcritical Global Education

In recent years, a range of critiques of GE have been articulated. Some of these represent the experience of practitioners and researchers who question the extent to which practice matches the rhetoric of policy. Others, from what might be called a postcritical or alternative perspective, question the limited (and sometimes damaging) ways in which knowledge, learning and global challenges are understood in technical/liberal and critical GE, and how these affect practice. While there are many criticisms, here I highlight just some of those that illustrate how and why GE needs to be more radical, meaningful and relevant for adult learners today.

Drawing on analyses of coloniality and her experience of working in GCE programmes with young people and in teacher education, Vanessa Andreotti has played an influential role in ensuring that decolonial critiques have become central to recent and popular calls for postcritical GE (Stein and Andreotti 2016). She questions types of GE that reinforce colonial attitudes and practices. Aware of the problems associated with presenting easy prescriptions in critical GE, she argues for education which enables people to deal with the complex, unjust, unequal and exploitative outcomes of modernity and capitalism. Andreotti (2014, 20) argues that postcolonial theory makes 'it impossible to turn our back to difficult issues, such as our complicity in systemic harm [...] the gap between what we say and what we do, or our own sanctioned ignorances'. Drawing on the work of Gayathri Spivak, she highlights the need to unlearn our damaging ways of thinking and knowing, and patterns of relationships and practices with people and the planet, which, she argues, involves deep reflection on all aspects of life, relationality, interdependencies and interconnections. She, along with others in the 'Gesturing towards Decolonial Futures Collective', has developed a range of cartographies or models for supporting critical reflexivity (deep analysis and reflection) among educators and learners on a range of issues. One of these, for example, she calls the *HEADSUP checklist* which offers a narrative prompt and a range of questions for exploring the potentially damaging dimensions of some forms of education and activism. These, she explains, are different

> patterns of engagement, flows and representation that are: hegemonic (justifying superiority and supporting domination); ethnocentric (projecting one view, one 'forward', as universal); ahistorical (forgetting historical legacies and complicities); depoliticised (disregarding power inequalities and ideological roots of analyses and proposals); salvationist (framing help as the burden of the fittest); uncomplicated (offering easy solutions that do not require systemic change); paternalistic (seeking affirmation of superiority through the provision of help). (Andreotti 2014, 21)

As such, educators need to reflect deeply and critically on what we are doing through our work, and in our lives, and to support learners to do so too. This includes reflecting on how we may be reinforcing status quo unequal and exploitative relationships and assumptions through GE in adult, community and further education practices.

This argument that critical GE approaches can reinforce existing damaging patterns (assumptions, practices, relationships, etc.) is developed by Karen Pashby et al. (2020) and Sharon Stein (2021). They argue that a tendency towards diagnosis and prescription in critical GE can promote fixed understandings of proper action, of the goals of GE, and fixed visions of the future. Stein argues, for example, that this is insufficient in our VUCA (volatile, uncertain, complex and ambiguous) world. 'Without the capacities for facing and navigating the complexities, contradictions, complicities, and uncertainties that characterise the contemporary world, people can quickly become overwhelmed, immobilised, and even nihilistic', Stein argues (2021, 484–485).

This concern about critical approaches to GE which are too solution focused and which emphasize fixed outcomes and understandings is also evident in the work of Sharon Todd (2009) and others. Todd calls for education that enables learners to critically engage with 'the messiness' (Leggo 2005) of what's happening in the world, enabling learners to face and deal with difficult and frightening realities. For her, this means refraining from the tendency to idealize so that we can 'imagine an education that seeks not to cultivate humanity […] but instead seeks to face it – head on, so to speak, without sentimentalism, idealism, or false hope' (Todd 2009, 9). In drawing on Hannah Arendt's work, Todd (2009, 14) argues that this involves 'embracing the very ambiguity that lies at the core of education; the task of teaching for a "world that is or is becoming out of joint"' (1956, 192). As such, she argues that education should be concerned with the 'complexities of the human condition, in all its pluralities' (Todd 2009, 16).

Sharon Stein also proposes an approach to GCE that might be better suited for VUCA times, which prepares learners to

> (1) confront the increasing volatility, uncertainty, complexity and ambiguity of our current system with more self-reflexivity, accountability, and discernment; (2) connect recent changes in this system to ongoing colonial legacies of violence and unsustainability, and implicate themselves as inheritors of those legacies – understanding that we can be both part of the problem, and part of the solution; and (3) approach the future in ways that do not presume either the continuity of this system (through various kinds of reform), nor its replacement with a prefabricated alternative system, and that understand the simultaneous indispensability and insufficiency of all knowledges in this process. (Stein 2021, 485)

But all of this is very complex and challenging for educators, who themselves are trying to grapple with the difficulties, uncertainties and ambiguities of life in this VUCA world. This is particularly the case for vulnerable communities who experience the brunt of our unequal, over-consumptive and exploitative economic system. Facing these challenges, with their real lived consequences and emotional implications, requires forms of GE that are up to the task. Audrey Bryan (2020) argues that GE needs to foreground emotions, but not in any superficial way, and for a pedagogy of the implicated where education engages meaningfully with complex problems and knowledge, 'particularly as it relates to learners' [and educators'] self-implication in the conditions that are being addressed' (Bryan 2022, 330).

Conclusion: Some Reflections for Global Education in Practice

This chapter opens up the different assumptions and practices associated with different types of GE for adult, community and further educators. Highlighting their strengths and weaknesses, I invite educators to reflect on their implications in different contexts in Ireland and elsewhere. I suggest that a liberal approach is inadequate for dealing with the complexities, imbalances and interdependencies of our world today. This GE can support individualized forms of activism, ethnocentric and colonial mindsets and relationships, and disconnected, apolitical and growth-based understandings of sustainability. Despite this, creating the space for GE in FET – albeit often starting with a technical approach – offers considerable opportunity for opening up more critical GE engagement. Critical GE is important in its focus on political and economic structures which cause many of the problems we face in our world today. It is also strong in its analytical potential and its emphasis on reflection, understanding and action. As such, it can support collective forms of critical engagement, transformative movements and global solidarity, while engaging learners with questions around wealth and privilege, structural power, human rights, complicity, coloniality and responsibility. Though international policy on GE has moved towards a more integrative, multifaceted and critical construction of the world and of the role of GE therein, it tends towards lofty and aspirational rhetoric, which can deflect our attention from less critical practice. We have also seen how the policy space for GE in adult, community and further education in Ireland requires significant change, especially in its support for critical and postcritical GE. Insights from postcritical GE also focus on power and coloniality, suggesting that there needs to be much more of an emphasis on the complexity, uncertainty, ambiguity, and paradoxes of modernity in GE and less of a focus on prescription.

Meaningful and relevant GE is not easy to implement in practice, but it is worthwhile. As discussed here, at least in its critical and postcritical forms, it is not about learning about global issues but education which supports us to deal in a real way with the complexity and implications of the lives we live, here and now, and the world we help to shape for the future. These perspectives cannot be adequately addressed in GE if it is confined to a stand-alone subject or module in FET programmes. Nor can they be integrated by inviting a speaker from an NGO to talk about their work. It needs deep integration across and within different adult, community and further education settings (and at all levels). This requires policy and implementation support for these types of critical and postcritical GE in curricula in different contexts. It also requires understanding and commitment on the part of education management to support these perspectives and cultures of learning. This is where education contexts and practices themselves become the subject of transformation and decolonization and where educators are supported to critically reflect on their own assumptions and practices through peer and other learning opportunities.

This chapter suggests that we need more GE which emphasizes the interconnectedness and interdependence of our multifaceted relations in and with the world. GE that is based on an understanding of relations and relationality (Lange 2016) at all levels supports us to see ourselves (learners and educators, our lives, relationships and actions) as deeply connected. This approach to GE presumes a political and transformative role for GE in terms of facilitating analysis of how power works at local and global levels and in interrogating the power of those involved in GE (Dillon 2022), and it supports analyses of power, positionality and relationships, such as Andreotti's '*HEADSUP checklist*' (2014). As such, it is about enabling learners to struggle with the complexities, inequalities and injustices in our world today and to forge connections beyond division. While it acknowledges the challenges of living with the discomfort of the intractability of the problems facing us, of our own complicity (as implicated subjects, Bryan 2022) in relation to them and our feelings of being overwhelmed by them, critical and postcritical GE support radical and meaningful hope through education, action and the creation of alternatives. Through supporting different practices of critical reflexivity (Andreotti 2014), ongoing reflection and creative pedagogies, for example, narratives, poetry, art, music and drama, learners and educators are encouraged to deeply question how our lives and realities intersect, interact, are interdependent with and shape those which appear to be 'in the wider world'. This relational approach is one of many critical and postcritical approaches to GE which goes 'below the surface, beyond binaries and certainty, and deep into complex realities and ambiguity [...] support[ing] empathy, solidarity and creative alternatives' (Dillon 2022, 409).

Practising critical and postcritical GE remains a significant challenge for FET educators, especially when policies, resources and training are mainly directed elsewhere and where the emphasis is still largely on GE for children. In 2019, for example, UNESCO highlighted progress in the provision of GCE in schools but expressed its concern that insufficient attention had been placed on the integration of GCE into FET settings (Oberdofer 2022). The challenges are great, but so too are the opportunities and the needs. Critical and postcritical GE are not only worthwhile but also necessary, now more than ever.

Chapter 7

A WINTER SUN: CREATIVE REFLEXIVITY AS PRACTITIONER RESEARCH

Jerry O'Neill

Part One: A Pedagogic Intervention of the Banal

It is December 2019 and a room full of twenty-six emerging adult educators and myself are coming to the end of the first semester. We've had a rich but dense enough morning in which we've been talking about ways in which we can gather feedback from students by using and adapting versions of Stephen Brookfield's *Critical Incident Questionnaire* (2015). We've also been exploring how certain technologies can enhance participation and gather voices that may not otherwise be heard in groups. There has been some discussion too on useful, and not so useful, planning documents and resources that are used in further and adult education settings.

We have covered a lot of ground. All interesting enough stuff in a way, but I am not, pedagogically, setting the world on fire.

It's now 12:30 and we have about thirty minutes left before we finish. There are a few things I'd like to touch on in terms of the logistics of placement but I sense that people are tired – we have been sitting and talking too much.

I feel the need to interrupt the passivity which seems to have crept up and enveloped us as the morning has progressed.

My recognition of this – this reading of the group – happens in a moment. And almost in the same moment of becoming aware of it, I know that I must address it somehow …

… my distracted gaze shifts out beyond the windowed-wall of our classroom to survey the campus landscape below us …

We are in a new building on the north campus of the university which dominates this small Kildare town to the west of a sprawling Dublin. The window looks out onto the older, ecclesiastically resonant, south campus – a place where generations of Catholic priests were trained safely in Ireland away from the more politically charged seminaries of France and Italy.

The winter sun is low in a clear sky and there is that low-intensity, almost ancient, light that I associate with this time of the year. A contradictory light that can be subtle and sharp all at once. A light that, today, plays with the droplets of fallen rain that cling to the bare trees on the south campus. The rain is non-discriminatory and settles equally on the assorted metallic building equipment which litters the north campus. Bark and steel glisten in an uneasy collegiate harmony.

Crowds of people pass below us – hurrying back and forth across the public road that splits the campus in two. A rush to beat the queues for lunch. The world is busy out there.

I see all this in a moment.

Thinking, possibly in action (Schön 2003), as I absorb this winter scene, I sense, rather than see, a pedagogic moment (van Manen 1991). Is it possible in those mere seconds that swirling ideas about slow education (Mountz et al. 2015; O'Neill, M. et al. 2014) and the cognitive importance of standing and moving (O'Mara 2019) somehow combine with thoughts about perspective shifts in transformative learning (Mezirow 2000, Formenti and West 2018) which, in turn, merge into an instinctive drive to do something different?

Maybe, but I do know that in those few seconds, the recognition of a need for a shift drew my gaze to a bigger picture – a perspective shift from within the class to the world outside. And in these few seconds of perspective realignment, a proto-idea forms about the possibility of how a slow, unforced looking might offer the opportunity for a deeper, critical engagement with the specificity of the educational landscape outside our window. A pedagogic desire to turn the outside in and the inside out.

Is this really how it happened? I don't know. But I will go on …

Something else is coming back to me now as I write through this pedagogic memory … I am remembering now (or did it come to me then?) a fragment from a supervision visit with a student in a community education classroom at the top of a creaking Victorian building in Dublin some years back.

The student had excellently facilitated a session on some dense and quite abstract sociological ideas about structure and power. The details escape me now, but I do remember a moment from our post-observation conversation. We stood side by side, looking out the small garret window which revealed the city skyline – both of us in momentary silence reflecting upon the session.

The steeples of Dublin's many churches punctuated that scene. But religion no longer held the high points in the cityscape – commercial buildings now stood tall enough to cast shadows on the church and, of course, on the people below. As we looked, I pondered aloud with her that there was much to be learned about the shifting structural power dynamics of Dublin over the last century by merely looking out this window. Seeing from this window.

What would it be like, I wondered with her, to stand with her learners where we stood in that moment and contemplate, to imagine, the sociological through a slow reading of a Dublin skyline (Mills 2000)? Could the window frame an urban image that could be read, revealed and known like a Freirean code (Freire 1972, Chapter Three).

And so, years later, here I am in a suspended moment with my own group sitting beside another window that is also emerging as a possible resource for critical reflection …

Before I know what I am doing, but operating purely on instinct, I find myself inviting the class to stand and face the window. Even as they move from their seats to come to the window, I am still unsure where I am going with this. But I am not panicking as it feels that moving, at least, and changing our perspectives is the right thing to do.

We arrange ourselves into an arc in a communal act of standing and looking … and, without direction from me, the initial quizzical shuffling settles into a more contemplative silence … after a bit, I hear myself pose a question …

What do we see?

The question, like the instruction to move, is unrehearsed but rather emerges from this moment. There is no other question to ask. It is the only thing that can be uttered.

There are some immediate responses which name the obvious … we see … trees … cranes … people walking … and lots of cars.

But after a bit, a deeper, slower looking invokes more conceptual, more critical responses – a 'looking' that shifts to a 'seeing'. Our collective *seeing* starts to connect with other things, other ideas, bigger structures, a revealing of the bigger picture … a rhizomatic discussion emerges and works its way around religion … the power, control and damage caused by the church in Ireland, the commercialization of higher education, the environment, the climate emergency … we stand, we see, we talk and, after a bit … we sit.

And that's it.

With a renewed and maybe slightly puzzled energy, we close the session and go our ways for another week.

Afterwards, as part of the blog that I write after each session, I seem to find myself drawn to the poetic rather than the usual prose format … until, again, without thinking too much about it, I find myself crafting a poem of sorts out of those few minutes we shared standing together, slowly-seeing …

Twenty-Six Adult Educators Gazing through a Dirty Window

So, here we are
        standing together in a slowly
emerging, collective arc …
    looking out the window
        on a mid-winter sunny morning.
Operating on the vapours
        of pedagogic intuition and
   ~~teaching~~ … facilitating out of
        my mundane practice
and into
        an unplanned moment.
And in our few unplanned minutes
        precipitated by
   tired bodies and a stuffy classroom
it seems all we do is
    gaze for a bit.
We gaze for a bit
        without direction or instruction
   out a dirty window.
We stand as an arc …
      or maybe a raised eye brow
   looking for a fresher, a deeper, perspective
        on familiar landscapes.
    We see …
   a dirty window …
        cars – too many cars …
people walking … tight and stiff in themselves …
        on a clear and bitter December day …
Our vision deepens …
      … we see
   high-vis workers in low-paid work ….

        .

We see …
    a church spire towering like
        Bentham's panopticon
   over centuries of learning
centuries of knowing.
      Soon, maybe, to be surpassed
        by a relentless shiny-glass building

                that will shoot upwards from
                              disturbed earth
                                          on this side of the road.
       An edifice constructed by a different religion.
We see ...
                    a wise winter light cut through
                                      naked trees
working the low horizon
                              in preparation for the solstice ....
      As our own sacred place
                                  channels this light -
     just for a moment -
                              in, and through, the arc we form
        our raised eye-brow
                                  our inverted smile ... :)

Part Two: Reflexivity as Pedagogy and Practitioner Inquiry

What I have presented so far is a narrative reflection, which moves to the poetic, on a pedagogic moment with a group of emerging adult educators on a postgraduate Initial Teacher Further Education (ITFE) programme in Ireland. What follows in this second section is a discussion on how I see such attempts at creative and engaged reflective practice as something that can be viewed as being an expression of research in adult education as much as pedagogy. Part Three will conclude with a return to a narrative and poetic reflection which emerged from a closing session with the same group of educators whose learning, professional and personal lives had, by that stage, been disrupted by the great disorientation of the first months of the coronavirus pandemic.

Critical Reflective Practice: Lens and Triskelions

Guided by adult education principles where meaning and knowledge can be co-created from a collective and critical reflection on common experiences (Freire 1972, Brookfield 2017), I endeavoured to create space each Friday morning where this group of emerging educators could reflect upon, and problem-pose, issues that were coming up for them in their further education teaching practice placements[1] which run for the whole year.

---

1 Students are required to successfully complete at least 100 practice hours in an accredited adult, community or further education centre in order to pass this postgraduate FE Teacher Education programme.

Stephen Brookfield (1998, 2017) has long stressed the importance of our openness and capacity to engage in authentic and considered critically reflective practice as a fundamental aspect of our always urgent work as educators in an inequitable and endangered world. His notions of critical reflection go beyond the more familiar ideas of reflective practice associated with various occupational fields that very often frame it as practice-enhancing processes that are somehow contained within the boundaries of a classroom, institution or professional field. Brookfield, drawing on a more political tradition, calls for acts of critical reflection to push beyond these boundaries into encounters with wider sociocultural and environmental terrains.

Acknowledging that individual acts of reflection are important but offer a limited perspective on our practice and world view, Brookfield, instead, proposes that we create opportunities for reflection, through four lenses: ourselves, our students, our colleagues and theory (2017, 61–77).

In my own work, I have drawn on Brookfield's four-dimensional reflective framework to develop an interconnecting triskelion model of reflexivity (Figure 7.1). In this fluid and always-pulsing reflexive meaning-making process, I collapse Brookfield's separate domains of 'students' and 'colleagues' into a broader practice or learning community. I also widen his 'theory' lens to suggest a Freirean prompt to 'read the world/word' (Freire, 1972, 2).

In my Brookfield-inspired triskelion flux, I imagine knowledge and meaning being constantly created and recreated through reflexive cycles where the personal, communal and careful readings of the word/world engage and inform each other (O'Neill 2015). Importantly, the energy of this reflexive flow

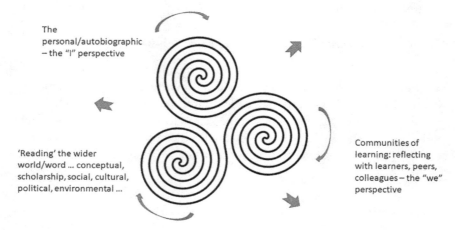

Figure 7.1 A triskelion reflexive flux.

doesn't just circulate endlessly in on itself but has a transformative capacity to act upon, to change, our inner *and* outer worlds.

Writing as Reflective Practice

And so, returning to my Friday morning class with a group of emerging further education practitioners, it was my hope that our learning space would not just be somewhere to work through some of the joys and challenges of always-developing practice but that also, in our slow-burning and interweaving acts of critical thought, we might create a sometimes critically fused space that stretched us a bit further in our reflective perspectives. As Camilla has pointed out in her discussion of engaged pedagogy in Chapter 1, the views that we encounter in such critical acts are not always comfortable as they can disturb long-held assumptions. These may be assumed perceptions about the purposes of education or the role of a teacher. More specifically for the group I was working with, it was not uncommon for us to unearth unsettling questions about what it might be to be an educator working in the tentatively forming professional spaces of Irish further education that vacillates with the tensions of performativity and precarity (Avis and Bathmaker 2004, O'Neill and Fitzsimons 2020).

Learning, constantly, from the likes of Jennifer Moon (2004), Gillie Bolton (2014) and David Mc Cormack (2010), one way that I make sense of a group learning experience, and hold some of these emerging discomforts, is by writing my own reflection of the session which I often share with the group as a pedagogic artefact. In the case of the pedagogic moments I am focusing on in this chapter, I did so through a blog on our online virtual learning environment. Over time, the accumulation of these reflective posts becomes one, but just one, narrative perspective of a learning group. Conscious of the epistemological damage that could be done by the heavy pen of the narrating subject of the teacher (Freire 1972, 26), I encouraged students to respond to my posts online and, in their own journals, to write their own learning stories. Invariably, as we wrote from, and around, our personal and collective experiences, we circled in this reflexive flux, drawing in other perspectives, wider readings of, and from, the world/word, which gave our learning narratives more critical depth, context and complexity to create an always-emerging critically fused curriculum.

Reflexivity as Research

These acts of reflective writing, this writing through to knowledge, are part of the episto-pedagogical performances of my practice – a space of persistent and labouring knowledge where research and teaching start to become indistinguishable. And so for me, the sites of research, as a critically reflexive educator, are most consistently the spaces where I work with and reflect on my pedagogic work with groups. We can expand the possibilities of these research encounters if we acknowledge that these groups may be students but also peers in wider communities of practice and the 'pedagogic' might be defined more broadly, as Zembylas suggests, 'as the relational encounter among individuals [and groups] through which many possibilities for growth are created' (2007, 332). The pedagogic experiences that we all share can be seen as the 'data' for the reflexive, praxis-charged inquiries that aid and ignite not just our own 'possibilities for growth' but, as is always the intention and hope, the world outside and its intersections with the classroom, institution or professional field of practice.

Grounded, as I am, then, in the value of critically reflecting on lived experience (Brookfield 2017; Dewey 1997; Freire 1972; hooks 1994), it is no surprise that I am drawn, through the pen of my scribbling pedagogic self, towards, and across, the various methodologies associated with reflexive inquiry (Etherington 2004), writing as inquiry (Mc Cormack 2014; Done et al. 2011; Richardson 1994) and autoethnography (Denzin 2014; Pelias 2019).

As I have argued elsewhere with colleagues, there is a common methodological purpose in the work of adult education and these forms of reflexive research (Mc Cormack et al. 2020). The starting point for much of this reflexive work is most often the self. But, again and as we are already aware from Brookfield (2017), starting with the self is just that – a start into an inquiry of much wider, sociocultural significance. As Pelias, commenting on autoethnography, claims:

> I write, not as an act of self-indulgence, but because I want to deploy myself, my experiences, as means for understanding how one might make sense of and change the world.[…] make myself present so that others might find resonance or points of resistance. (Pelias 2019, 32)

Pelias goes on to pose the various 'selves that carry the potential for autoethnographic work' (2019, 37–39) and lists, non-exhaustively: the disrupted self, the diminished self, the confessional self, the joyful self, the critical self, the complicit self and the testifying self. For me, the self that carries the potential for critically reflexive inquiry is the pedagogic self – a self that loses interest in maintaining its unitary boundaries as it dissolves and combines into the intersubjectivity of the group in a move towards a collective authorship of meaning and transformative learning. Or, to put it another way,

I see my voice as just one element in a group that, as a collective, will always offer richer insight into our experiences together.

I am drawn, particularly, to the kind of creative and intersubjectively porous poststructuralist-influenced reflexive methods that are sensitive to the (inter)play of the self with context and environment. One such methodological ally is Gannon who sees her poststructuralist-informed autoethnography as 'performance of the self in embodied social spaces in (con)texts that promote an ethics of care and that foreground the limits and fragilities of self-knowledge' (2006, 492). Again, such an approach may use the self as a problematic starting point but soon opens up the inquiring-pedagogic space for a collusion of collective talking and listening learning subjects in the transformative spaces of adult education (Ryan 2001). The pedagogic centrality of such a collective is something noted by Hoggan et al. (2017) in their critique and reinvigoration of transformative learning when they stress that they see the human experience that fuels transformative learning as being 'first and foremost intersubjective' (54).

Emboldened, then, by the conceptual spaces opened up by reflexive researchers and adult educators who are thinking critically and intersubjectively, I am always on the lookout for small spaces (a crack would do) to practice play (St. Pierre 2013). This serious playful work for me is, I suppose, the collective labour that 'we' must do to dislodge the 'I' in the participative, co-creating knowledge sites of adult education. As with my practice, my research and this chapter upon which it inscribes itself, the 'I' is always a way to shape the story of the 'we' and, indeed, the bigger story outside the space where we gather.

In this critical play with practice, I am drawn very often to framing writing itself as a methodological space for reflexive work.

Writing as Inquiry

Traditional approaches to research tend to see the act of writing as part of the technical process that happens after the work has been done. But for the more process-sensitive epistemologies of adult education pedagogy and research that I'm sketching out here, we can start to see writing itself as a significant part of the learning or research act. Writing, for me, is very much like the group processes that are at the centre of our adult education practice – it can become a place where knowledge emerges from the process. And just as participative and dialogic pedagogy can sometimes disrupt traditional ways of teaching, writing, as a form of inquiry, can disrupt traditional notions of how research is done and, furthermore, what the product of that research looks like.

My main concern here is to reflect on and present the narrative and poetic acts of writing knowledge that emerged from work with a group of emerging educators. But, of course, the act of writing this chapter may also be something to reflect upon briefly as an instance of non-traditional knowledge-making.

This text, in various forms, has laid mostly idle on my virtual desk for a few years. Every now and then I returned to it – to play with it, to shape it one way or another. This sense of letting something settle, allowing a slow knowledge to emerge, works against the fast time of performance and outcome-obsessed work in both further and higher education. Yet, I sense, as others do, that there is a value and a need to take radical steps towards slowness in allowing meaning and knowledge to work its own way through the sedimented layers of our practice (Cullinane and O'Neill 2020; Mountz et al. 2015; O'Neill, M. et al. 2014). Taking the time to craft something over time in our practice can, in itself, start to be seen as a critical or disruptive act.

This chapter, then, may be seen as a modelled invitation to adult, community and further education practitioners to embrace unrushed, collective and creative processes of reflexivity as moments of qualitative, or even post-qualitative, inquiry (St. Pierre 2013). Such work(ings) are valuable contributions to knowledge in our fields of practice wherever that may be in the diverse landscape of further education.

But to return, again, to the writing that emerged from the reflective acts of my work with this group of students on their teaching practice …

On the surface, there was nothing extraordinary that happened that winter morning that warrants inclusion as a chapter in a book. It is more accurate to say that a lingering glimpse into my own limited and banal practice has acted as a catalyst for this slow-burning and persistent reflective act. Although I am pretty sure that most of the students walked away that morning with a feeling of nothing more than, at best, bemusement, there was something that seemed significant in the session – something not quite in my line of sight that I couldn't let go of. And something that I obviously felt compelled to return to over the last few years.

The reflective space of the blog that I kept for the group was often the space where I worked the puzzling or disorientating things through – this writing process and product became the group's emergent curriculum. But sometimes prosaic reflective writing doesn't feel like the adequate vessel to hold what is struggling to emerge …

… sometimes, in the spaces that are at the very edge of my peripheral meaning-making vision, and as I revealed already, I find myself drawn to more poetic forms and modes of reflexivity. In, and with, those moments, I might try to craft a textual something from the 'found' words of a session (Walsh 2004). I find poetry useful for working on, and into, the hard-to-see places in practice. And, drawing again, on Pelias (2019), I'd agree that there is something in the way that '[t]he poetic can enter into the heart of its subject with language that crystallizes everyday life in an evocative manner' (96).

I suppose this is what creative writing, and a poetic practice specifically, is all about – the *writing through to* knowledge rather than *the writing it up* (Bolton 2014; Cixous 1976; Richardson 1994). Of course, these are not new ideas – McCormack sees the epistemological potential for an adult education practice in Keats' 'negative capability' of Romanticism's poetic imagination:

> Negative capability refers, then, to the capacity to hold and contain feelings of distress and disturbance from not knowing and allowing knowing to emerge from that place. It requires the capacity to sit with not knowing and trust the process of coming to know. (McCormack 2014, 169)

It is, for me, the irresistible draw to sitting with, and working through, 'not knowing' that lies at the heart of the very occasional richness and perennial tensions of my own adult education practice. Maybe it is no surprise, then, that a kind of poetic-reflexive practice often seems to be the best methodological fit for me to work through the not-infrequent times of epistemic and pedagogic uncertainties that I experience in my life as an adult and adult educator.

This reflexive inquiry – this open and creative writing *into* and *through* moments of practice – is just the kind of research and professional development that I am interested in (Done et al. 2011). There is so much to be revealed in our practice-knowledge in the spaces where research/inquiry, reflective practice and creativity are permitted to dance a little bit together … to dance on the edges of what we see, feel and think we might know as we contemplate the personal and wider world possibilities for growth …

Part Three: A Poetic, Covid Close

And now we jump forward from the solstice into a new year, through spring, and land in the first week of May 2020. I am with the same group. But we are no longer in our glass-walled classroom. Instead, I am over 70 km away, sitting in an old, precariously balanced caravan outside my house in Wicklow.

The group of emerging educators has come together again with some of the other lecturers on the programme for a final, closing session. But this is no normal close. We gather online; still reeling from the great disorientation of the Covid-19 pandemic. Our working, learning and personal lives have collapsed into uneasy, disordered days where we feel we should have time to get things done. But, instead, we are all struggling to think and act coherently.

Most of the students have made it for this final online session which we host on this new and now-ubiquitous space called Teams. But there are absences. I am reminded of the words of my friend and colleague, Camilla, who opens the session – she frequently asks us to think in various ways about 'who is not in the room' when we come together as groups.

The absences today are largely due to the problems that have emerged during the pandemic – increased workload for practitioner-students, poor internet connectivity, lack of suitable spaces, anxiety of lost incomes, care commitments and, of course, illness (AONTAS 2020). We name these as we open.

In preparation for this close, I have asked everyone to think of a word or image that, in some ways, captures their experience of the programme as they come to the end of their course.

Two of the students have agreed to lead the group in a grounding exercise to help us all be as present as we can in whatever spaces we are in. As we move through the grounding exercise and into the sharing of words and images, I find myself, as I often do, scribbling down many of the words that are being shared.

But halfway through the session, I get a call from my brother to say that my father, who is in a nursing home, has tested positive for Covid. I make my apologies and leave abruptly to attend to this new familial crisis.

Later, much later, I come back to my notebook and scribbled words. I am very worried about my father. But as well as having a pedagogic and research potential, there is also a therapeutic capacity, for me, in writing (Mc Cormack 2010) – I find solace in writing and playing with words in critical and creative ways. So, before I know it, it seems, again, I am crafting a poetic found something (Walsh 2004) from the words that I harvested from the session in my notebook ...

Twenty-Six Adult Educators Staring into Shimmering Screens

And so I sit with a strange sadness
                    precariously balanced in my
                            pedagogically-charged caravan
somewhere on the outskirts of Wicklow.
It's not quite 2pm
                    and the group is gathering
      somewhere, out there around
                    laptops, tablets, desktops, phones -
rearranging the domestic to get some space to think, to reflect -
            coming together for a kind of a close.
It's near summer but still the light seems

A WINTER SUN

    to cut into the space with the same
   sharp subtlety of our winter sun …
And I'm trying to get my head
    into the space.
Trying to tap into the feeling, the memory of what
    it is like to sit with a learning group in the flesh.
   I am finding this hard – this intense
       communion with a screen.
I realise, now, how much we need,
      as educators,
  to listen to the unspoken.
How much we rely on reading
     the silences, the subtle shifts
  in bodies …
   the ways we read, we sense
  the tensions in a group.
     The unsaid things that
   alert us to a need
to follow up with someone quietly after class
    or
     make a subtle shift in our process.
We need to see-hear-feel-sense
  all the little things
     as one collective, embodied presence.
  All the little things that are not the little things.
But the ringing of a small bell
  through the digital noise draws me
    into a different state …
  and two familiar student voices
     speaking from the initialled-discs
that stand in for them on Teams
   invite me, us all, to …
  Breathe in …
    Breathe out …
   Breathe in …
    Breathe out …
And I do just that …
  and even as my ever-wandering mind
    does its wandering, I am reassured that is ok …
My students teach me that
  all I need to do is to bring it back to the breath

                              ... always the breath
in ... out
                          in ... out
in ... out
          And before I know anything else the small bell rings again.
          The silence of the student-led opening slips away and
                    we settle back into a
                                digitally crackling presence.
Crackling and disconnected ... but a presence all the same.
                Camilla invites us to share the words,
                        the images which speak to
      where we are as the programme comes to this strange end ...
And, as it turns out,
                  we are in lots of places ...
We are ....
        half-way up mountains
                    half-way through wild gardens
We are ... ship-wrecked.
        But we stand on our ship-wrecks hopefully
                            gazing at horizons.
And horizons may be emerging – even shifting.
                                  Despite our disorientation.
              Despite our sadness.
We are ... pushing rocks up hills
      and watching them roll down.
We are ...
                    catching lightning in a jar.
And deeply worried as we face into already
        precarious career futures that are now
    laced with all the additional uncertainty that
                comes with Covid.
We balance the loss, the difficulty, the slowness,
      the disconnection, in this
            moment of Ramé.
                    Or is it Ramé we are mourning?
The students' words and images keep coming ...
            But suddenly I am drawn away by another ringing bell ...
a phone that
            insists on ringing.
      And stops.
                                 And rings again.

I sense, on that second ring,
                        that there is something amiss ...
I answer ... something is amiss ...
          Suddenly I have to leave ...
          I have to leave this virtual close,
                  this tenuous moment ...
But I step away with a delicate hope
          that might just see a possibility for something better
     in the cracks that have appeared in the
          inequity of the familiar.
                    A delicately-poised possibility.
And I know that I only have the capacity
              To work the cracks with others,
         like those I have left behind in my
                  precariously-balanced caravan
                          somewhere in Wicklow ...

Chapter 8

OLDER THAN THE INTERNET: DIGITAL WORLD LITERACY AND ADULT LEARNING

Leo Casey

This chapter introduces 'Digital World Literacy' as a useful framework for digital literacy educators. The learning challenge posed by digital literacy is more complex than might first appear. Tempting as it is to reduce digital literacy to an itemized list of skills and know-how, the experience of many adult educators suggests there is more to it than that. Digital World Literacy is intended to promote an understanding of digital literacy from a lifelong learning perspective. A set of five statements of learning need are proposed with discussion on how these may provide a basis for digital literacy education.

It is certainly the case that as technology is increasingly embedded in our homes, workplaces, and communities, it has significant impacts on the lives of people of all ages. Many adults strive to maintain the ability to manage functional aspects of their lives such as travel, banking, shopping and connectivity as digital technology transforms these practices. This is particularly true for people like me who are 'older than the internet', hereafter referred to as 'older adults' (50+). For most of us, the technology-mediated world of today was unimaginable in our youth. Put simply, we did not expect the world to change so much.

In an everyday sense, we talk about the digital world as a collective term for the impact of new technology on our lives. The term has become a placeholder for all that is changing around us. This is somewhat justified as technology appears to be driving much of the change. People often say, 'whatever did we do before internet and mobile phones?' For many, digital tools have become so ingrained in their lives that they would be 'lost without them'.

The persistent development of new technology continues to challenge and change the social fabric of our world. However, not everyone is ready or willing to embrace the latest innovations. New technology can give rise to difficult decisions and unavoidable choices for older adults. Many are set in their ways and simply do not wish to change. Such is the ubiquitous nature of digital transformation that resistance or reluctance to embrace the latest gadget or innovation is often the most difficult path.

There are reasons why it makes sense to be reticent. As more and more technology companies provide services such as streamed entertainment, health and fitness monitoring, and on-line banking, they are positioned to collect and analyse data on our daily lives in ways that were unimaginable a few years ago. Technology is also being used as a mechanism of social control. For example, complex algorithms are increasingly used to surveil migrants and in some cases, these technologies contribute to life defining determinations (Bradley and De Noronha 2022, 123). There are also growing concerns about the power of giant Artificial Intelligence (AI) 'digital minds'. In March 2023, over 1,000 AI experts urged a delay in development so that the capabilities of systems such as 'ChatGPT' can be fully understood (Hearn 2023).

As adult educators working across a range of disparate spaces, we are particularly concerned with the empowerment of older learners to manage their lives and succeed in the digital world amidst these fast-paced changes. At times this means supporting people to acquire skills and know-how to leverage digital technology to their advantage. At other times, it may involve reassurance and affirmation as they strive to cope with the relentless impact of the colonization of new technology on their way of life.

Introducing the Digital World

There are two ways in which we can regard the digital world. First, it can be taken to mean the collective term for the impact of new technology on all our lives. The digital world signifies change and transformations that can be externally observed and objectively measured, for example the number of people with smartphones, or those that shop online or engage with social media. Measures such as the European Commission's *Digital Economy and Society Index* (DESI) (2022) provide valuable metrics for economists and policymakers to track the growth and transformations of the digital world. These metrics are used to inform planning and policy such as evidenced in the Irish Government's *Adult Literacy for Life Strategy* (2021).

In contrast, there is another way of regarding the concept of Digital World (note capitals) that may be more useful for educators. This is to think of the Digital World as part of our personal working model of the world as it evolves through life experience. This conceptualization of the Digital World emerged as a category from grounded theory research involving adult learners' perspectives of the impact of new technology on their lives (Casey 2009). Based on these findings, the Digital World was seen to encapsulate the preconceptions, feelings, imagined models and anticipated impacts of technological change on the way we live our lives. In this sense, the Digital World is a phenomenological construct. Each person, including you and I, has our own constantly evolving Digital World.

The proposition here is for greater appreciation by educators of Digital World as a basis for working with older adults and consequently positioning Digital World Literacy as a focus of learning need. The remaining parts of the chapter provide a brief overview of digital literacy responses in the current Irish context, a more general and at times personal account of the evolution of terms and approaches to digital literacy, followed by further consideration of Digital World Literacy through typical adult learner personas. These establish a basis for introducing Digital Word Literacy as a foundation for five statements of learning and discussion on implications for educational practice.

Digital Literacy in the Irish Context

Good evidence of the extent of the impact of the digital world on the lives of older people is available from the Irish Longitudinal Study on Ageing (Doody et al. 2020). Several of its findings are worth noting by way of background to this discussion.

- Sixty-four per cent of adults aged 50+ have access to a smartphone/tablet (and therefore to apps).
- Access to smartphones/tablets similarly decreases with age. Only 30 per cent aged 80+ have access to a smartphone/tablet, compared to 80 per cent aged 50–69 years, and 60 per cent aged 70–79 years.
- Internet use for any purpose declines with increased age, with social media use experiencing the largest of these age-associated declines from 47 per cent in those aged 50–69 years, 30 per cent in those aged 70–79 years, to only 20 per cent aged 80+.
- Of adults aged 50+ living alone, 30 per cent do not have internet access in their homes.

While noting the high levels of uptake of digital technology across the population, the report also states that a relatively large section of the population aged fifty years or over do not have home internet access. 'For these individuals, and in particular those living alone and older age groups, more traditional forms of communication and information distribution, e.g. telephone, radio, television, and the national postal service, in combination with ongoing family and community support, are likely essential' (Doody et al. 2020, 11).

In Ireland, basic digital skills courses are provided across many FET settings as well as by the National Adult Literacy Agency (NALA), community education providers and public libraries. *Adult Literacy for Life* is the Irish Government's (2021) ten-year adult literacy, numeracy and digital literacy strategy. It was developed through extensive consultation with stakeholders across adult, community and further education and this is reflected in its learner-centred approach. The introduction sets an aspirational tone: 'Literacy is a form of power. It offers a person the opportunity to carve out a place for themselves in the world. The ability to read and write, work with numbers and navigate the digital sphere can unleash an individual's potential' (Government of Ireland 2021, 21). The strategy is underpinned by actions centred on four pillars enabling people to (1) understand their needs, (2) access content, (3) expand their learning and (4) be empowered to make a difference to their lives.

Adult Literacy for Life uses a digital literacy measure based on DESI, with a specific target to 'decrease the share of adults in Ireland without basic digital skills from 47% to 20%' (Government of Ireland 2021, 13). The most recent DESI country profile for Ireland (2022) shows the share of adults without basic digital skills as 30 per cent, this compares with an EU average of 46 per cent. The strategy identifies older adults (55+) as one of the potential vulnerable cohorts for targeted funding (European Commission 2022, 59).

The complexities of the digital divide in Ireland is further evidenced by the findings from a survey of over 1,000 adults where motivation and access were identified as two key obstacles for people who described themselves as 'below average' digital competency (Accenture 2020). With respect to motivation, 40 per cent of people with poor digital skills did not see a need to improve, while 33 per cent reported not knowing how to access local learning support. The report comments how 'in the last decade, the educational focus within formal and informal education has been on the functional side of digital literacy' and goes on to recommend 'the next decade must be about teaching transversal skills, critical thinking and higher-level cognition, which are increasingly recognised as vital building blocks for developing digital skills' (Accenture 2020, 73).

Like many other countries Ireland is endeavouring to close the digital divide and facilitate all citizens to benefit from the economic and social dividends of digital transformation. Older adults, more likely to lack basic digital skills, are further disadvantaged as access to services such as welfare, health and citizen information are increasingly provided through online portals. Further education has a part to play in reducing the disadvantage. However, it is not simply about supporting skills and know-how, the learning needs are much deeper and holistic.

Approaches to Digital Literacy

My experience as an educator has spanned several iterations of policy and pedagogy, each seeking to address the challenges of learning with, and about, new technology. The account provided here is part of my Digital World and as such is based on my experiences in educational television and development of e-learning in support of basic literacy and digital skills.

During the 1980s and early 1990s, most users of computers and information and communication technology (ICT) were working in universities and multinationals. It is only since then, with the advent of home computing, internet connectivity and the introduction of smartphones, that the requirement for the general population to upskill in relation to ICT was advocated in national policies.

Energized by the internet and relatively cheap access to technology, the new economy required a well-qualified workforce and a consumer population capable of taking advantage of what it had to offer. Before digital, everything new and connected with computers was described by the addition of 'e' as a prefix. Thus, we had e-commerce, e-content and e-mail. Educators were quick to jump on board with e-skills (McCormack 2010) and e-learning. Throughout the 1990s, the education sector response focused on enabling learners to develop technical skills such as those associated with using personal computers and ICT. It was the late 1990s before digital skills became part of the education vocabulary and it was around that time that the notion of digital literacy began to emerge.

The European Computer Driving Licence (ECDL) epitomized the educational approach at the turn of the millennium. New technology was impacting our lives and the idea was to package essential know-how for entry-level users of technology and software. The driving licence motif is revealing, it connected learning with the ability to use technology for your own purposes. The education sector quickly embraced the ECDL as well as similar branded offerings by technology companies. This led to a proliferation of certification options for everyday ICT users. By 2009, ECDL had grown worldwide with 9.7 million candidates in 121 active countries (Leahy and Dolan 2010).[1] These initiatives went some way to meet the needs of adult learners and their tutors.

It is worth noting that most adult educators were not ICT experts, so the structured content of the modules provided the best available guide for tutor and learner. Recalling my own experience as a designer of

---

1 The ECDL has more recently been rebranded as the International Computer Driving Licence, and continues to be rolled out across the world.

digital skills courseware at the time, the early optimism was quickly dispelled as several drawbacks began to emerge. Tutors soon realized that many students were not interested in completing all parts of a course. As adults they self-directed their learning to what they perceived as immediately useful. Furthermore, developments in technology began to outpace the standardized curricula as the introduction of smartphones, camera technology and social media opened new possibilities for content creation and sharing.

These changes corresponded with the increased prevalence in the use of the term digital literacy. The starting point for its popularity is generally regarded as Paul Gilster's (1997) book of the same name. Prior to then, formulations such as computer literacy, ICT-literacy and e-literacy were considered in the literature. Several sources provide useful overviews of the origins and conceptualization of digital literacy (see Bawden 2008; Bacalja et al. 2022; Lankshear and Knobel 2008).

Two questions to be considered in relation to the widespread adoption of the term digital literacy are why 'digital' and why 'literacy'. Dealing with the latter question first, it has always been obvious to me that conflicting definitions of literacy reflected contested epistemologies and there has never been a clear and universally accepted definition of literacy. Literacy definitions ranged from skills orientated (such as Moser 1999), through the work of the New London Group (1996) and to what Gee (1999) calls the 'social turn'.

From an adult education perspective, the most useful theoretical lens is provided by a view of literacy as a socially situated practice (Barton et al. 2000; Papen 2005; Tett et al. 2006). This approach sees literacy as embedded in the activities of everyday life (social practices). Proponents of situated literacy would argue that there is little value in thinking about literacy independent of the context in which it is encountered. This paved the way for educators to shift their focus from measurable skills to context-based competence. As these functional contexts such as shopping, banking and finding information moved online, the scope of situated literacy extended beyond text and print to encompass capabilities associated with new technology.

The word *digital* is often used as a synonym for all aspects of our technology-mediated world. It is useful precisely because it is imprecise and therefore widely applicable. Scientists may point to the digital binary code that underpins the workings of technology, but for most people digital simply means the stuff that changes our world. Digital literacy therefore seems more in keeping with the deeper sociocultural understanding of literacy and situated practice.

Reflecting on thirty years of the dramatic impact of digital technology and building on the sociocultural approach, we consider a fresh formulation of the concept of digital literacy and its connection with adult learning.

In this regard, an assertion by Mezirow (1996) still resonates today. Mezirow argued that literacy is associated with the development of communicative competence and therefore is 'centrally concerned with the crucial and neglected distinction between instrumental and communicative learning, the development of critical reflection and participation in rational discourse - all essential to adult learning' (Mezirow 1996, 115). Mezirow's comments were in relation to print literacy and much in keeping with the ideas of critical literacy theorists such as Freire (1972). They argued that meaningful reading involves more than a straightforward transfer of ideas; but rather it also involves an understanding of context, power relations, genre, history and critical awareness. In a similar way, digital literacy is concerned with these same factors and as such, it encompasses instrumental and communicative learning.

Looking back to the turn of the millennium, we may ask why the communicative aspects of digital literacy were overlooked. From my recollection, the full extent of the transformative potential of the digital world was not fully appreciated. Educators focused on teaching skills and technical competence because that's what learners wanted. Like other appliances, home computers were simply regarded as presenting technical learning challenges; 'show me how to switch it on and I'll take it from there'. The idea that communicative learning might be required would have been considered far-fetched by many educators at the time.

In contrast, from the perspective of today's digitally mediated world, the value and need to develop capabilities for communicative rationality and discourse (Habermas 1984) can be more fully appreciated. Meaningful participation in social media discourse involves skills and abilities that extend beyond the functionality of a device or software platform. Literacy as the capability to make meaning through participation in our shared social practices, quickly becomes digital literacy when the shared social practice is Facebook, Instagram or TikTok.

Digital World

How then can we come to know the Digital World of our learners? Adult learners who participated in a previous study I conducted (Casey 2009) described encounters with technology in terms of the interplay between the traditional world and the Digital World. In many cases, these encounters were associated with feelings of alienation and a sense of being overlooked. One participant, who did not use social media, depicted how friends discussing their conversations online, left her with a sense of isolation and insecurity. For her, the Digital World presented itself as a new social space where her friends congregated without her. As a response, she decided to learn the necessary skills to enable her to be with her friends and engage with the group online.

The phenomenological concept of a lifeworld, introduced by Husserl (2001) and subsequently developed by Habermas (1984), may provide an additional perspective to consider the Digital World. For Habermas, the lifeworld is made up of a storehouse of background assumptions that frame our interactions. While the experience of the world remains as expected, these assumptions go unchallenged. At times of change and upheaval, the resulting disorienting dilemmas (Mezirow 2000) will cause us to question our prevailing assumptions and thereby disrupt the lifeworld.

A case can be made that Digital World forms part of the lifeworld. People don't perceive technology in a passive or neutral manner; economic, social, age-related and gender-related patterning of the lifeworld are all brought to bear on technology-mediated interactions. For instance, an elderly person might say that digital technology is 'out there', associated with practices by others but not part of their world. If that person's circumstances change, for example they begin to use a smartphone, they will experience transformations in how they see themselves through the eyes of others, as participants in the world. This can work both ways; they can be framed as heroic transformations for embracing the new or as regret for lamenting the loss of the traditional.

Digital World Literacy

Digital World Literacy (DWL) is introduced here as a wider and more useful concept than digital literacy. Digital World Literacy is concerned with enabling appropriate levels of participation to allow people to fulfil their life goals. It may be defined as our capability to deal with the ongoing challenges of sustaining personal choice and agency within the changing contexts of our lives. Digital World Literacy therefore enables us to manage our affairs, maintain relationships, achieve lifegoals and fulfil our wishes as we negotiate our practice in the social situations of the modern world.

For many older adults, the dynamic between traditional and digital worldviews is a source of challenge and tension. Everyday tasks such as shopping, banking, booking holidays and finding information, are shifting to equivalent digital domains. These transitions present learning challenges, not just in terms of skills and competence but also in terms of protecting our worldview and identity. Much adult learning is incentivized by our need to participate (Casey 2015). However, the process is not straightforward in relation to DWL; our desire to remain effective and involved competes with the relentless demands of new technology and the changing ways of getting things done. As the digital world becomes increasingly embedded in our homes, workplaces and communities, familiar sites of competence become contested ground between digital and traditional practices. This is also the case for adult and further education teachers where new technology such as artificial intelligence, simultaneously gives rise to opportunities for enhancement and threatens the quality of established practice. Older educators may struggle to keep up and may even find themselves being leapfrogged by more digitally competent students.

The following examples illustrate how DWL facilitates wider appreciation of choice and agency among adult learners. The profiles discussed here are based on composite personas developed from previous research and subsequent informal discussions.

Ben is sixty-eight and retired. He has a sixteen-year-old mobile phone that does not connect to the internet, nor does it have a built-in camera. He uses the text feature to stay in touch with his friends. He also uses the device for online banking and from time to time, he gets text reminders from local services such as the pharmacist to remind him to pick up his prescription. Although Ben does not see himself as anti-technology, he is reluctant to change his ways unnecessarily. For Ben, DWL is about balance and the maintenance of his identity; he regards technology as a means-to-an-end, but he is also wary of the way he sees it as impacting on others. He does not want to be the kind of person who lives their life through their smartphone.

Mary is also in her mid-sixties and she and her smartphone are never apart. She is a frequent user of a range of social media apps and is in regular contact with friends and family. She takes pictures, posts comments and likes to share updates within her social circle. For Mary, DWL is the ability to maintain her social presence and to continue to be part of an ongoing dialogue among friends. Mary regards the smartphone as an essential means of social connection. She feels sorry for people like Ben who miss so much by being unconnected.

From a functional skills approach, the learning challenges for Ben and Mary seem quite different. Mary must master the functionality of her up-to-date smartphone. Ben's is a simpler device but it is used only for text information and telephone conversations. Thinking about digital literacy in terms of technical skills is not very helpful. Put simply, Ben chooses not to require the kind of skills that Mary finds essential. However, they both exhibit high levels of DWL in that they are each capable of living their lives according to their own choices.

In contrast, there are many people and situations where DWL presents a learning challenge. For example, some adults find social media protocols bewildering; concepts such as 'friend', 'trending' and 'following', have specific meanings on social media. Digital World Literacy certainly involves developing a sense of understanding the hidden code of online discourse. It goes deeper, it may also deal with critical awareness of vested interests, questioning evidence, assessing assertions and vigilance for false news, conspiracy theorists, scams and online fraud.

Many older adults describe the sense of being left out and excluded from effective participation in situations that are important and often unavoidable. For example, some people struggle to come to terms with online banking and cashless transactions. In keeping with a situated view of literacy, digital service providers need to be aware of the assumptions they make about the abilities of their intended users. There are many cases where the digital literacy problem resides in the situation rather than the participants. Most but not all people can meet the learning challenges presented by technology-mediated functions such as internet banking, digital healthcare and other services. Often those who find it most difficult to access a service are the same group who are most in need of its benefits. It is unreasonable to problematize those who find it difficult to adapt and learn, the onus is also on the provider to facilitate multiple means of engagement and accessible support for learning.

An experience of Ben (the persona introduced earlier) will help illustrate this point. Ben qualifies for a free public transport pass because of his age. He lives outside the local town and therefore needs to drive to the station to take a train to the city. Customers are required to pay for parking at the station; however, the only visible means of payment is via an app that must be downloaded from the internet using a QR code. Ben does not have a smartphone.

Consider the conflicting messages Ben takes from the situation. On the one hand, he feels valued by a society that provides a free travel pass to people of his age; on the other hand, the parking arrangement clearly signals how he, and many others who do not use smartphones, are overlooked and thereby considered unwelcome. The literacy deficit is not with the individual but with the situation. Notice how the disadvantage for Ben is two-fold, not only is he denied the cash option to pay for his parking, but he is also made to feel this is due to his own inadequacy.

Implications of Digital World Literacy for Educators

Having introduced the concept of DWL, it is worth considering how this may be useful for people working across FET. Digital World Literacy as proposed here, would involve learning in the tension field between all three dimensions of learning – cognitive, social and emotional (Illeris 2003). It would be made up of what you do (skills), how you think (knowledge) and how you value and identify with digital practices (disposition). Disposition may also mean opting to be 'ok as you are'.

The teaching tasks for DWL would imply extending current frameworks such as the Digital Competence Framework for Citizens (Vuorikari 2022) to include topics such as nurturing personal choice and agency, responding to the changing practices of our world and coping with the alienating impact of the digital world. Teaching for DWL would be underpinned by respect for the autonomy and self-determination of adult learners. Digital World Literacy may therefore be positioned within the context of each person's lifelong learning journey.

A pedagogy of DWL may be characterized by the following five statements of learning need:

1. The impact of the digital world presents a significant challenge for adults and is therefore a legitimate topic for learning.
2. The preservation of personal choice and agency is a valid learning goal for adults of all ages.
3. Adults are encouraged and supported to self-determine their goals and adopt multiple learning pathways to enhance their desired digital capabilities.
4. Development of critical awareness of the powerful influences that shape the digital world (including artificial intelligence, algorithms and data mining) is an essential learning task.
5. Advocacy for wider appreciation of how digital world situations can, intentionally or unintentionally, exclude and alienate certain groups from full participation, should be nurtured.

In conclusion, adult, community and further education has an important role in shaping how the benefits of new technologies can be experienced by people of all ages but especially with older adults who were not born into a world where the internet was the norm.

As educators, we should contribute to wider debates on how to meet the needs of these particular students. Ultimately, learning for literacy is about enabling fuller participation in the social practices of our world. Participation does not mean the same for everyone.

The policies and funding structures of further education continue to assert powerful influences on adult education provision. Much of this is helpful and supportive of the work that needs to be done. However, there is also a responsibility on educators to challenge the disproportionate emphasis on skills supply for labour markets or for the development of digitally capable consumers. Older adults, vulnerable to being on the wrong side of the digital divide, should equally be empowered to navigate the digital sphere and unleash their potential. As educators, we are not neutral in this process, we are well placed to work with students to empower them to identify their appropriate learning needs. There is also an onus on us, as adult educators, to extend our own digital literacy to ensure it extends to a critical analysis of the often underappreciated, power of corporations, algorithms and predictive technology in determining our life choices and opportunities (Bradley and Noronha 2022, 123; Táíwò 2022, 72).

Teaching and learning for DWL can provide an alternative framework to skill-based curricula, based on the values of lifelong learning and adult education. The five learning statements outlined above may form a basis for such a revised approach to allow adult educators play their part in creating a better world where the advantages of digital technology can be shared by everyone. We have our own Digital Worlds and, for each of us, a personal sense of where we fit within the dynamic of change.

Chapter 9

TOWARDS A GROUNDED PRACTICE: COMMUNITY EDUCATION IN IRELAND TODAY

Eve Cobain, Susan Cullinane and Suzanne Kyle

We begin with the story of a typical community educator whom we have called Mary. She works for a long-established community organization which receives a variety of funding from state agencies including the local Education and Training Board (ETB), the Health Service Executive (HSE) and the Social Inclusion Community Activation Programme (or SICAP for short) among other smaller funding sources. She is on a two-year contract and pays into the organization's pension scheme.

What drove Mary to work in community education was a commitment to changing the world for the better along with a sense of injustice about how inequalities and poverty hold people back. She knows community education can positively impact on people's lives, both at a personal and collective level and thinks that everyone gains from more equal societies. For Mary, the purpose of education is to enable people to understand the world so that they can be active participants in shaping it for the better. Consciousness-raising dialogic education is an important aspect of her work so that people can address the issues that are negatively affecting them and understand the forces that shape their lives. Together people can build understanding, relationships and social solidarity.

She is also committed to reflective practice and spends time each week thinking on how things went, what she learned and how she might approach the following week. Little wonder she gets frustrated with the policy discourse which sees education primarily as a tool for the development of skills for employment.

With a busy work and home life, she often feels overwhelmed but feels steadier in herself when she can work in a way that is congruent with her strong beliefs. When she is able to see the bigger picture and focus on the things that make the most difference. Why does it sometimes feel like being busy is the most important and valued thing rather than considered action? Why does she often feel a tension between what the organization says are its values – and the reality on the ground? Relationship building, communication and reflective practice seem to go out the window when there is a deadline or when funders change their requirements. Trying to find the cracks to do the work that is needed and meeting the organizational demands is a constant pressure and worry. It's as if she is split in two.

In other words, she is conflicted between what she thinks her priorities *should be* and what her priorities *actually need to be* to keep things ticking over. Mary supports outreach, meaningful planning, needs analyses, relationship building and one-to-one support as the key features of her work. Instead, she often has to prioritize keeping abreast of funding opportunities, filling out funding applications, knowing about policy developments, responding to consultations to make sure grassroots opinions are captured, collecting data for funders and meeting quality assurance requirements so they can keep offering accredited courses. Long-term planning is not an option because of the heavy administrative requirements or short-term funding streams.

There is also this constant pressure to achieve more *outcomes*. But relationship and trust building take time and cannot be rushed. Sometimes it feels like if she just ran lots of IT courses life would be a lot easier. She would like to do more informal courses that engage marginalized people and meet their needs – where learners are often nervous and downcast at the beginning but can blossom and have increased confidence and aspirations for themselves at the end.

She gets frustrated with the amount of time she spends on recording data in a centralized database to 'measure outcomes'. And there is nowhere for her to capture the wider benefits like the 'blossoming' described above. That has no place in the database. The people who take the courses she runs also deal with paperwork, especially a lengthy enrolment form regardless of the length of the course. Mary hates how this impacts how most groups begin. Instead of focusing on needs and ways to address these, producing the enrolment form puts a damper on the work and people often don't understand why so much information is needed. Some people have told her that these forms stop them from doing courses and that they worry about what their data will be used for.

On top of all this, recruiting colleagues to work alongside her is a nightmare as there is a high turnover of staff due to short funding streams and poor working conditions. Overall, staff meetings seem to be continually focused on budgets and funding opportunities to keep the different projects afloat, rather than the practice of education. While colleagues within her own organization are friendly, it is those doing similar critical education work in other organizations that she feels most affinity with. These are the people that share her thoughts on working together to address the issues community education has been facing. They talk about how they can build resilience and capacity, strengthen solidarity and strengthen community education values and principles.

She can see that government policy is getting better at framing community education as part of addressing some really important global issues like widening inequalities, the growth in divisive far right movements, climate change and the fallout from Covid-19. But she worries this is just lip service and is tired of community educators having to work hard to prove their worth and value. She is also tired of pressures between her responsibility to the organization (admin, outputs, meeting targets and delivering work-ready courses) and her responsibility as an emancipatory educator (caring for students, focusing on quality and critical skills for communities). She is walking on a tightrope between her own personal values and principles and the organizational constraints she endures. She doesn't know how long she can sustain this.

This chapter presents primary research that addresses the current state of publicly funded *community education provision* in Ireland. In particular, it seeks to uncover some of the challenges faced by those working in the field by reflecting on practitioner responses to a fictitious profile of a 'typical' community educator, which was developed by the authors and served as a tool to spark reflection, discussion and debate.

Our understanding of community education can be best described as an *approach* to education. As outlined in *Learning for Life: White Paper on Adult Education* (hereafter referred to as *The White Paper*), a landmark government policy publication for community education in Ireland, community education is 'a process of communal education towards empowerment, both at an individual and a collective level' (Department of Education and Science 2000, 110). AONTAS, the Irish national adult education organization, has a definition of community education that likewise affirms its political nature when it states that 'it differs from general adult education provision due to its political and radical methodologies' (AONTAS 2011, 3). According to AONTAS, engaging in this type of learning should support the development of 'a strong capacity for social action, a sense of collective empowerment and an ability to tackle issues of social justice' (AONTAS 2004, 19). As such, we view community education as a form of 'popular education' whose *raison d'être* is 'facilitating critical understandings of the underlying causes of increasing inequalities and social deprivation' (Mayo 2020, 58).

This understanding of community education, as a vehicle for social change, is built on the theories of Brazilian educator and theorist Paulo Freire who advanced a model of education based on principles of dialogue, consciousness-raising and co-creation of knowledge. As other contributors to this book have also pointed out, it is the opposite of the 'banking' model of education, criticized by Freire, which places the educator as the expert at the top of the room with all the knowledge which s/he must impart to the students (Freire 1972, 45–47).

About Us

What motivates the authors of this chapter is a shared commitment to community education provision that can respond to the challenges of our times while remaining true to its roots and values. Both Suzanne and Susan have worked within state and community and voluntary sector community education provision over the past two decades. In our roles we have experienced, and have had the opportunity to observe, the daily challenges faced by practitioners on the ground. We have engaged with significant adult education policy and structural changes over many years. Susan was one of the first appointed state-funded Community Education Facilitators, roles which came about under one of *The White Paper* recommendations to support and resource community education provision in local areas, and has been an active member of the Community Education Facilitators Association (CEFA) since its inception. Her background in education, equality studies and psychotherapy was instrumental in shaping a type of community education provision in County Kildare that had an ethic of care and a culture of human flourishing at its heart. In her previous roles in community development organizations in different parts of Ireland over sixteen years, Suzanne gained an understanding and appreciation for the impact and wide-ranging benefits of community education. Subsequently, as coordinator of the AONTAS Community Education Network (CEN) for almost seven years, she acted as an intermediary between community education practitioners and policymakers, relaying the realities facing both practitioners and learners to the AONTAS team in order to collectively advocate for the sector. Eve, though newer in the adult education space, has regular contact with practitioners and learners engaging in community education. In 2021, Eve led the development of the first census to examine the state of community education in Ireland (Cobain et al. 2021). This research, conducted by AONTAS, highlighted many sustained challenges within the sector in terms of funding and administration, which at the height of Covid-19 came into new relief.

The authors have also coalesced as members of a community education focused group called 'The Three Pillars group'. The group's mission is to raise the profile of community education and build on its history of inclusive and social justice focused adult education practice. Collectively, the authors represent each of the key stakeholder groups that make up the three pillars; namely, practitioners, advocates and academics, from organizations such as CEFA, the AONTAS CEN, ETBs and universities. In 2021, the Three Pillars Group developed a charter which reasserts the radical nature of community education and the belief that it 'is about social inclusion in its broadest sense'. Overall the charter states that:

Community Education ...

... is rooted in equality, justice and empowerment.
... creates voices for those who are furthest from the education system.
... is about social inclusion in its broadest sense.
... is needs based, driven by the community and reflective of lived experiences.
... recognizes the value of accredited and non-accredited learning.
... promotes critical thinking.
... is learner centred, flexible, supportive and developmental.
... is facilitative, group focused and open to new things.
... centres on relationship building.[1]

It is this radical vision of community education that the authors wish to reaffirm and reclaim for these times.

While the community education space is characterized by social justice aspirations, this approach has, in many instances, been curtailed by increasing administrative burdens for staff, and the lack of sustainable funding for a model of education that places a premium on social justice agendas.

Our Approach to Research

Methodologically, this chapter was borne out of a number of conversations between us about these issues and the impact they were having on the ability of practitioners to be value-led in their community education practice. We believed that our discussions had broader resonance, yet felt our ideas needed further exploration in order to represent a truer picture of the experience of

---

[1] The charter can be viewed at https://communityeducationkwetb.ie/2021/05/12/a-charter-for-community-education/.

those working in community education. In writing this chapter, we wished to uncover how other practitioners had experienced significant structural and policy changes to community education over the past decade, and the impact that these have had on their day-to-day practice. As a means of illuminating the experience of others, we developed the profile of a fictitious 'typical' community education practitioner named 'Mary' by drawing on our collective experience of working in this area over many years. An abridged version of this profile opened this chapter. Mary is an attempt to give voice to the experiences of people who are navigating the tensions of working within a policy landscape that has often been at odds with their values.

Six purposively selected colleagues working in a community education leadership role within an ETB setting and/or the community and voluntary sector were invited to respond to the profile as a means of better illuminating the aspirations and lived experience of practitioners. We felt that purposive sampling was a way to use our limited resources effectively to increase the depth of our understanding of the issues at hand (Palinkas et al. 2015). As such, the respondents selected were those that were 'most likely to yield appropriate and useful information' (Kelly 2010, 317). Participants were invited to 'write into the document' or respond in 'whatever way makes sense for you'.[2] The approach sought to create a kind of textual dialogue and provoked a variety of creative responses. Indeed, the research process was consistent with the critical and creative ethos of community education as described by Grummell and Finnegan (2020, 2–3), in that it embodied many of its key features and characteristics including reflection, dialogue, and the co-creation of knowledge.

In line with the methods adopted, this research does not claim to speak for all community educators, but to use the insights from a sample to deepen our understanding of their experience within the current landscape. While it was beyond the scope of this research to carry out a detailed analysis of the experience of an extensive number of practitioners, the exploratory nature of our methods helps further our understanding of a sea change within community education that we believe needs urgent attention.

History and Evolution of Community Education in Ireland

As we begin to consider some of the challenges facing community education organizations and practitioners today, it is helpful to trace the radical roots of

---

2 The research document circulated was longer than the abridged version that we have reproduced here. The full document is available from the researchers on request.

Irish community education and name the social movements which form part of its blueprint.

Grassroots literacy movements, which began to emerge in Ireland in the 1960s (Fitzsimons 2017a, 73–74) are one important strand of community education's radical history, and a strong example of its approach to tacking social exclusion. In response to high demand, adult literacy classes were set up on an *ad hoc* basis around the country (Ward and Ayton 2019). The influence of Freire is felt indelibly on this movement, and his work became a shaping force for Irish community education more broadly.

As community education grew through the 1980s, it was rooted in community life and was responsive to high levels of poverty, unemployment and emigration, challenges acutely felt by women (Connolly 2008, 44). This was highlighted in one of the earliest studies of women's community education in Ireland (Inglis et al. 1993) which focused on what were called daytime education groups run by local voluntary groups of women educating themselves. The authors describe these groups as 'the major phenomenon within adult education in Ireland' (Inglis et al. 8) and the groups provided women with companionship and confidence (Kelleher and Kelleher 1999). These groups recognized that learning had to be supported by childcare and underpinned by other practical supports if it was to be successful in building participation; many operated therefore on a 'no crèche, no class' basis. *The White Paper* also acknowledged the outsized role of women's groups in the evolution of Irish community education, stating that they had 'been central in the defining character of Community Education in Ireland and merit particular recognition for their contribution to date' (Department of Education and Science 2000, 111). Moreover, *The White Paper* (2000, 111) applauds these community-based women's groups for taking 'lived experience' as their starting point. It states that:

> In starting from that point, as opposed to a syllabus or institution-driven agenda, Community Education assumes a different character to all other forms of formal education, not merely in terms of its content but in terms of the relationships between the participants themselves; between the participants and tutors; the learning process and outcomes and the modes of assessment.

This model is distinctly Freirean, in that it strives to adopt a dialogic and reflexive approach to learning, as opposed to promoting the aforementioned 'banking system' of education where the tutor 'fills' the student with the 'contents of his narration' (Freire 1972, 45). Within the Freirean process learning spills through the boundaries of the classroom, and through a process of conscientization, both tutors and participants become more aware of the power structures at play in their daily lives, and their potential to disrupt them.

Another important pillar of an Irish community education tradition has been community development. In its early days, the community development model in Ireland took a reformist approach based on the principles of empowerment and social change through equality of participation in democratic structures and processes. This was also led and influenced by the growth in women's groups, demonstrating the interrelationship of these various movements. The Combat Poverty Agency, which was established in 1986 to raise awareness and promote evidence-based measures to combat poverty in Ireland, defined community development as 'a process whereby those who are marginalized and excluded are enabled to gain self-confidence, to join others and to participate in actions to change their situation and to tackle the problems that face their community' (Combat Poverty Agency 2000, 2). According to social researcher Brian Harvey, what emerged in Ireland through the 1980s and 1990s was regarded as at the cutting edge of community development and anti-poverty work throughout the European Union (Harvey 2015, 8). In 1990, the emergence of the Community Development Programme, under the then Department of Social Welfare, led to recognition and resources for a social change model of community work, central to which was community education. It was under this programme that funding was provided for independent community development groups working with communities throughout the country who were considered the most disadvantaged. *The White Paper* also acknowledged the strong links between community development and community education including the 'common goal of the collective empowerment of the participants based on an analysis of the structural barriers to people's life chances' (Department of Education and Science 2000, 110).

The publication of *The White Paper* in 2000, as stated earlier, was a landmark for community education in Ireland more generally. The policy document allocated an entire chapter (Chapter 5) to addressing the role of community education and defined it as a means 'whereby marginalised groups formulate a process of user-driven, learner-centred and communal education' (Department of Education and Science 2000, 28). *The White Paper* made a commitment to support the growth of community education, proposing the appointment of a national team of thirty-five Community Education Facilitators who would be 'required to demonstrate a deep-rooted knowledge of the communities they serve and a clear understanding and empathy with the philosophy and processes of community education' (115). The role was designed to facilitate the funding of independently managed and non-statutory community education organizations (AONTAS 2004) and to nurture and support the development of new community-based learning groups (Department of Education and Science 2000, 114).

The New Adult and Further Education Landscape

In the years following the global economic crash of 2008, the adult education policy landscape shifted dramatically. When the new national further education body, SOLAS, was formed in 2013 and launched by then Minister for Education and Skills, Ruairi Quinn TD, his government saw it as a means of addressing 'skills gaps in our labour force' (Frawley 2013) and providing integrated, flexible and cost-effective programmes that would be responsive to individuals and the economy. This led to the replacement of thirty-three VECs, which had been the main providers of further education (McGuinness et al. 2014), with sixteen regional ETBs. This happened in tandem with the establishment of Quality and Qualifications Ireland (QQI), an amalgamation of the previously operational Further Education and Training Awards Council (FETAC), the Higher Education and Training Awards Council (HETAC), the Irish Universities Quality Board (IUQB) and the National Qualifications Authority of Ireland (NQAI). At national and European policy level, the emphasis was now on building skills for the economy over social and community development and the renaming of the Department of Education and Science to the Department of Education and Skills in 2010 was indicative of this new focus.

While the vast majority of stakeholders in Ireland viewed adult and further education as addressing both social inclusion and labour market agendas (McGuinness et al. 2014), the policy discourse shifted dramatically in Ireland to one of labour market activation, with the term Further Education and Training (FET) replacing that of Adult Education as the umbrella term for the field (Shannon 2019). All these changes led to a new approach to community education policy, new accountability mechanisms and financial restrictions. The political climate at this time was one in which the Community and Voluntary Sector had, only a few years earlier, been hit by funding cuts of up to 41 per cent (Kelleher and O'Neill 2018, 23) and civil society organizations such as the Combat Poverty Agency were closed. Patricia Kelleher and Cathleen O'Neill (2018) describe how this constituted a significant blow to community education and development as this body had built strong alliances by bringing together personnel from a research institute, universities, voluntary organizations, working class and rural communities to combat social exclusion and poverty. Moreover, the language of community development, and local projects themselves, had been colonized and replaced with a training and work activation programme with 'repressive bureaucratic procedures' (Kelleher and O'Neill 2018, 24). As such, while community education providers were responding to the fallout from the recession in communities that bore the brunt of austerity, they were also required to navigate new further education structures, build relationships with their new regional ETBs and deal with new funding systems and competitive tendering processes for community development funding (Magrath and Fitzsimons 2020). Targets and outputs based on individual progression, such as certification and employment, became the priority, and notions of what constituted progression at policy level were very often at odds with what practitioners on the ground were aiming to achieve. The individual learner gaining employment and coming off the 'live register' (i.e. register of social welfare recipients) was given precedence over community building and long-term collective outcomes aimed at reducing poverty.

Perspectives from the Ground – Navigating the Contradictions

A Clash of Values

The responses to our practitioner profile unearthed some major tensions in terms of the realities of working within the confines of what equality theorists have called this 'care-less' neoliberal state (O'Grady 2018). One the one hand, responses strongly emphasized a politicized or politicizing view of community education, which was seen as 'an alternative, a radical approach that democratizes the learning space and empowers learners' (Respondent 2). Yet on the other, they highlighted many challenges that divert practitioners from this approach. Many of these tensions have gradually surfaced over the years since the publication of *The White Paper*. As one respondent explained,

> The practitioners that were originally appointed under *The White Paper* had a space for reflection and developing a deep understanding of community education, and a space for networking and critical reflection. The absence of this cannot be underestimated. (Respondent 3)

Moving practitioners away from a Freirean approach, it was felt that funders were taking a short-sighted and atomizing approach to learner support, resulting in a 'focus on one to one and family provision rather than [supporting] a collective, group or community solution to local issues' (Respondent 3). This tension was echoed by another respondent who stated that while she was 'led by collectively identified community priorities – "nothing about us, without us," these localized issues and priorities were often quite different to funders' objectives' (Respondent 6). In line with this, another respondent described how they were struggling to practice 'emancipatory, transformative education while [also] addressing the skills gap' (Respondent 4) often prioritized by funders.

A key tenet of community education is its grounding in an analysis of unequal relations of power and resources (Shaw and Crowther 2014, 395), but the responses to the practitioner profile indicated that administrative requirements of the work are leaving little time for analysis and reflection on work practices. Practitioners are therefore left concerned about the extent to which they are promoting social inclusion and democratic learning spaces or, in fact, inadvertently colluding in the maintenance of existing inequalities. One respondent, concerned about outcomes for participants of accredited community education courses, highlighted this dilemma:

> We send people into the world of work with no concept of what trade unions are – we don't include this in preparing people for the world of work. The sector has bought into it by not reflecting on issues like this. People aren't told that the collective is stronger than the individual. The neoliberal mindset is about the individual and this makes people less powerful. (Respondent 5)

As such, while community education courses have traditionally placed a premium on consciousness-raising, there is sometimes little room left for critical reflection in the classroom. Another respondent likewise described the 'increased administrative burdens reducing our capacity for the quality and depth our work needs to be effective' (Respondent 6). Another expressed even deeper ambivalence: 'Are we becoming more bureaucratic – a service – language that's turning us in to bureaucrats?' (Respondent 4). These perspectives are consistent with other research in this area (Fitzsimons 2017a; Kyle 2018) which has uncovered considerable frustrations among those working in the sector as they navigate the bureaucratic demands that come with data collection, funding applications and a disproportionate focus on short-term quantitative outputs over long-term, qualitative community and social outcomes.

Moreover, data collection, particularly in the shape of learner enrolment forms, and other bureaucratic requirements were felt to pose a great threat, removing the organization 'from the centre of the community' (Respondent 6). The salt to the wound in the case of enrolment forms was that numerous consultations took place in the design of data collection processes (Aontas 2023), yet submissions made by those with experience of working on the ground – who anticipated the consequences of such heavy enrolment requirements – did not seem to be taken into account. The result is that while government say they wish to engage so-called 'hard-to-reach' learners – including target groups such as 'Travellers', 'one parent families' and 'migrants' (Department of Education and Science 2000, 13) – it is the centres that become hard to reach with their exhaustive enrolment procedures creating a barrier between learners and their educational aspirations.

These requirements have resulted in many practitioners feeling unable to cope with demands. As one respondent noted:

> I would say that many CEFs [Community Education Facilitators] left the post due to disillusionment or were promoted into roles that were part of an oppressive system that introduces computer-based systems that counted numbers and savaged the previous gathering of essential data. [...] The Networks and Partnership that had been developed with community based groups and other organizations were also severely damaged. [...] Community Practitioners in community/voluntary sector and statutory providers were left with the task of relaying the changes and the paperwork requirements to their groups [...] this was a very demoralising task. (Respondent 3)

The requirement to endlessly prove the value of the work was also a source of frustration, with the same respondent describing their need to constantly defend community education, and 'value for money for courses without accreditation' (Respondent 3). Another described 'huge pressure around accreditation as the only measure' (Respondent 4), highlighting the problem of having to measure what matters to policy rather than what matters to people (Crowther 2018, 22). Yet another respondent protested: 'you could spend your whole life ticking boxes and not giving people what they need' (Respondent 6). For those responding to the profile, then, the focus of policymakers is almost always given to that which can be quantifiably measured over that which cannot, a point captured by Solnit and Fernandez (2014, 97) who talk about the danger of prioritizing 'the utilitarian over the mysteries and meanings that are of greater use to our survival'.

Our research also uncovered the work that is rarely if ever captured; the everyday challenges and additional labour that result from the under-resourcing of the sector. One respondent suggested adding to the profile a piece about:

> the days Mary sets out to do something important ... and gets side-lined dealing with the blocked toilet/internet outage/paper-jam in the photocopier/receptionist out sick/etc. Dealing with mini-crises on a regular/daily basis can be draining. (Respondent 1)

Helen Colley does not hold back in her assessment of the psychological implications of such challenges when she speaks of the 'chasms between practitioners' ethical values on the one hand, and economic value on the other' (Colley 2012, 332). These chasms 'halt them in their tracks and threaten descent into a void. That void is one of existential crisis [...] the game, as it now has to be played' notes Colley, 'makes little sense' (332). This 'game' can take its toll on practitioners at a personal and professional level through work-related stress, exhaustion and disillusionment (332). A dilemma therefore exists around how practitioners can support learners in reflective practice and self-care if those practices cannot be modelled among practitioners themselves.

Precarity and Working Conditions

Despite having an in-depth awareness of issues affecting the communities with whom they work, as well as trusting relationships within those communities, practitioners spoke of powerlessness and limited autonomy in their practice. This is connected to the precarity and insecurity that often comes with working in adult education (O'Neill and Fitzsimons 2020) and within the community and voluntary sector. On the subject of individual job stability, some went so far as to say that they would fear for their future employment prospects if they were to bring too much of themselves to their role. Reflecting on Mary's situation, one respondent added the following text into the profile:

> Most of all, she feels [her two-year contract] limits her autonomy in the role as she feels vocalising her beliefs or putting her head above the [parapet] in any way, could jeopardise future employment with the organization. (Respondent 2)

The contradiction between the precarious nature of employment conditions for those working in adult and community education (O'Neill 2015, 34) and the expectation of 'professionalism' was also evident in our findings, with one respondent stating the following:

> I never had a two-year contract – it was always a one-year contract. [...] While I had a pension option in some places I worked in (but some of my community sector employers did not make employer contributions making it almost worthless), I could honestly never afford to pay into a pension as the pay rates were so low in comparison to ETB/public sector rates of pay. There were no increments. Trying to support a family while being a community worker in Dublin is not easy, especially if you are renting! (Respondent 6)

Another added: 'while Mary feels very lucky to be employed, her two-year contract causes much anxiety and uncertainty' (Respondent 2). There were further concerns regarding the broader impact of these working conditions for the sector – 'precarious work doesn't encourage new people', it was noted, so 'it's an aging sector' (Respondent 4).

Existing challenges within the community education space became even more pertinent in the height of, and in the wake of, the Covid-19 pandemic. The under-resourcing of the sector as a whole came into sharp relief at this time, with research highlighting an urgent need for sustained multi-annual funding for independent community education providers (Cobain et al. 2021). Many providers lost access to funding sources and revenue streams that had been crucial to their provision during the initial stages of the lockdown. As one practitioner, interviewed as part of the CEN Census conducted by AONTAS during this period, noted, 'those of us who operate under the social enterprise model now have no income streams. [Our] education income stream ceased overnight (course fees, room rental)' (Cobain et al. 2021, 41). At the same time, providers had additional financial needs in providing necessary supports to their learners.

The CEN census found that practitioners during this time were confronted by a great deal of change, and felt a duty of care to learners that in some cases added significant strain at a time when many were themselves experiencing challenges around health and job security. As Colley (2012) highlights, being confronted with unfamiliar ways of thinking, relating and behaving creates deep disorientation that makes learning very difficult. 'Disorienting dilemmas' (Mezirow 1991) can also activate older defence mechanisms, including omniscience or omnipotence (Formenti and West 2018), which were evident in the surfacing of a 'hyper productivity' in the early days of the pandemic and lockdown (Ahmad 2020). Practitioners interviewed as part of the AONTAS CEN Census highlighted the exponential demands that they faced in supporting learners during this time. During the period of emergency remote learning, this support entailed over '200 calls a week' to learners for one organization (Cobain et al. 2021, 36). A staff member noted that 'when the office closes at 5 o'clock the phone is switched over to my phone. Technically we're on call seven days a week'.

These changes and additional demands were happening within the context of an already overstretched sector, further reducing the ability of practitioners to engage in any kind of reflexivity, a practice described by one respondent to the practitioner profile as a means of teasing out the 'dilemmas' that come with 'increased administrative burdens' (Respondent 6). Naturally, this lack of reflective space poses a challenge in terms of adapting to perpetual change while remaining grounded in the values of community education.

Building Networks

To begin to address or reflect on the challenges discussed above, the importance of building networks of support and communities of practice was highlighted in one response to the practitioner profile: Mary wonders if other practitioners have the same experience as her [and] would love to be able to talk to other practitioners (Respondent 3). Such networks may present themselves as an opportunity for democratic deliberation, where the values of community education highlighted in this research may be reasserted and rediscovered. Strengthening formal and informal networks is crucial, even more so in the wake of the disorienting dilemma of the coronavirus pandemic.Networks help 'legitimise practice, provide spaces to learn from each other and validate experiences' (Fitzsimons 2017a, 234).They can be used to share information, showcase, consult, collaborate, campaign and advocate for the sector. In this way, practice can start with lived experience, placing it within collective structures and building solutions based on solidarity and common goals.

The AONTAS Community Education Network (CEN) along with the Community Education Facilitators Association (CEFA) and the more recently established Three Pillars Group, are spaces valued by practitioners where the struggles they encounter in their practice can be shared and solutions developed. In such a way, as the title of one of our Three Pillars webinars suggests, the politics of community education can be reasserted (Connolly et al. 2021). This reassertion will involve disrupting 'established patterns', as Fitzsimons describes, 'in a way that unlocks the potential for groups to become spaces for cultural, educational and psychological openness' (Fitzsimons 2017a, 239).

It is also worth exploring other fields of interest, since stepping outside our comfort zones can allow for creative flashes of insight and the formation of supportive cross-sector alliances (Daft and Marcic 2013). Initiatives in which academic institutions build relationships with community education organizations, and become collaborators in their work provide opportunities to do this, as would international alliance building with popular and critical education providers across Europe and further afield. More alliances could also be formed between community education organizations and non-state–funded grassroots groups organizing around issues of racism, migrant rights and housing, to name a few. As highlighted in this research, consciousness-raising activities have been a driving force in Irish community education since its inception, and reasserting alliances with organizations with a broader educational remit could be one step towards re-asserting the disruptive, Freirean objectives that are at the roots of the practice. Samantha Power popularized the term 'upstander' as someone who, rather than being a bystander, stands up for what they believe in, (Power 2002).Community educators can be upstanding by choosing our level of compliance in response to ethical dilemmas. Fitzsimons (2017a) and O'Grady (2018) also describe ways to resist, cultivate scepticism and work through disorienting dilemmas in order to remain true to the roots of community education.

In Ireland today, *The White Paper*, which espouses a grassroots or bottom-up approach, remains a policy for community education, whether or not these principles are broadly upheld at national policy level. We are also witnessing, in more recent times, a mobilization of anti-racism groups, showing solidarity with refugees in response to far-right, anti-immigrant protests. We can use this backdrop to re-invigorate the critical, Freirean approach that locates personal experience within wider societal structures (Shaw and Crowther 2014), and involves an awareness of injustice and unequal power relations. In this way we can turn again towards a grounded, equality-focused and inclusive community education practice.

Conclusion

This chapter has highlighted the tension at play between the often radical and social justice-oriented values of community education practitioners working in state-funded organizations and the realities of working on the ground. Since the restructuring of the sector post-2008, organizations have faced many difficulties in terms of navigating insecure funding, increased administrative burdens, reporting demands, and a lack of job security. Moreover, organizations who seek to be 'led by collectively identified community priorities' (Respondent 6), and who foreground an 'emancipatory, transformative [model of] education' (Respondent 4), have increasingly struggled to justify their work, particularly their non-accredited offerings, to funders. For those faced with these daily challenges, particularly in the wake of Covid-19, these tensions can seem insurmountable at times.

In researching and writing this chapter, we were motivated, however, by the responses of those engaging with the profile, and took inspiration from the following comments on the value of sharing 'Mary's story':

> It's very effective and gives us all a voice, expressing our frustrations and lived experience of CE [community education], which unfortunately isn't always pretty! (Respondent 2).
>
> The profile is really good, captures voice of all practitioners. There isn't anyone that would say 'that isn't me!' It captures the pressure and the guilt. (Respondent 5)

Collectively revisiting the history, practice and ethos of community education, as well as unapologetically naming the issues facing those working in the area, are mechanisms for building solidarity among practitioners and shaping the future of community education in a complex global climate.

Chapter 10

IDENTITY (TRANS-)FORMATION IN SECOND-CAREER FET TEACHERS

Brendan Kavanagh, Francesca Lorenzi
and Elaine McDonald

This chapter will consider the process of identity (trans-)formation among second-career teachers within the Irish Further Education and Training (FET) sector. Mezirow's Transformational Learning Theory is used to provide a lens through which to view the processes of career change and professional identity (trans-)formation. Career change and the resultant identity (trans-)formation can be a challenging time involving many transitions and radical changes. Recognizing the heterogeneity of the FET sector, the focus of this chapter is on Further Education Colleges.

The uniqueness of the FET sector in Ireland brings about a tension as one of its strengths, its diversity, is also its Achilles heel. The continual misunderstanding regarding college-based, Further Education (FE) provision is made apparent in its close connection to the post primary sector and in the lexicon used when discussing it. Language has power, the power to describe, the power to acknowledge, and the power to denigrate. Unfortunately, the language used regarding FE is often somewhat derogatory and misleading, resulting in low expectations regarding the sector and those therein (O'Leary and Rami 2017), which ultimately may negatively affect the identity (trans-)formation process.

The chapter begins by providing a brief overview of the FE college structure, highlighting the negative perception of FET which is evident through the language used regarding it. It then progresses to explore the complex motivations of those who move into teaching within the FET sector as a second career. Second-career teachers bring a wealth of experience from their previous career into teaching. The chapter then moves to focus on how these teachers differ from their first-career colleagues, exploring some of these differences. In the final section of the chapter, a number of these challenges and the supports which assist in the identity (trans-)formational process are presented.

The Irish Further Education and Training Sector

The Irish FET sector is frequently described as being unique. This uniqueness is evidenced through its diversity, namely the variety of locations, educational courses provided, the ability and the age range of learners. As an educational sector it has grown rapidly, essentially being the amalgamation of disparate educational environments, which had worked and developed independently, in uncontrolled and unstructured ways (Department of Education and Science 1995). Prior to 2013, responsibility for post second-level education and training, in addition to administration and policy development, was distributed between separate authorities. This *ad hoc* arrangement continued until the passing of the *Education and Training Boards Act 2013* and the *Further Education and Training Act 2013* which unified the sector.

The FET sector today exists in an educational space which is neither secondary education nor higher education, and yet it is drawn between both. It provides a unique and widely disparate context in which to work and learn. It is expansive in nature, casting its educational net far and wide and, more recently, the government have started to position it as being part of what they have started to call a 'unified tertiary system' encompassing further and higher education (Department of Further and Higher Education, Research, Innovation and Science 2022). The FET sector seeks to provide education and training, and to counter social exclusion through supporting marginalized groups (McGuinness et al. 2014). To accomplish this, it encompasses multiple areas which results in the creation of an educational sector that escapes neat categorizations. This community of educational provision includes Youthreach, apprenticeships, Senior Traveller Training Centres, adult literacy programmes and Post Leaving Certificate (PLC) courses (Department of Education and Science 2004). For clarity, in this chapter, use of the term 'FET sector' will specifically refer to PLC programme provision within the FET sector, which provides post second-level education leading to employment or enabling access to higher education. McGuinness et al. (2018, 8) consider PLC programmes to be 'the cornerstone of further education and training (FET) in Ireland'.

Language as Power

Grummell and Murray (2015) noted the existence of negative perceptions regarding further education. Moreover, there is a continuing misconception that those within it, students and teachers, are somehow less capable and of a lower calibre when compared to other educational environments. The addition of unhelpful names reinforces such misunderstandings, with Edwards (2009, 3) noting that:

> names are important, as are the 'naming narratives' by which we describe ourselves. Consequently, the misuse or the appropriation of names […] can be both an insult and an attack on identity.

An example of this lies in a prefix 'second' which is frequently used when describing FE. In some instances, it is legitimately used to describe what is happening. The students who take the opportunity to study in this sector are sometimes seen as partaking in 'second-chance' education. This education is delivered by 'second chance educators' (Hickey et al. 2020, 2). While there is limited research regarding the Irish FET sector, it would appear that many of the academic staff working within the sector are 'second-career' teachers (Bates Evoy 2017). We interpret second-career teachers as individuals who left a previous occupation and subsequently entered the teaching profession, bringing previous experience and identities with them. The word 'second' can carry with it an inherent stigma which the sector does not deserve. Typically, 'second' implies inferiority, lesser value and subordination within the hierarchical educational structure. Second-career teachers have chosen to enter the teaching profession later in life for numerous reasons. They are not, nor should they be considered as being, second-best or somehow less.

Another aspect of negative perceptions is the use of unhelpful tags that can reinforce misunderstandings and creates unhelpful distinctions which have the potential to cause disquiet and affect the process of identity (trans-)formation for educators entering the sector. For example, the very use of the word 'teacher', which is the official word used when describing the academic staff working within the colleges of further education in the FET sector, is somewhat problematic. Within the Irish educational structure, tertiary education includes education provided at FE and Higher Educational (HE) levels. Both provide post secondary school education, albeit at differing levels on the National Framework of Qualifications (Quality and Qualifications Ireland 2021). However, despite the association with tertiary education, teaching staff within colleges of FE are in actuality more closely connected to the post primary sector than to HE. One example of this disconnect is in the use of the title of 'teacher' in FE college contexts in Ireland which, it must be noted, compares with the usage of 'lecturer' or 'tutor' in FE in the UK. While academic staff in universities may teach, they nonetheless understand themselves as being more than a teacher. Teacher is a title most often associated with primary and post primary education, and its usage is perhaps indicative of the perceived inferior status held by FE educators, and the sector in general (Boland and Hazelkorn 2022).

This relegation from tertiary level to secondary level was recognized by O'Sullivan (2018, 319) who contends that FE 'operates within the post-primary sector but has not been integrated within it'. He further argues that FE colleges, many of which follow a second-level model are essentially just 'post-primary schools staffed with post-primary teachers delivering FET courses'. The perception of FE as being somehow different from post primary education is further compromised by the fact that FE teacher contracts and conditions are the same as those for second-level teachers (McGuinness et al. 2018). In addition, Section 30 of the *Teaching Council Act* states that all teachers must be registered with the Teaching Council in order to be paid their salary, with FE teachers being separately classified as 'Route 3'. This requirement, while providing a means of safeguarding standards, also poses a challenge, as it restricts the recruitment of individuals who have industrial expertise but who do not meet the necessary requirements to register. In contrast, registration with the Teaching Council is not a requirement for those working in higher education.

The stigma of being 'lesser', which is borne by the further education teachers may be reduced through a conscious choice concerning the language used when discussing it. The continued presence of terms which give rise to negative perceptions may act as a deterrent to those who have an as of yet unfulfilled desire to teach, regardless of their motivations to join the teaching profession. The application of negatively toned language by journalists such as 'Cinderella of the broader education system' (McGuire 2013), 'the backwater of the education system' (McGuire 2013), as 'the black sheep of the education system' (Flynn 2012, para. 1) and 'the backdoor to higher education' (Sweeney 2016, 1) reflects an overall lack of awareness and recognition of FE. This language, coupled with continual under-funding and under-resourcing (O'Sullivan 2018) may inadvertently imply that further education is somehow second best within the hierarchy of Ireland's educational framework. In actuality, certain aspects of the FET sector explicitly aim to promote progression to higher education and are not merely a surreptitious route into higher education.

While its diversity is undoubted, it is a mistake to view FE as a disconnected educational sector which provides learners with a stand-in, safety-net education. It is a valid educational route for those who, for whatever reason, choose to take it. In addition to the phrases previously mentioned, further education is often subtly burdened with contentious, negatively loaded terminology.

For example, 'alternative' is used liberally when describing or discussing any of its constituent elements and has the potential to negatively influence public opinion of the sector and the identity of its teachers.

'Alternative' is a word used to describe something which is removed from the mainstream, different from the norm and implies separation and inequality. Within the context of education in Ireland, the norm is considered as the traditional route, moving from primary to post-primary and then onto higher education. The use of the tag 'alternative' alludes to a divergence in the educational path being taken, signalling a move from the traditional to the unconventional. Of late, within the broader social context, alternative has become synonymous with falsity and deceit, through the use of phrases like 'alternative facts'. The use of phrases like 'alternative pathways', 'alternative routes' (Conway et al. 2009) and 'alternatively certified teachers' (Newton et al. 2020, 3) suggests that there is a 'correct' route into the teaching profession. Consequently, there is almost an implication that those who do not follow this career path are in some way intruding into a profession.

Complex Motivations to Join the Teaching Profession

While further education is widely recognized as being diverse, the teaching staff working within it add a further element of complexity, being broadly categorized as either first-career or second-career teachers. First-career teachers are those who may aspire to teach from a young age and have chosen to pursue teaching as their first career. In contrast, second-career teachers have changed career, entering the teaching profession from multiple professional backgrounds and bringing with them a rich mix of professional skills and experience. Individuals enter the teaching profession, particularly in FE, for a wide variety of reasons and at different stages of their career journey, which may be viewed as being both horizontal and vertical in nature, and develops over an individual's lifetime (Phillips 2015). The horizontal element comprises a linear, past-present-future movement. The vertical journey relates to position within a specific area of employment, frequently referred to by terms like 'climbing the ladder' and 'glass ceiling'. Both journeys are important in this context, as for many FET teachers, education is a second career. This entails a change in both the horizontal journey – the change in career – and the vertical journey, as the move means returning to the position of novice, albeit with experience.

Richardson and Watt (2010, 139) recognized the 'centrality of teacher motivation' with regard to career decision-making. Motivators may be viewed as essentially pushing or pulling an individual away from a career or drawing them into one. Push motivators are frequently subjective in nature, while pull motivators are most often objective, and are related to external factors. For the purpose of clarity, these elements will be examined independently. However these 'push' and 'pull' factors should not be seen as mutually exclusive, given that they may occur simultaneously, to a greater or lesser extent.

In some cases, individuals aspire to teach at an early age, and given the choice, they would enter the profession as a first career. However, due to a variety of circumstances, they may not be able to follow this career path. Only in later life were they able to fulfil their desire and pursue their preferred, first-choice profession as a second career and not as a second-best option (Anthony and Ord 2008). Career change may be voluntary or involuntary and goes beyond normal career progression. Ibarra (2006, 77) considered it as being:

> a subset of work role transitions that include a change of employers, along with some degree of change in the actual job or work role and the subjective perception that such changes constitute a 'career change'.

Career choice and career change are not passive, impetuous events. Instead, they are dynamic and complicated processes which are influenced by multiple factors and bring about change in profession, and ultimately in the person and their perspectives.

One perception of second-career teacher motivation may be summed up in Shaw's Maxim 36 phrase which is often misquoted and used in a derogatory manner: 'those who can, do; those who can't, teach'. The use of a phrase like this undermines those who are entering teaching later in life. It suggests that second-career teachers are somehow inferior, and differently motivated when compared to those who chose teaching as an initial career path. Perhaps there is an inevitable inference that necessity was the motivation for turning to teaching as a second career, which does not acknowledge the career change as being a normal part of the career process. It may raise questions as to why an individual changed career. Was it due to failing in their previous career as a consequence of a lack of ability or general incompetence? Did they leave because of career paralysis, or was it that they just want an easier life owing to advanced age? Fallacious thoughts such as these may give rise to unwarranted hostility and encourage the misconception that second-career teachers are predominantly extrinsically motivated. In reality, Baeten and Meeus (2016, 173) recognized that second-career teachers frequently possess 'strong intrinsic motivation'. High levels of intrinsic motivation are indicative of an individual searching for 'someone to be' (Waterman 2004, 210), and their transition into teaching is the result of the appeal of teaching, and a desire to share their knowledge and not the quest for extrinsic benefits such as longer holidays, salary or job security. The aspiration to teach may stem from previous, personal experience within an educational environment, or arise from an apparent ability to teach. This interest may also be the result of feelings of responsibility towards students or the apparent challenge, enjoyment and internal satisfaction brought about by teaching.

For Anthony and Ord (2008, 364), the motives of those entering teaching as a first or subsequent career are considered to be 'multifaceted, complex, at times emotionally charged and contradictory'. Motivations, like other contextual factors, can positively and negatively influence the process of professional identity (trans-)formation, with 'self-realization values' (Waterman 2004, 216) being key elements to both motivation and identity (trans-)formation. A purely intrinsically motivated desire to teach may lead to frustration and stress if the individual's ideals are overwhelmed by the reality and the challenges of teaching. In contrast, motivation, which is predominantly extrinsic in nature, may affect levels of commitment and positive relationship building with others. The decision to work as a teacher in the FET sector illustrates that while there may be differences between first- and second-career teachers, which includes their motivations, the individual is committed and willing to assist students as they engage with the FET sector.

Attempting to Profile Second-Career Teachers

Career changers are an intriguing and disparate grouping who are not confined to any one specific discipline. Their diversity of life histories, professional backgrounds and experience contribute significantly to the wealth of knowledge within the further education teaching profession. This professional experience adds a richness and credibility to the classroom, and to FE colleges. However, while being an advantage, this experience is sometimes not acknowledged or undervalued, perhaps due to negative perceptions of second-career teachers. Second-career teachers are often presented as being different and they may view themselves in the same way. When compared to other teachers, these differences may be 'subtle but significant' (Chambers 2002, 212). Frequently, these differences lie in the elements they bring into the teaching profession, which they have gained through previous work and engagement in real-life experiences. These skills and professional knowledge may accentuate the difference between first- and second-career teachers. The result may be that second-career teachers, regardless of their novice status within education, may believe they offer new perspectives which connect the real world and the classroom in a way in which first-career, professionally inexperienced teachers cannot. This perception of difference may also give rise to a subtle elitism among second-career teachers. This may manifest itself where second-career teachers who had graduated with a degree identified themselves as being 'scholars' (Laming and Horne 2013, 334) whose primary purpose is the sharing of their knowledge. In contrast, those without a degree were viewed as better suited to focusing on students' social development. Differences in knowledge and expertise may inadvertently establish a hierarchy within the ranks of second-career teachers, creating what may be considered as second-class, second-career teachers. Being different does not mean second-career teachers are somehow 'less'. They do not possess less ability, less skill, less enthusiasm or less motivation when compared to their first-career colleagues. On the contrary, they have attained specific competences and experience and bring elements of authenticity into the classroom, enhancing both the quality of their teaching and the wider profession.

The skills possessed by second-career teachers may be classified as being 'soft' or 'hard'. Soft skills are considered as being implicit in nature and include social and cognitive skills while hard skills are more explicit and include industry-specific practical skills. Some of the skills second-career teachers bring to the FET sector are considered to be 'hard' skills, with McGuinness et al. (2018) noting that course provision in the FET sector is frequently determined by the skills of available teaching staff. The practical, hands-on experience gained by second-career teachers in previous employment may provide them with a greater knowledge base than first-career teachers. Moreover, continuity of skill usage, between past career and the teaching role, may make the change of career and status easier to navigate.

Some of the skills possessed by second-career teachers may be complex, specialist technical or cognitive skills, which diminish over time through lack of practice. The degradation of these skills may potentially have a negative impact upon the quality of teaching being provided. To keep these skills up to date, periodic refresher training may be needed, which may require returning to areas of professional practice. This continual need to return for upskilling and retraining may prove problematic for the process of identity (trans-)formation, as this cohort of second-career teachers may find it more challenging to fully form a new clear professional identity while having to remain closely connected to previous identities. Additionally, there may be issues with returning to engage in retraining for second-career teachers whose move into teaching was strongly motivated by 'push' factors, such as redundancy.

The move to a second career as a teacher within the FET sector essentially results in an experienced professional becoming an (in)experienced novice. This occurs because simultaneously they bring professional experience into their new career, but they lack teaching experience. This change in status (vertical career) from what was potentially a successful position within another career to the position of beginner, may be a stressful time. Those with previous career experience may not be able, or agreeable, to all the changes expected or required. Those entering the teaching profession from careers or positions in which they were highly experienced and respected may find change more difficult to accept. In addition, the loss of camaraderie which had been experienced in a previous career setting, may lead to feelings of isolation within a new career. Second-career teachers may not be able to let go of all elements of previous career identities, which makes the transition to the positions of student teacher and novice teacher more challenging. This is particularly true when their previous careers entailed high levels of independence and required the performance of leadership or managerial roles.

Tigchelaar et al. (2008, 1546) noted that the identities of second-career teachers, who were given greater autonomy, underwent 'surprising experiences of change'. However, it would be a mistake to assume that leadership in non-educational careers transfers seamlessly into a teaching environment. The autonomy given to second-career teachers, by virtue of maturity and subject expertise, can be daunting for the novice teacher. Recognition of inexperience in the classroom setting may be appropriate, although difficult to accept. Not all the skills possessed by second-career teachers will be easily, or automatically transferred into the new classroom setting. Teaching is a specialized area and may be vastly different in regard to nature, culture, familiarity and expectations, when compared to previous positions of employment. Consequently, not all competencies and skills, regardless of their value, are necessarily relevant to teaching. Some elements of their expertise may not be appropriate for, or transferable to, this new context. For example, specialized accountancy or computer skills may be too advanced for use in an FET classroom setting, and the ability to tailor these skills in an appropriate manner may not be readily obvious. Regardless of any differences which exist between first- and second-career teachers, the move into teaching requires the formation of a new professional identity, that of teacher.

Challenges to Professional Identity Formation

Struggles adjusting to the complexities of a new position and experiencing imposter syndrome, whereby an individual experiences self-doubt and feels like a fraud (Clance and Imes 1978), can also adversely affect professional identity (trans-)formation. Imposter syndrome is a pattern of behaviour in which people have an ongoing belief that they are a fraud, and their deception will be exposed. They frequently doubt their ability, despite objective evidence of their proficiency in an area. Anderson et al. (2011, 39) recognized transition to be 'a turning point or a period between two periods of stability'. This implied instability can be more or less challenging, depending upon factors including the individual's mindset and coping mechanisms, current situation and their support network. Regardless of prior experience, embarking on a new career as a teacher brings with it challenges, particularly when the reality of working as a teacher does not match up to expectations. While these challenges affect individuals differently, those moving into teaching from another career may possess previously developed coping mechanisms which enable them to cope with additional, work-related stress.

As a consequence of entering a new profession and new environment, in conjunction with having no previous experience in teaching, second-career teachers may encounter obstacles. In spite of having previously acquired many skills, they need time to acquire the pedagogical strategies which will allow them to appropriately implement these skills. Challenges to professional identity (trans-)formation are not confined to issues relating to discipline or classroom management. Adapting to a new position may give rise to difficulties, particularly in the areas of increased responsibilities and additional workload and administration demands. Expectations regarding the transferability of skills may also place an extra burden on second-career teachers which their first-career counterparts do not experience. Skills may not be readily identified by the novice teacher, or they may not be appropriate or versatile enough to be utilized within an environment as unpredictable as a classroom.

While professional challenges may make identity (trans-)formation more problematic, so too can personal challenges. Moving into a new, unfamiliar teaching career may require additional hours of planning and preparation for classes. This, in addition to increased work responsibilities, may result in increased stress levels if the balance between private life and career is upset. Sacrifices may have to be made by student and novice teachers, as they find they have less free time and less time for being with family and friends. The move from a successful career into a position as a novice teacher may be challenging and may involve radical change for the individual directly involved and for their family. The decision to change career may initially have been distressing and the process of undergoing that career change, and the process of identity (trans-)formation, may result in increased levels of stress. Mature students may have family and financial responsibilities and returning to education may necessitate a move away from paid employment. Undertaking the financially uncertain life of a student may add a financial burden if income is not adequate to meet financial commitments.

The decision to change career and the process of identity (trans-)formation may be difficult. While career changers may face a variety of challenges, there are often supports available from personal and professional quarters to help with the process.

Identity (Re)formation as Transformative Learning

Professional identity is the dynamic manner in which individuals understand, define and ultimately give meaning to who or what they are, in the context of their career. It is 'an amalgam of personal biography, culture, social influence and institutional values which may change according to role and circumstance' (Day 2007, 609). Frequently, teachers within FE colleges have been employed in non-educational settings prior to taking up these jobs. Here they accumulate a wide array of knowledge derived from life experiences, high-level education, expertise gained and activities carried out on the ground. These elements are incorporated into their life in such a way that they form a complex network of connections, the result of which is that the boundaries between the individual and their professional identity become so blurred that they may be said to practically become one and the same thing. Professional identity (trans-) formation and the resultant meeting of new experiences and information may create what Mezirow (1994, 223) referred to as 'meaning perspectives'. These provide a frame of reference, affecting how an individual thinks and acts, how the world views them and ultimately how they see themselves. These are fundamental elements of their professional identity that they transfer from their previous to their new professional role. Those changing career bring these deep-seated and valuable elements of expertise and professional identity with them. The transition into a new profession requires the reconciliation of new knowledge with knowledge previously acquired, and the formation of a new professional identity. To facilitate this, a process of identity (trans-) formation occurs, which involves negotiating what Mezirow (1978a) referred to as the ten Phases of Perspective Transformation (Table 10.1). This process

Table 10.1 Mezirow's ten phases of transformative learning. Adapted from Mezirow and Produced in Kitchenham (2008, 105).

Phase 1	A disorienting dilemma
Phase 2	A self-examination with feelings of guilt or shame
Phase 3	A critical assessment of epistemic, sociocultural or psychic assumptions
Phase 4	Recognition that one's discontent and the process of transformation are shared and that others have negotiated a similar change
Phase 5	Exploration of options for new roles, relationships and actions
Phase 6	Planning of a course of action
Phase 7	Acquisition of knowledge and skills for implementing one's plans
Phase 8	Provisional trying of new roles
Phase 9	Building of competence and self-confidence in new roles and relationships
Phase 10	A reintegration into one's life on the basis of conditions dictated by one's perspective

entails the simultaneous connection of past and current experiences, the critical assessment and adaptation of long-standing perspectives, the retention of aspects of past identities and the formation of a new identity. These elements ultimately meld and settle into one new hybrid identity.

The Irish FET sector is unique, and teachers working therein frequently have a distinctive profile and professional identity. For many, this is a consequence of their maturity, occupational backgrounds and experience gained prior to entering the teaching profession. However, the overall positioning of FET has the potential to adversely affect the identity (trans-)formation process, by eliciting feelings of uncertainty and vulnerability among academic staff, particularly those who are new to the teaching profession.

The process of professional identity (trans-)formation, of essentially 'becoming a teacher', occurs through a potentially challenging process of evolution, in which identities are allowed to connect, integrate and finally to settle. However, numerous elements may result in tension and resistance, which may negatively impact the (trans-)formational process as both student and novice teacher.

One issue regarding the process of 'becoming' is the possession of an erroneous, unrealistic image of what it is to be a teacher. If reality differs from perception, the individual may struggle to adapt. Other issues which negatively impact the (trans-)formational process include context, prior possession of a strong occupational identity and fear of identity loss. Second-career teachers may not be able to let go of all elements of previous career identities. Consequently, if previous identities remain dominant due to the inability to form a new identity, they may inadvertently end up engaging in an unsuccessful attempt to straddle two contexts, namely their previous profession and teaching. This may be worsened within an ambiguous context like FET; there may be uncertainty or insecurity and a tendency to hold onto or return to a stronger, previously held identity. This inconsistency and uncertainty may potentially result in a fragmented identity (Ibarra 2023).

The process of career transition, and professional identity (trans-)formation may be viewed through the lens provided by Mezirow's Transformational Learning Theory (1978b). This theory holds that transformational learning is learning which goes beyond acquiring knowledge. It challenges the learner and brings about significant change in an individual's perception of 'self', which is internally and externally identifiable. For Mezirow, those changing career are transformative learners, and the transformative process often follows ten phases, which essentially cover two stages, the process which guides actions and the outcome. The overall process may be initiated by experiencing 'push' factors, which may act as a catalyst to career change, being essentially 'motivations to leave' (Coppe et al. 2021, 3). Experiencing these push factors can occur at any stage in life. They may be the result of a long-held aspiration and intention to follow a specific career, or what Mezirow (1990) called a 'disorienting dilemma'. This dilemma may take the form of one specific acute crisis or challenging event, such as illness or redundancy. Conversely it may be the consequence of steadily increasing feelings of frustration, boredom or isolation, chronic issues that have not been resolved, eventually becoming overly intrusive. These disorienting dilemmas may eventually result in a disconnection from a current career and be the catalyst which initiates the process of change and transformative learning. These dilemmas, however, are not simply causing disquiet. They are severe enough to initiate a radical change in career path, which potentially will give rise to a variety of positive and negative emotional responses, in addition to feelings of guilt and potentially feelings of failure. Consequently, individuals may require a period of time to recover from the physical and/or psychological effects of the causative issue prior to considering embarking on any new career.

For Mezirow, transformative learning involves critical reflection, wherein an individual reviews, analyses and evaluates their priorities, life goals and their career path. It leads to the questioning of assumptions and may identify areas of discontent, potentially leading the individual to investigate available options. One such option may be to continue coping where they are, even embedding themselves deeper into their current career. Another reaction may be to seek an alternative, potentially moving into teaching as a second career. To achieve this move, Mezirow recognized the necessity of planning a course of action, which ultimately leads to the desired outcome. This strategy involves testing out new beliefs and for those who choose teaching as a new career, they must undertake a process of teacher education which necessitates the move from experienced professional to student teacher. In quick succession, their identity must (trans-)form, from that of professional to student, and then from student to novice teacher. This novice state necessitates the building of relationships within a new professional setting, in addition to growing confidence and competence, which ultimately result in professional identity (trans-)formation. The formation of a new professional identity is profoundly influenced by context and the extrinsic expectations placed upon the individual by society, the institution and by its members.

For Irish FET teachers, this process occurs within a complex educational environment and includes personal context and the strength of formerly held occupational identities. As previously noted, those entering into, and indeed those currently working within, the Irish FET sector find themselves working in a sector which is unsure of its own identity (McGuinness et al. 2014). This uncertainty makes the process of role identification and teacher identity (trans-)formation more problematic.

While second-career teachers face many challenges, they also bring numerous strengths and benefits derived from real-world experience into the FET sector and the teaching profession as a whole. Frequently, individuals moving into teaching in later life have gained both professional and social maturity, in addition to significant content knowledge. This combination of subject expertise, experience and self-confidence can be incorporated into their teaching, positively impacting student learning by bringing a broad perspective into the classroom. This is the result of their ability to move beyond theory, forming unique connections between the professional world and the classroom through the provision of real-world examples and practical applications of concepts.

While skills transfer and usage may make the career change process easier to negotiate, issues with identity (trans-)formation may be resolved through a process of self-knowledge and reflection. This practice, which draws on the work of Schön (2003), facilitates identity renegotiation, allowing a balance to be achieved through acknowledgement of previous expertise and experience. This occurs through the lens of the new professional context and expectations. This permits the process of identity (trans-)formation to occur in a manner in which the new teacher identity is not formed at the expense of any previously held identities. Instead, through the (trans-)formation of old identities, the development of a new, hybrid, multidimensional professional identity may occur.

The process of becoming a teacher, and forming an appropriate professional identity, involves the integration of perceptions, beliefs and previous experiences. Beijaard et al. (2004) noted that the professional identity of teachers, which is influenced by life experience and a variety of relationships, is an ongoing process which initially formed while they themselves were students. Professional identity is affected by elements including gender, relationships, previous experiences and prior career choices. Each individual has a unique life story and professional identity, and teachers need to be understood within their individuality, which Day (2012, 14) classed as the 'personal in the professional'. The (trans-)formation of identity may be influenced by the opinions of others regarding the FET sector as a whole and teaching therein. This diversity of opinion may mean teachers are not afforded the recognition and respect that is given to other professions and may result in disparaging phrases such as 'anyone can teach' (Buchanan 2020, 80) being used.

Perceptions of difference may affect how a new identity develops and how this is integrated into previously formed professional and personal identities (Mezirow 1978a). Changing career, and the (trans-)formation of a professional teacher identity may be difficult. However, it should be recognized that the move into teaching as a career is not the first transition experienced by career changers. Previously, they have moved into a career in which they have built up 'a repertoire of adaptation mechanisms for responding to the opportunities and constraints of a different occupation' (Crow et al. 1990, 200). Following this, there was the potential challenge associated with the transition from experienced professional to mature student teacher.

Career changers may have to acknowledge their own vulnerability, with Lasky (2005, 191) holding that 'vulnerability is one of the most fundamental of all human experiences'. This vulnerability may arise from experiencing positive or negative feelings. Positive feelings often relate to developing relationships, building trust, expressing emotions and emotional growth, or from negative feelings such as anxiety or insecurity, exacerbated by the new role and new environment. Vulnerability begets authenticity, which allows an individual to work through the emotions which accompany change, and ultimately facilitating the process of identity (trans-)formation.

This new environment may be radically different to, and more challenging than, any previously encountered. 'Novice' teachers (a term which an adult education lens would contest for educators with significant prior experience) may experience learning environments as unpredictable, even hostile. This may be a consequence of unreasonable expectations. The complex, and sometimes chaotic nature of a classroom may not offer the same levels of courtesy and respect when compared to previous, orderly, working environments. For Lee (2011, 4), this move into the classroom 'involves a shift away from idealism and naiveté toward survival mode'. While all novice teachers may encounter problems, frequently those transitioning from other careers bring with them skills and strategies which may make them more adaptable and flexible, making the transitional process less traumatic. Initially, the professional identity of teachers is that of a novice teacher, an individual who is moving from outside to inside the teaching profession. This identity is shaped, maintained, negotiated and reshaped by a number of elements including an individual's abilities, environment, agency and context, in addition to the opportunities and challenges they encounter.

Career change and the resultant need for professional identity (trans-) formation may begin as the result of an acute incident or a chronic issue. The (trans-)formational process requires older professional identities to diminish which will allow a new hybrid identity to emerge. This hybrid identity is the result of the interaction of identities which are considered as being 'distinct in each context' (Iyall Smith 2008, 4). This process, however, is not necessarily straightforward and challenges may be encountered.

Supports to Identity Formation

The move out of a career in which an individual is established, and into a career in teaching, can be a daunting experience but it is not a completely bleak time. During a period of career transition, new relationships are formed which shape how an individual perceives their place within this new profession. These interactions are essential to personal growth and the development of professional teacher identity. These new relationships, in addition to previously established relationships, may offer appropriate supports to novice teachers entering the FET sector. Peer support for second-career teachers is perhaps most appropriately provided by those who have faced similar situations and it may be most beneficial during the initial part of the transitional phase. Those who have undertaken a similar career transition potentially have a greater understanding of the issues that may arise. They can tailor the support to the distinctive needs of second-career teachers, being particularly aware that, during this initial stage, the novice teacher may encounter numerous challenges, including adjusting to a new environment in which they are developing in both teaching confidence and competence.

While the support of peers is important, so too is the support offered by college leadership and knowledgeable teaching staff already working in the sector. These groups can offer assistance to novice teachers, relating to areas of concern regarding administration, course work, pedagogy and teacher practice. This mentoring process, in addition to a positive college culture, helps to empower the novice teacher. A positive mentoring experience reduces feelings of isolation and fosters a sense of collegiality among staff members, helping to foster a sense of belonging, improving the integration of the novice teacher into the college community. In addition, it provides novice teachers with the space in which they can establish connections between the previously acquired personal and professional skills and their newly acquired teaching skills and their still developing teacher identity. This assistance also aids the novice teacher in settling into the college culture and helps in the development of both positive feelings regarding professional well-being and professional teacher identity. Peer and mentor supports are important throughout a teacher's career. Professional supports can make suggestions or offer advice and assist in making an individual feel respected and secure.

In addition, the emotional and social supports offered by family and friends, while more general in nature, cannot be underestimated. They offer support to the individual prior to, while undergoing and in the recovery period after experiencing a disorienting dilemma. Families may offer practical supports through the provision of supplementary finances or by taking care of children for the period of time spent in teacher education or during the initial period of being a novice teacher. Additional supports offered are perhaps more modest and yet they are extremely significant, being as straightforward as offering encouragement and providing a listening ear, and these assist in building confidence, and are significantly valuable during transitional periods.

Conclusion

The Irish FET sector is diverse, misunderstood and in need of further study. Many of the teachers working in FET do so as a second career and bring with them previously gained industry-specific expertise and professional identities which greatly enrich the sector and ensure its vocational integrity. Identity (trans-)formation is a complex process in which an individual grows to understand themselves within a specific context. Career change necessitates embarking on a process of adapting previously held professional identities and integrating these with a new teacher professional identity. The negative image of the FET sector affects its attractiveness and may adversely impact the identity (trans-)formation process of teachers. Moving forward, enhancement of the sector's image may be supported through the acknowledgement of it, not as a competitor to higher education, but as a sector with great value in its own right. Governmental advocacy and recognition of the capacities of teachers are constructive steps in creating a positive awareness of the sector. These may assist in moving the FET sector from the alternative space it currently occupies and into one which emphasizes its relevance and supports the process of professional identity (trans-)formation.

Chapter 11

A PRECARIOUS PROFESSION

Camilla Fitzsimons and Jerry O'Neill

Toni[1] likes her job. She's been doing it for nearly fifteen years and has worked with so many groups that she'd never be able to remember them all. It's autumn 2023 and she's just about to start with a new group. Eight people have signed up to a course called 'key skills' which is delivered by her local Education and Training Board (ETB). Among other things, they'll work on their reading, writing and spelling. One of the things she likes most about her job is sitting at her kitchen table the night before a course like this begins and putting the finishing touches to the next day's plan. She loves the nervous anticipation of a new group, and she can't deny that it is convenient that she can do parts of her work when the kids are in bed. She wouldn't be able to pick them up from school if she had to clock in, nine to five.

But there's lots she doesn't like about her job, such as having to use her own computer which has definitely seen better days. She also doesn't like having to fork out for other equipment like flip charts, pens and even paper. During the coronavirus pandemic she had to buy a webcam that cost her €70. There was no mechanism to claim this money back from her employers. Her job is to show up at a certain time and deliver her class, something she's been doing for eight years now, even though she's not a permanent member of staff with the ETB. In fact, Toni doesn't have any contract at all – she gets paid, by the hour, for the classes she teaches. Just last week one of her friends jokingly commented she'd have better terms of employment in Amazon who are notorious for below par working conditions (Davis 2020).

'Key skills' isn't the only class Toni is due to teach this year and the ETB isn't her only employer. She also works for a community group that is funded

---

[1] Toni is a composite of our own shared experiences as non-permanent staff in FE and the stories of many others we have met over the years.

through the government's Social Inclusion and Community Activation Programme (or SICAP for short). Here she teaches on a community leadership programme and has worked on this for twelve years now. She got the gig because she was recommended by someone already working in the ETB, a common way for people to end up working in adult, community and further education (O'Neill and Fitzsimons 2020, 11). Toni supplements both jobs – the ETB work and the SICAP work – with a third job in a different ETB where she teaches 'communications'. When she pools the money she earns from these three jobs, it's enough to get by, although she always dreads the looming holidays when she needs to sign on for social welfare unemployment benefits.

These 'bits and pieces of work', as she calls it, has pretty much been the shape of her professional life so far. Sometimes she wonders if she can even call it a 'professional' life. It's certainly not how she imagined things would pan out when she started the journey into adult education, especially given the money that she had to invest in her own learning. At the last count, she'd forked out almost €11,000. She spent nearly €7,000 on the post-graduate diploma she needed to register with the Teaching Council of Ireland and then another €4,000 on a Masters. She loved these courses and especially enjoyed university life but she hates the debt it has left her with. She always wanted to be a teacher and, having returned to education as a mature student herself, she knew this would be with adults.

But Toni's biggest challenge is the impact this precarious occupational existence has on everyday life. When she needed a credit union loan for a car last year, she had to fudge the application form to give the impression her work was more regularized. It was also stressful getting a mortgage and her partner had to front the application.

During the coronavirus pandemic of 2020–2022, a whole set of other concerns emerged that she hadn't considered before. She constantly worried that if she got sick, she wouldn't be eligible to sign up for the dedicated social welfare payment. To this day, she can't help worrying about another pandemic or something similar that would prevent her from going to work. She loves her job, but these sacrifices are big, and she sometimes feels despair as there seems little hope of anything changing.

Toni's situation isn't unusual – in fact it's typical in the precarious professional world of Further Education and Training (FET) in Ireland. Both of us know this from our own experiences of working precariously in FE as well as from extensive research we have carried out into the issue. This includes a previous study on graduate outcomes from initial teacher education specific to FE (O'Neill and Fitzsimons 2020) and a more recent study that looked at the impact of the Covid-19 pandemic on non-permanent workers who, like Toni, are employed in post-compulsory education (Fitzsimons et al. 2022).

This chapter reflects on some of the challenges and critical opportunities for the increasingly professionalized and precarious field of adult, community and further education teaching. As well as highlighting the case of Toni, we draw on the experiences of thirty-six other educators working in further education settings who took part in primary research we carried out in 2021 (Fitzsimons et al. 2022). All of the voices you will hear work on a casual, occasional or temporary basis and often (44 per cent) for more than one employer. These employers include FE colleges, Youthreach Centres, Vocational Training Opportunities Scheme (VTOS) and community education.

Professional Isolation and Invisibility

Most (66 per cent) of the participants we talked to worked part-time, often not by choice. And as many as 46 per cent were only paid for term-time, meaning they often supplemented their income with social welfare payments in the summer months, a situation that is not unique to casual workers in FET (Bobek et al. 2018). Some also reported taking up other non-teaching work to tide them over. For example, this participant shared:

> The nature of insecure employment means I am forced to take on as much work or sometimes more work than I am able to do. I have managed to work all year round as I have found alternative work (non-teaching) for the summer period. I am now forced to do this because we are paid holiday pay and this makes it very difficult to claim unemployment benefit during non-term times, summer, Christmas, etc.

This sense of having to say 'yes' to everything is highlighted by Lopes and Dewan (2015, 33) who describe the extreme pressures people sometimes feel for fear of missing out on future work. They also report disproportionate workloads between permanent and non-permanent staff as 'a highly contentious issue', something that, again, is evident across the experiences of Irish-based precarious staff.

Another practitioner, John[2], also works for more than one employer and tells us 'I am extremely disillusioned with the system I find myself in. [...] This is not something I would choose. My preference would be to work in one

---

2 Pseudonyms are used throughout for research participants.

job'. His is not an isolated example. Another educator, Clara, who works both in an FE college and in community education, shares:

> I love working in the field of adult education and have been doing so for the past 15 years. However, I do not like the uncertainty of working part-time, do not feel valued and feel that adult literacy is being forgotten about. I also dislike having to sign on during holidays - it is difficult to make a living wage.

As this example shows, these aren't people starting out in teaching – rather, over 60 per cent had been working under these conditions for more than three years with a quarter working on a temporary contract for over ten years. Another person, Sara, and who, again, works across several public providers, described a battle to eventually receive the contract of indefinite duration (CID) she is legally entitled to and which provides limited security of employment. Sara recalls how underwhelmed she felt by this eventual recognition because, as she puts it 'I am still considered a part-time worker and am only paid for the hours I work'. Like most of these workers (56 per cent), Sara is registered as an FE teacher with the Teaching Council of Ireland and is one of 75 per cent of participants to hold a post-graduate qualification. But when she compares her situation to other registered teachers, she is not happy: 'If a secondary school teacher can be awarded a full-time contract and paid a salary then further education tutors should also be paid in that way. At least divide the hours awarded between the months worked for a more stable income'. The impact on her professional identity becomes clear when she adds,

> I hate that I am listed as a part time tutor. Coordinators and staff resent the fact that tutors 'are off' during school holidays. My hours are so unpredictable I have to cram as much as I can in during term time. This means constant preparation and creating teaching resources even over the summer. I feel I never get a break or holiday because of this. I feel my co-workers think I have it easy. I don't have an office, I don't have stability, or a regular dependable income. It does not reward hard work and innovative practice. I feel I am exploited because I constantly try my best for my learners.

The findings from our study are not unique. A number of other researchers have also evidenced negative social, psychological, educational and career impacts of non-permanent employees including educators (see, e.g., Bobek et al. 2018; Courtois and O'Keefe 2015; Lopes and Dewan 2015; Bobek et al. 2018). One British study by Lopes and Dewan (2015) identified four key issues relating to the rights of educators employed on casual contracts: precarity; exploitation; lack of support and lack of career progression. They also highlighted poor levels of communication between employees and their bosses, writing 'respondents spoke about feeling isolated and not being part of the teaching team in which they worked' and continuing 'for the most part, they were not invited to department meetings and were excluded from decision-making processes and planning of the curriculum' (Lopes and Dewan 2015, 36). The researchers argue that excluding these workers from everyday power renders discussions and decision-making as only ever partially informed and reduces the efficacy and quality of work by education providers. Meanwhile, in extensive research on working conditions within universities, Sara Ahmed identifies how many precarious educators are locked out of complaints processes and have no support if they are treated badly by peers, managers (Ahmed 2021) or, in our experience, even students.

The Gendered Dimensions of Precarity

O'Keefe and Courtois (2019), who write about Irish universities, point out the gendered dimension of precarious work, where institutions rely on women's labour but create working conditions that increase their vulnerability to harassment in the workplace and where there are repeated career disruptions and a lack of salary progression. Some of the thirty-six practitioners we reached out to also talked about being disadvantaged as women. One wrote, 'I feel the profile of tutors is generally older females who can work under precarious conditions because they have a partner who can support them', continuing:

> [...] I kill myself working throughout the year so I can live off savings throughout the summer. [...] Sadly, most who have the best of intentions leave because it is not practical or sustainable to live in such precarious conditions. I have written to Minister Harris [government Minister for Further and Higher Education, Research, Innovation and Science] to outline these concerns but have received no response.

Other women also talk about relying on a spousal income and of a sense from their employers that being precariously employed was in some way more acceptable or tolerable because of the care commitments they also hold. One tells us:

> It's typical. I've gone from a female dominated care workforce (early childhood) to a further education workforce where I worked for little pay and recognition and never in 18 years was even offered a pension to pay into and I'm still left in a position where I'm employed precariously, never knowing what income will come in or stop, and still no pension with 20 odd years left to retirement

age. Again, as with early childhood, I love what I do, and I put my heart into it but so much is expected for so little in return. I often think about what would happen me if my husband died or had an accident or left us. Myself and the children would not be financially secure.

Precarity and the Pandemic

The Covid-19 pandemic starkly revealed the hidden realities of working precariously. Whilst the global pandemic affected the working conditions of all employees, research by Matilla-Santander et al. (2021) found that, worldwide, workers trapped in precarious employment were among those most affected. The FE practitioners we spoke to repeatedly shared examples of how they too had been disproportionately impacted. Many had to rely on their own equipment without access to technical support. One woman told us about being 'really anxious' that the poor quality of her laptop could result in her losing her job: 'If I didn't have the up-to-date equipment […] I felt like another tutor would be preferred over me if I didn't have access to an up-to-date laptop, a printer etc.' These problems are certainly not insignificant but, arguably, pale when compared to Matilla-Santander et al.'s (2021, 227) assertion that precarious working conditions actually increased the spread of Covid-19 by forcing people into work as they didn't have sick-leave entitlements.

In her own account of being precarious in the pandemic, Whelan (2021, 581) draws attention, with full ironic awareness, to the constant flow of communication laced in the language of care from her employer as the reality of working in Covid settled in. In our study, Sara complained about an increased workload because of the pandemic, something reported by 49 per cent overall. Additional tasks included endless webinars, higher demands from students and a continued pressure to get your work done regardless of your personal circumstances. Two people lost their job. To illustrate, 'My FE work with ETB has completed dried up. The students I was teaching are now being taught by an external company. … I have been chasing my contacts in the ETB and they are not getting back to me'. In the wake of the pandemic, many of these posts did not return.

There are other lingering shadows too including the lack of communication between employers and their casualized workforce, something 58 per cent reported as problematic.

The Long and Wide Story of Precarious Work

Further education teachers are not the only people impacted by what is a global increase in the casualization of many jobs and a growing incongruence between what the United Nations (2015) and the International Labour Organization (2019) frame as a right to 'decent work' with the values, aspirations and practices of labour markets in late capitalism (Finnegan et al. 2019; Mercille and Murphy 2015). Many critics link this broad casualization of labour to the international dominance of neoliberal policies that seek to transfer economic risk onto the shoulders of workers through flexibilization, casualization, self-responsibility and financial insecurity (Jaffe 2021; Lopes and Dewan 2015). Although much of the initial attention on casualized work focused on low-paid, low-status work that was often done by the most economically marginalized members of society, there has been increasing focus on the precarious work in so-called professional occupations including education. In extensive research on the topic, Sarah Jaffe tracks an ideological shift within advanced capitalist societies where job satisfactions, in other words 'loving our job' (Jaffe 2021, 10), is now supposed to be enough to sustain ourselves despite the continuing erosion of once basic protections such as a pension, a contract, paid holiday, and illness and maternity leave. The reason why work has so dramatically changed for so many people is succinctly described by Amelia Horgan (2021, 51) as the implementation of a post-Fordist 'new work' model that is part of 'a conscious, political project, undertaken to break the power of organised labour', individualize and marketize our social lives, and deconstruct the welfare state. We agree.

And just as precarious work is depressingly common on a global scale, it has always been a common thread in the field of adult education (Murtagh 2015). Yet, despite its persistence, it has never received the same levels of attention as education workers' rights in secondary and primary education. In part, this is because of the uneven and diverse history of the sector which this book highlights through many of its contributions. Some historical changes to adult, community and further education are worth re-emphasizing in the context of the casualized nature of the FET workforce. These include many of the people working in these colleges being either qualified secondary school teachers or having industry experience of some kind, be this hairdressing, construction work, from the business sector, or the arts. As public provision for adults grew outside of these college settings, which have always had a high percentage of adults attending (Hardiman 2011), job opportunities arose on locally based evening and daytime courses for people who had left school prematurely (Fitzsimons 2017a, 74). Education and Training Boards, then, remain the primary employer for most adult educators in Ireland although their working contexts and ideological sense of educational purpose will determine job titles: for example, adult educator; teacher; trainer; tutor; facilitator; coordinator and organizer are just some of the more generic professional titles that are used.

It was a push from below by this fledgling adult education sector that led to the slow emergence of government support, at least in principle, for professionalization. The state commissioned Murphy Report (Committee on Adult Education 1973) and the subsequent Kenny Report (Commission on Adult Education 1984) both promised sectoral development and professional recognition for educators. This slow move started to crystallize in the form of policy influence in the 1990s with the Green Paper: *Adult Education in an Era of Lifelong Learning* (Department of Education and Science 1998). This Green Paper, written in consultation with lead adult educators, called for an inter-agency group to make recommendations on how best to recognize adult education qualifications, including a practitioner forum and in-service training and career progression (Department of Education and Science 1998, 112–113). It acknowledged 'the sector compares poorly with the other education sectors in terms of the stability of employment, career options and structures for ongoing development of practitioners' (109). Two years later, the *White Paper Learning for Life* (Department of Education and Science 2000) repeated many of these assertions.

These documents were written in the shadow of a growing discourse which stressed the human capital functions of education and an accelerating tendency to align education with employability (Finnegan and O'Neill 2016; Grummell 2014; Hurley 2014). Although an inter-agency group did meet, this was suspended soon after its inception and there were no real outcomes from the process (Fitzsimons 2017a, 204). Instead, professionality came in the early 2010s from outside the adult education field as the newly established Teaching Council of Ireland created a third space within their professional regulatory structure alongside existing primary and post-primary ones for further education teachers. This shift to a more accountable and regulatory professional structure than that which was imagined by the White Paper was not unconnected from a broader European and international concern to enhance professionalization, standardization and accountability in teacher education and, more generally, concerns about the quality of education (Conway and Murphy 2013; Murphy 2015; Research voor Beleid [Alpine] 2008). The Teaching Council of Ireland's role is not just to safeguard standards in teaching but to support structures for career-long professional development and promote teaching as a career. It's original and core focus was, and remains, on primary and secondary teaching. The Council has twenty-two representatives from primary and post-primary teaching but none, explicitly, from further education.

As a result of this development, where the Teaching Council assumes at least some of the responsibility for standards and accreditation in FET, several post-graduate programmes sprung up across Ireland (including the programme we both work on). Since 2013, anyone applying for work in the Irish FET sector must be registered as a teacher; either a secondary school teacher, or under 'route 3 – Further Education'. This is only possible where a person holds an honours degree (or equivalent) and an approved post-graduate qualification which typically costs around €7,000 to obtain.

The State of Play Today

Despite these advances towards professionalization, it is clear from the findings presented in this chapter, findings from an earlier study (O'Neill and Fitzsimons 2020) and our ongoing observations on how graduates are faring, that little has changed for the precariously employed adult educator. Government promises continue. Ireland's most recent national strategy for the sector *Future FET: Transforming Learning. The National Further Education and Training (FET) Strategy 2020–2024* repeats earlier commitments to address uneven staffing structures (SOLAS 2020, 56) but, as before, the strategy offers no coherent pathway on how this might be advanced. Furthermore, despite the welcome creation of a dedicated government department for further education (DFHERIS), it remains, as yet, unclear what its role and responsibilities will be in relation to the development of professional structures and opportunities that teaching colleagues in primary and post primary enjoy under the leadership of the Department of Education and Skills.

One welcome development was when, in 2017, Education and Training Boards Ireland (ETBI), the national representative body for Ireland's sixteen ETBs, published work on the professional development of those working in publicly funded FE settings. This strategy promises to build on 'targeted professional development' through creating and supporting integration and consistency across the sector (ETBI 2017, 1). It is heartening to see that ETBI are thinking carefully and developing practices to support cultures and structures for Continuous Professional Development (CPD) and some programmes have indeed been developed in partnership with the university sector. However, despite acknowledging an ageing workforce (ETBI 2017, 19–20), current developments are principally aimed at existing, permanent staff and less attention, it seems, is paid to its high dependence on a causal workforce and the impact of this on sectoral sustainability and growth on a longer time scale.

It is unclear, from the ETBI strategy, how new graduates can embark on their next steps in developing their professional identity as educators. Although there have been recent claims made in public spaces by policymakers (ETBI 2022) that the issue of FET professionality 'is being looked at', there remains a lack of clarity on what such professional structures and futures would look like for emerging educators in FET. It is this sense of what the sociologist Richard Sennett (1998) calls the 'futureless' occupational spaces of precarious work that makes the current conditions of many practitioners incompatible with the future-orientated nature of professionalism, as is implied in any CPD discourse.

This sense of professional inequity across the teaching professions is made clear by even a cursory look at structures and opportunities for colleagues in other educational sectors. In particular, the situation is very different for teachers working in the school sector where there are clear early career, professional induction pathways that are not only supported but required by the Teaching Council of Ireland. Moreover, many people who commit to becoming further education teachers are non-traditional students themselves and have often come through FE as students and/or completed their degree as mature students (O'Neill and Fitzsimons 2020). Like most non-traditional graduates, these teachers can lack the access to the networks to 'get a foot in the door' – the absence of this social capital can become a major barrier in career progression (Finnegan and O'Neill 2016).

If the existing FE structures, then, don't appear to create opportunities for genuine professional growth and equity, it is little surprise that practitioners have begun to push for change from below through an upsurge in grassroots activism mostly through the 'Adult Education Tutors National Campaign' which was formed in response to the government's failure to adhere to a 2020 Labour Court recommendation that the Department of Education address the contract and pay-related concerns of 3,500 precariously employed tutors working within the City of Dublin ETB. In February 2023, the campaign's national expansion was marked by a demonstration outside the Dáil (Irish houses of parliament) by tutors from across the country. Protesters called for an end to what they described as 'abusive' working conditions characterized by the absence of contracts and the ongoing reliance on top-up social welfare payments outside of term time. They also highlighted difficulties in securing tutors for the growing number of programmes on offer to Ireland's growing refugee population, arguing that the precarious posts remain vacant because the terms and conditions are so dire. As has been touched on earlier, the issue of precarity is brought up through questions and contributions from the floor at public events organized by ETBs and community education providers as practitioners seek to force the issue onto the national agenda.

The Role of Unions

Of course, another recourse for any workers who are struggling with the consequences of precarious work is to seek support as a collective through a trade union. Everyone has the right to join a trade union and each union's right to engage in collective bargaining is protected in The Universal Declaration on Human Rights, which recognizes 'the right to join trade unions and the right to collective bargaining' (Article 23.4). Collective bargaining is where people with a shared grievance negotiate their concerns through their trade union who enters into discussion with the employer on their behalf. Trade unionists believe collective bargaining is crucial to a fair and equitable workplace.

The reality, however, is that precariously employed staff typically fall outside of collective bargaining agreements. It is also hard to get a coherent sense of union organization and membership in FE in Ireland – again, this is due in no small part to the heterogeneous organizational and professional structures of the field. Of the thirty-six practitioners we engaged with in our most recent study into the issue, just 35 per cent were members of a trade union. This is likely a lower number than the overall population of FET teachers given the presence of secondary school teachers, especially in FE colleges. These teachers typically bring their unions (and pedagogies) with them, meaning the predominately post-primary focused Teachers Union of Ireland (TUI) which is one of the largest unions in FE. However, these FE teachers are a drop in the ocean when compared to the overall membership of the TUI and our own experience has been that the principal focus of TUI representatives is the terms and conditions of employment within post-primary schools, not FE spaces.

It is also the case that there have been persistent attempts by neoliberal governments to restrict the actions of unions and to sully their reputation (Horgan 2021, 130–131). There is also a persistent gap between ordinary trade union members and union officials and a bureaucratized trade union structure that has left many senior officials out of touch with the realities of its members and co-opted by the lure of social partnership arrangements that have ultimately failed to deliver for most workers (Allen 2013, 134–136).

We've also heard reports of people finding it difficult to join a union – indeed one of the thirty-six educators we researched told us: 'I would like to be a member of a trade union but found any queries met with condescension and rudeness'. The recent report by the think tank TASC points out that precarious working conditions strive in areas of weak worker representation (Bobek et al. 2018) and although it can hardly be argued that teachers have weak representation, those working in the FE field, without a dedicated union, have justified concerns about the centrality of their plight within a large secondary school teachers' union such as the TUI. For those working in community education, Services Industrial Professional and Technical Union (SIPTU) has been the most active union and was central to a 2012–2015 'Communities against Cuts Campaign' that sought to respond to a downsizing of the Community Sector that resulted in many job losses (Harvey 2012).

It is also important to note that the struggles faced by further education staff in securing decent working conditions, remuneration and some sense of career security are not dissimilar to the ongoing, and probably more public, plight of early years educators who are represented, in terms of unions, again mostly by SIPTU. There may be alliances that could be forged with unions that represent similarly exploited workers in the early childhood education sector. There have also been some criticisms of trade unions themselves and there is no denying trade union membership has shrunk across the board more broadly. However, although precarity in the university sector remains a chronic problem, trade unions representing lecturers have had some success. It was because of trade union pressure that the government commissioned a *Report to the Minister for Education and Skills of the Chairperson of the Expert group on Fixed-Term and Part-Time Employment in Lecturing in Third Level Education in Ireland* (commonly called the Cush Report). In 2016, the Cush report recommended CIDs for anyone teaching in higher education more than two years, and that additional teaching hours should be allocated to existing part-time lecturers. The Irish Federation of University Teachers (IFUT) have successfully advanced workers entitlements through Cush.

In 2022, IFUT identified the ongoing plight of precarious post-compulsory educators as a priority matter. At the time of writing, they are finalizing a charter on precarious employment for all union branches which asks them to locally prioritize a number of demands including: clear career pathways for educators and researchers, a regularization of contracts, supports for casual staff facing redundancy, non-cooperation with exploitative practices, proactive campaigns to seek to reduce non-compulsory education's reliance on casual staff and reserving the right to take collective action to defend the rights of precarious staff. Also, at the time of writing, IFUT are preparing a report on a national study on precarity carried out in 2022–2023. It may very well be that FET educators would benefit with union representation that was sensitive to the diverse sector-specific nature and challenges of working lives in adult, community and further education.

Conclusion

Education providers not only benefit hugely from the dedication and efforts of the many of their staff who are employed on non-permanent contracts, they rely on these educators to deliver the programmes they advertise. Although while we acknowledge that it isn't always easy, and there are certainly layers of power dynamics at play, there is a case to be made that permanent educators should take the lead from university-based campaigns and play a role in advocating for the enhancement of the terms, conditions and experiences of their non-permanent colleagues. Could they too stand up for their colleagues who may not be protected by collective agreement or are non-union and fight for better working conditions for others?

As is clear from our own research, precarity is much more than about terms and conditions of contracts – it is also a psycho-social phenomenon that has a profound impact on the internal world of workers. Precarious working lives can have a detrimental impact on professional and occupational development and identity formation and, ultimately, contribute to the emergence of precarious subjects (Worth 2016). Until the government, as the principal employers of non-compulsory teachers stop avoiding the issue and start embracing the benefits or remunerating people as they should, little will change. Without addressing this fundamental right to sustainable professional working conditions and opportunities, the state risks relegating people to a continual cycle of uncertainty that has a very real impact on a person's mental health, and their capacity to earn a decent wage, engage in meaningful professional development, borrow money to pay for their housing and transport, and other essential features of everyday life (Bobek et al. 2018; Courtois and O'Keefe 2015; Irvine and Rose 2022; Lopes and Dewan 2015; O'Keefe and Courtois 2019; O'Neill and Fitzsimons 2020; Pembroke 2018; UCU 2016; Whelan 2021).

For people like John, Sarah, Tara and Clara, it seems likely that their love of, and commitment to, connecting and working with adult learners must, eventually, be depleted by their long struggle to find permanent, stable work. And it is also important to remind ourselves that, along the way in the slow and complex growth of FET, choices have been made, or maybe more accurately not, to create certain professional structures and experiences for educators working in the sector.

We agree with Susan Ferguson's (2019, 118) assertion that 'precarious workforces do not come into being magically or naturally. They are *produced*' (italics in original). And within a global system that is differentiated along gender, class and racialized lines. If the political will was there, governments have the means to create structures where people like Tara would be better supported and valued in her work. It is more likely these changes will come from below. Our immediate ambition is to be part of the growing collective efforts that seek to make this happen.

'AFTERWORDS': A CONCLUDING CONVERSATION

Sarah Sartori, Jerry O'Neill, Jane O'Kelly, Lilian Nwanze, Francesca Lorenzi, Suzanne Kyle, Brendan Kavanagh, Camilla Fitzsimons, Eilish Dillon, Sarah Coss, Bríd Connolly and Leo Casey

In an effort to stay true to the participative and dialogic values which many of us write about, we conclude this book with re-crafted fragments of an online conversation between the authors that started with a collective reflection on the passions and motivations behind what we wrote. This surfaced some challenges and opportunities facing adult, community and further education which we address. We then conclude by contemplating possibilities of hope.

Why Did We Write What We Wrote?

Camilla

… it's really fantastic to have everyone in the same space – albeit online …

Let's talk about the 'why' of what we wrote … it might unearth some of that passion beneath the chapters that is so evident …

Jane

I might kick off then … what I'm looking at in my chapter is neurodiversity in FET in the context of inclusion. But it really comes from a very personal viewpoint because both my children – adult children, have autism.

And the 'why' behind my chapter … well … really, I think over the last number of years, just before Covid and through Covid and beyond Covid, I have this sense that I'm getting older myself … and I'd like to make some sort of an impact or support people much more so in the number of years that I have left in academia. So, hopefully in getting into more community activism and working with like-minded people.

I'm very aware of the complexity and diversity of people, of learners and of staff and of people involved in community, adult and further education across the board and am slightly, as always, concerned – and 'concerned' is probably too strong a word, but I'm going to use it anyway – around the push into tertiary education and the wholehearted grabbing hold of the linkages of [QQI] levels five and six into seven and eight and higher education.

And even though I'm working in higher education, I've concerns for everybody else, across the country, in our society, in our communities and in our families.

So, it's a very personal thing for me to try and explore and it's a challenge for me because I'm not an academic 'expert' in autism or neurodiversity, but I'm learning more every day by talking with autistic people, people who work with autistic people and the hopes and dreams of everybody involved.

So, I was trying to bring together a reflexive kind of overview of what's happening around neurodiversity and FET ... how people are trying to develop their own potential and move through their lives with autism. And the challenges and the strengths that they bring into further education and how they're experiencing that.

Sarah [Sartori]

If it's ok for me to come in there, Jane ... you mentioned that you're concerned about the push into tertiary education? And I was just wondering what your concern was because when I look at it at face value, I think that the move to a tertiary system looks great.[1] I hear students say that there's not clear pathways into universities beyond traditional routes ... that they can't see the connection between their FE awards and how that's going to get them to where they want to go so ... to me it looks great, but then I'm always a bit concerned about what looks great on face value. So yeah, what *are* your concerns?

---

1 In May 2022, the Irish government launched a consultation process on the creation of what they called a 'unified tertiary education system'. The policy vision behind this further realignment is to create a more coherent alignment between FET and higher education.

Jane

Yeah, thanks. And Sarah, I appreciate all the really good work that's going on there and the support and the research ... including College Connect (Sartori and Demir Bloom 2023), and also the work that AONTAS are doing, examining the obstacles for diverse populations coming through education (Meyler et al. 2023).

In theory, it's all wonderful. It is great. I'm all for access of opportunity and for support for people to make choices around what they want to do and removing obstacles. It's just ... I worry about the very linear and siloed approaches to things and this focus with always moving upwards ... I do worry that basic certificates and all the work that goes on in non-formal and informal education gets overlooked in the rush to higher ed.

I would just like to see more balance and more acknowledgement of what's going on across the board, for all of members of society. And more equality around how that is promoted and marketed.

I know I'm not deeply immersed in it. I'm probably on the periphery of it, but as someone who values the quality and respect and dialogue and communication and conversation, I worry about the way it's presented through the media and the constant push into the higher education space. I came into higher education in my 30s. I was one of those people intimidated by it. I thought it was elitist and I thought it wasn't a space for me. I see that changing, but, I hate to see the rush into the promotion of it. I'd like to see much more community emphasis rather than the emphasis on the individual having to succeed and achieve. I'd love to see it going both ways up and down through our system.

Suzanne

I would share the concerns that you have Jane. And I think just at the end there where you talked about it going both ways, the different sectors learning from each other, is important. I think that that's probably one of the positive aspects of this new unified tertiary education system.

But I would be concerned, and I know other people working in community education who probably have concerns as well, around the idea of community education, within this model ... a concern that it's not just seen as a stepping stone to further education or employment and not as something to be valued in its own right.

And I think that this new tertiary education model could potentially feed that discourse or image of community education ... whereas community education can often just stand in its own right ... as you know, having an end in itself, whether it's social, community cohesion or people just engaging for confidence building, making connections with others, learning a new skill … engaging in local community initiatives and all the other things that we talk about all the time.

So, I think it's good to tease out those questions and not necessarily going blindly into this new model because community education is different and there are reasons why it is different and why it needs to have its own particular approach ….

I probably should have said at the beginning that I'm representing Susan Cullinane of KWETB and Eve Cobain, from AONTAS. The three of us wrote the chapter together.

And when Susan and I came together to think about what we'd write … well … that conversation and the opportunity was very timely because we were in the middle of Covid and lockdown when we started talking first.

We were trying to navigate the pressures that had come with working online and all the different challenges that had arisen. And so what we were thinking about was the responses to Covid – this kind of crazy pressure that was on practitioners to be really productive and immediately responsive to huge challenges … people who were working from home … minding their children … or had elder care responsibilities. […] And in some work environments, there seemed to be this pressure to almost make the most of the lockdown and be very productive. People were really feeling the pressure. And then in our initial conversations about what we might write, that led into further discussions about the ethos and the practice of community education and how it is really necessary to take time to reflect on what was happening around us and to have conversations about that and think about appropriate responses.

So, in a way the process we had in writing the chapter was useful because we were using that space to talk, to reflect on some of the challenges that had led to what some saw as a kind of 'toxic productivity'. And it wasn't just Covid … some of these challenges and moves towards hyper-productivity can be traced to the government-led changes that happened since 2008 – the focus on outputs was not just since 2008. This constant focus on outputs … whether it's in relation to funding or accreditation and all those different areas … all that pressure on practitioners was minimizing the possibilities for them to incorporate community education principles into their work.

We had a strong sense that practitioners were frustrated, are frustrated, and we wanted to capture that in the chapter.

Camilla

Thanks Suzanne … and I love that notion that you wanted to capture that frustration. I think it is a very strong.

Sarah [Coss]

It was really interesting that Jane started the conversation by talking about neurodiverse learners. And then it began to move into looking at the diversity of the work that we do. I'm just reminded of how diverse this is.

And there has been so much talk recently about pathways and this idea of progression. Progression forward and progression into employment. Progression into further and higher education. But it's very interesting to hear people talk about all of the range of different reasons why people participate in adult education and what they're hoping to get ….

So, for example, most of our work in our adult education service would be involved in those, so-called, 'lower levels'. And what's interesting is the huge range of learners that we see over the years. We've had people with doctorates, masters and degrees. They're all here for all sorts of reasons; not always for progression at all. Instead, it would be the range of things we offer as an adult education service, some accredited, many non-accredited. […] And I do think that bit sometimes gets lost. You know it is always this idea of progression and pathways and the idea that the higher levels somehow offer more. The higher levels offer something different but it's not always what learners want or need.

Camilla

And coming to the idea of what we think learners need – when we get focused on outcomes. […] I don't know how many times I've said to students who are developing as practitioners in various adult and further education spaces that maybe the most important outcome is that people make friends … particularly for younger people that have been locked away for two years with Covid. Maybe that is the learning outcome that is needed – that people, you know, have fun, laugh, socialize, challenge themselves.

Sarah [Coss]

I suppose what I thought, and coming back to Suzanne and Jane, we need to make sure that we have the community education and adult education principles [of democracy, participation, dialogue, criticality and person-centredness] to ground our work. I don't always see that across adult and further education spaces.

In terms of the chapter that I wrote – I was focusing on how we work creatively with curriculum – but really, I think it's important to stress that we need to maintain and keep hold of the principles that we have regardless of what and where we are teaching and who we're working with.

Sometimes when we're in spaces like this we take things for granted. I think sometimes when you're working in other spaces, we can see people who are working in FET and they don't embody the same ethos, you know, and they are working in a different way and from a different perspective.

Francesca

Sarah ... you put forward some ideas that I think are very important, really about ethos, but also the principles that inform adult, community and further education. And I think that the striking thing is about valuing these principles and valuing people: students and staff. And that probably doesn't happen.

And obviously diversity is another elementary aspect of values and ... giving a voice to anybody regardless of who they are, whether they're teachers, students or organizers. It's really seeing that the sector has a value *per se*, not as a pathway, but that it has its own value ... because it's doing something good for those who take part, not as a stepping stone.

Brendan could say more about valuing those in the sector because that's what our chapter is really about ....

Brendan

Yeah, of course, so it's about second career educators ... and I'm one of those. A second career educator is somebody who's had a career previously that's not education based. Later in life, they have decided to move into education within the FET sector. So, in a lot of the FET subjects, like health care, which is the area I'm involved in, there is a reliance on a professional understanding of the environment – it's taken as a given that you will have that background in that area.

When you change career in such a way, you're classed as a second-class teacher. Myself, Elaine and Francesca look at the language that's used around the sector and the big word that really gets to me is the word 'alternative'. Or 'alternative' paths. Why isn't it just a path? As Francesca was just saying, why doesn't it just have its own value as opposed to as a way into something else, or as a veering away from the norm?

Sarah [Coss]

Thanks, Brendan ... I may have picked you up slightly wrong, but I don't think so .... When you talk about people coming into education as a second career. The term you used, I think, was 'a second-class citizen' ... I thought that was interesting .... When we look at adult education and the importance of experience and how much we talk about experiential learning and everything that people can bring into the room and, you know, making that the centre of the learning ... I just thought it was very interesting when you talked about 'a second-class citizen'. To my mind, when you were describing it, I was thinking, wow, what a fantastic educator, you know, somebody who has had a career and all this experience and all this knowledge who is then able to work in an education space. So, I just wanted to pick up on that ....

Brendan

And it's just basically because sometimes the question is asked and it's not asked explicitly, but why? Why did you go? Why did you fail in your last career? Maybe the perception is that education is the easy route to take ... that you couldn't hack it, or you just wanted an easier job. Sometimes that what's levelled at people – I haven't experienced very much of that but other people say that they have ....

Camilla

... myself and Jerry have written a chapter on precarity, that seems relevant to our conversation at this point ...

... from Jane through to Suzanne through to Sarah, through to Francesca, Brendan everybody is showing so much passion and concern for the people that we're working with. But what about the educators? What about their terms and conditions of employment? ... So many people are on shitty contracts. People can't buy a car because they might have to lie on their applications to the bank, if they are brave enough. The amount of people on precarious contracts of one form or another who were simply ghosted by their institutions during Covid (Fitzsimons et al. 2022, 631) – it was shocking.

And now we've a situation where we have ETB tutors standing outside the Dáil [Irish Parliament] ... some of them with up to fifteen years work behind them and all they are looking for are some very basic terms and conditions of fair employment ....

Sarah [Sartori]

Can I just respond to something Brendan said about the word 'alternative'? Why further education or community education is described that way or, you know, 'pathways as being alternative' and it just struck me ... what came up when I was working on my contribution with FE students was how they saw FE as an alternative space and how they saw it in relation to higher education....

I was interested in if they see it as just a different space as opposed to alternative. And I remember that these students commented that they were sitting in the middle of an industrial estate … they were telling me to look around … 'look at the building', they'd say, 'when we go to university, we see big fancy buildings there. If universities and further education colleges are equal and part of one big tertiary system, why are we in prefabs?' They thought they were done with prefabs in school.

So, I just think that the buildings and our spaces we create for learning say so much about what we put value on. And I keep hearing again and again from FE students that I work with that it's not 'real' college.

And just on precarity. What really struck me or really shook me was moving into universities and realizing that the precarity is just as bad if not worse than the FE sector. I've been working for the university since 2014 on either zero or temporary contracts.

And I know this book isn't a comparison between further and higher education, but if we talk about precarity in FE, we also really need to discuss the precarity in our own HE institutions … because I think it's getting worse.

But look I could easily go down a rant rabbit hole … so yeah, I'll shush.

Camilla

Rants are often where the knowledge is. … So, Lilian, Bríd or Leo … any of you want to jump in?

Lilian

I wrote from personal experience as a fulcrum to write. I looked at myself wearing two hats, a Black student and a Black academic, and I fused and merged these two to propose, I suppose, tips that academics, mainly white academics, could take on board to embody an anti-racist ethos.

I remember sitting in classes as a Black student and being really isolated. Camilla spoke, earlier, about how maybe the most important outcome for a learner may just be to get to speak to one another in a group, to make friends. Part of my job with Maynooth University is that I visit student teachers on placement in FE spaces. I see the Black student or the minority ethnic students sitting on their own for one full hour then just walk away on their own after class. And the educator doesn't even see it because I ask them afterwards. Some say to me 'This is where the student wanted to sit'.

I wore these hats and used my own experiences to propose things that I thought white educators needed to know. I explain how, because of Irish laws, there's a large body of Black students in further education. I'm not saying all Black people are refugees or all refugees are Black. I'm just saying there's a large cohort there – as well as the fact that migrants, Black migrants who come into the country cannot get any other job apart from, most often, low-paid care work.

And so my chapter was just saying, look we can't shy away from talking about race we should talk about race ... but beyond talking we should do XYZ ... you can read the chapter to see what XYZ is!

Camilla

As you talk, I see similarities with one of the chapters I wrote which is about applying bell hooks' ideas of 'engaged pedagogy' in educational environments... flick back to Chapter 2 if you want to know more. But Lilian, tell us, why was it important for you to say that to white educators? Why aren't they doing this already? What's going on? What's going wrong?

Lilian

There is a lot of talk ... and I think 'anti-racism', 'diversity', 'inclusion' have become buzzwords. And once we attain buzzword status, there isn't any commensurate impact on the people that we claim. I have seen a lot of people talking about how they are so anti-racist, how they are appalled by racism, but their classrooms are still very much structured, the way I saw it or the way I experienced it as a student – with the Black students sitting miles apart. The structural issues are still there. There's a lot of talk about inclusion and diversity, but a lot of people are not embodying it.

And maybe I should also say that when I talk about ... and the things I talk about, even though I talk using Black as the lingo, what I am saying can apply really to any minority group.

Camilla

What's this sparking for people? What Lilian is saying?

Suzanne

I didn't want to jump in before others but it did spark something, which is when you talked about the buzzwords Lilian ... because I actually think that that's connected to, again, the productivity and the outputs thing. So we have all our written policies. And they're all about diversity. We're all about inclusion. But taking the time to actually have those conversations and reflect on how we are actually doing with all this doesn't really happen often – it's just sometimes about the optics.

Sarah [Coss]

Lilian, it's really great to hear you say as well that you have included things that people can use in their classrooms because I think that there are a lot of white educators that really just don't know what to do. Don't know how to approach this. Maybe they do see it, but they don't know that it's their place to do anything, and I think it's important for people to hopefully to get that confidence to be able to tackle these issues and name these issues and to raise them in their classrooms ....

Bríd

Well ... I think that the conversations are just amazing and I suppose I'm listening and thinking about what everybody is saying. It's so important that FET isn't just categorized in this slot between one level on a qualification framework and another because in many ways what adult educators really do is to try and model something that's really quite different from teachers and who have been trained to be teachers ... and also that idea of colour blindness or gender blindness is all part of those kind of biases really that have to be interrogated by anyone working with adults as an educator.

So I really do appreciate what you're saying, Lilian, but also what everybody else is saying. [...] Education has been obscured in many ways by having these categories of levels – of imagining education as levels from one up to level ten – when education really is about something really so significant and the kind of diversity that we're trying to embrace in FET is really the kind of diversity that was part of why community education was developed in the first place – an acknowledgement that the formal structures and the formal provisions really wasn't doing anything. And of course what we have seen over time is that an idea would be developed in community education and the next thing it would be tamed and corralled. And constrained by a policy, by a new term ... by something.

One of the things that I would have hoped from my own chapter – which is coming from the place of hope – is that when we are immersed in the problems of education, sort of perpetuating the status quo, that we really do have to have hope. That we can, as educators and as students, change things.

One thing that occurred to me so strongly really when I reflected first on being asked to contribute was that the pandemic threw up huge inequalities, but we were saying like, for example, people working at home and having to take care of their children, having to educate their children, having to turn up for work and so on. That's the kind of inequalities that really emerge so strongly during Covid and are the ones that are there all the time. Just that they're covered up by the normal everyday living.

So the precarity, the ghosting, the disdain for students or for our learners, and so on. That's always been there. There all the time, except that we can see it, I think, more clearly, since Covid.

And I suppose one of the things that strikes me today really is the television presenter Gary Lineker standing up.[2] I think that was so hopeful. And it really shows what a sentiment of the heart can do. That it really can uncover other things. And that's really what I would hope for when we're talking about the critique of education through that FET lens, I think that it is.

Education really has to be about changing people, and the people's knowledge base in terms of how they view the world. So it's not about completely adhering to the policies … it is really about transgressions in an awful lot of ways, and this really is enough.

And I think, Leo, you should say something …

Leo

Thanks Bríd and … actually, I've been enjoying that conversation.

My chapter introduces two ways in which we can look at digital literacy. The first is the almost traditional way in which you'll find in the policy statements and it's a list of skills … things you need to know. And there are many definitions. So, for example, we now call something cyber literacy … we have new literacies coming out all the time.

And that's really unhelpful and not very useful to us as educators because the ground keeps shifting. And also, from a personal perspective, I've always worked at the interaction between technology and education – I've always

---

2 In March 2023, Gary Lineker tweeted criticism of the British government's policy on preventing migrants crossing the English Channel in small boats seeking asylum. He compared the government's approach to those of 1930s Germany. He was criticized by the government and admonished by the BBC, his employers, for allegedly breaching social media guidelines. When he refused to apologize or remove the tweet, he was suspended. This led to a wave of other presenters refusing to go on air in support of Lineker's stance. After a significant media storm, the BBC apologized and he was re-instated. He tweeted his relief that the matter was over, thanked his supporters and said what he had been through was nothing compared to the experiences of the many displaced people who continue to seek safe passage and refuge.

felt very comfortable with both. But actually, I'm getting older. In terms of technology, I'm experiencing some of that sense of being left out or overlooked.

And that's a very powerful means of exclusion. And it's also something that maybe we're just not as aware of as we should be.

Even when you interrogate some of the policies, of what it is to be digitally literate ... it's like an obligation of citizenship. We need more consumers, we need the efficiencies of digital economy. We need to be able to access the skilled labour force. But that's not decisions that people are making for themselves – people are making decisions about 'how do I live my life more effectively' and 'what's good for me', and in some cases, some aspects of digital technology. Other aspects they may choose not to embrace and not to move forward with. And that's the problem for adult educators, because we need the voice of our individual students to be recognized and respected in that process. I introduce a concept called 'Digital World Literacy' and this digital world is that personal construct that we all have of the world, that as we see it, the changing technological world.

I argued that our most important contribution we can make is to have conversations with our students about that relationship they have with technology.

Jerry

I might just bring Eilish here to give us a sense of the 'why' behind her chapter ....

Eilish[3]

Thanks Jerry, I would like pick up on what Sarah [Coss] said about the principles of the education we are engaged in, and Bríd's point about our views of the world and transgressions. My background has been in the area of development and global education. That is about where we are in the world, the impacts of how we live in it and education which supports us to create a better world. Basically, I see global citizenship education as a powerful tool to support understanding and commitment to creating a more just, equal and sustainable world. One of my frustrations has been that it is not as critical or questioning or meaningful in practice as it aspires to be. I have been very influenced by the work of Vanessa Andreotti who shows that many

---

3 Eilish was unable to make the synchronous discussion so, instead she has answered questions put to her at a later date.

of us, often unintentionally, reinforce problematic thinking, relationships, patterns of practice and stereotypes which support inequality, injustice and exploitation in the first place. That's a big challenge for me and for all critical educators, I think. In my chapter, I try to explore how we can apply more critical approaches to global citizenship education in adult, community and further education contexts, ones that are radical, meaningful and relevant to participants and to the challenges we're all facing globally today.

Jerry

Thanks for that Eilish ... I know it's hard to get into the flow of the conversation when you aren't here ... but Jane ... you wanted to come in on a few things said previously?

Jane

Thanks ... it's really exciting stuff and I'm delighted to hear Bríd talking about hope because I think that's the engine of community education – hope for each other, our society and our communities. Lilian, I saw your 'the anti-racist educator' piece on EPALE with Stephen Brookfield (Brookfield and Nwanze 2022). It was such a catalyst for me to really reflect and think about what I'm doing and how I can perhaps use my voice and take action and be much more forceful around these things. And when I don't understand, to ask questions of the people who know and who are living their lives in front of me and I see students, people of colour in our own university, and they are very isolated.

And the precarity thing, we've just done a professional identity module, and it was a way to talk to some tutors about their status as educators and how they see themselves and there was real isolation and a feeling of a lack of respect coming through. That the status isn't there and that they're not recognized in the same way as others, particularly those in formal education settings, are. And that they sometimes have a status that is different to the person they're working alongside with – it is infuriating.

Back in the 1930s, that the Catholic Church stepped in and stopped vocational education from having the same status as higher education. One hundred years later we are still in the same place where there's no value placed on vocational or further education.

How do we make a change there? I think it can only be through action and using our voices and doing what we're doing here, gathering evidence, talking to the people involved and pushing it back to policy and legislation. I don't believe there's any malice in it, but it's conforming to these neoliberal metrics, siloed funding lines ....

Francesca

Lilian, part of my in job teaching in higher education, is that I teach a module on intercultural education. One of the things we found over the years that there's very little literature about racism in further education, particularly with relevance to Ireland. Your chapter is fundamental in pushing the issue. Thank you for that.

Camilla

So, Jerry, It's your turn.

Jerry

Just to pick up on something that Sarah [Sartori] said first about the built environment reflecting a lack of value or status. It's a similar theme in professional structures ... that lack of attention to the professional structure for further and adult education says something of its lack of value or status too within government.

Camilla and I dwell on the whole idea of naming of the FET landscape, and, of course, the term 'FET' itself as term. We connect 'naming' with 'taming' and the power dynamics of language in naming and renaming – not just further education but across the adult education field more widely. We also talk about how hard it can be to even organize, to have collective voices when all your energy is going into trying to keeping your feet steady on the ground.

I also wrote something that *performed* a critical and creative reflective practice as opposed to telling people what that is – there's enough of that out there. I took an instance in practice – I tried to write into and around a banal moment in practice – a very everyday kind of teaching moment with a group ....

Coming back to the point about interweaving the personal with the structural ... I think I was trying to do this.

I'm also trying to draw attention to slow processes that can interrupt the kind of accelerated, fast time of work that we're talking about here too – the productivity that Suzanne talks about. Myself and Susan Cullinane have written before about slowness as a radical, almost political, act (Cullinane and O'Neill 2020).

I wanted to propose for practitioners that to write from the personal but to move outwards to a collective and wider context can be seen as a form of inquiry and research that's very congruent with adult education ... that research isn't always something where FE needs to rush to university for expertise – maybe to see the chapter as an invitation to imagine reflexivity as a type of research.

And so I draw on autoethnography as a way into creativity and writing from a personal in a spiral out into the structure as a legitimate form of practitioner inquiry.

Hope

Jerry

So ... as we've been reflecting, a lot of our concerns, our challenges have really surfaced ... but I wonder, as a way of talking this book to an end, if we could follow that thread of hope that has also being mentioned more cautiously ... so, where are we seeing the possibilities for critical or radical hope in the work that that we're all involved with? ... Does anybody want to take up on the invitation to speak about hope or possibilities of hope in any kind of way?

Bríd

Can I? ... If I might just say that I listened to a podcast by Margaret Atwood this morning and she really was speaking about how hope is central. We actually cannot let go of hope. And if we really want to keep motivated ... to have any philosophy of change or working towards equality ... well, without hope we will just lose.

Without hope we will just become passive because we will feel that there's no point of doing it ... and I do think that David Attenborough has also highlighted the importance of hope even in the middle of complete and utter crisis and catastrophe that we really still need it ... and of course Greta Thunberg and Mary Robinson. [...] So there's people that are really talking about how central hope has to be.

And then when you do see the role that education has played in liberation movements of all kinds that even bad education is better than no education. And I suppose that's why the Taliban really wants to completely ban education because it is such a dangerous tool in spite of the flaws within it. So, I really do think that without hope that we will just become immobilized.

Suzanne

Yeah, I agree, Bríd. There's hope in these spaces. I always feel more energized going back to work after conversations like these when there's no bells or whistles. So I'm just really grateful for this space today. And the whole process around the development of this book – it wasn't just writing in isolation ... you can sense the commitment and that it's not just another piece of work to be produced and churned out.

The word 'oasis' was used at the start. And, Jerry, I remember being at a walking dialogues session you facilitated for the CEN. The word 'decadent' was used at the time by a participant about having the opportunity to get away from her desk and talk to a colleague in another part of the country on the phone while going on an outdoor walk. If we could move away from a situation where these spaces are a luxury or decadent and, instead, have them embedded in our work. Keep asking ourselves what does it mean to be productive? Maybe we need to reframe that too ... this space, to me is productive: it's producing knowledge and we will go back to our other work more energized and more creative.

Leo

I agree with the sentiments of hope and it would be easy to be overwhelmed with despair. If we become overwhelmed, our students become overwhelmed and it's not a good outcome ... but I'm a little bit worried about the potency of hope because ... 'I hope it stops raining'. But there's nothing I can do about it. Whereas actually, as educators, we usually can do something better than hope, we can have hope with action or something. You won't act unless you have hope. But you need both of them to make the difference ... Just wishing won't work for us. We need something more tangible. We can make a difference. We have been making a difference over the years. There's no measure of that and usually the best differences are not measurable.

Sarah [Sartori]

About hoping the rain would stop. I was thinking of this concept, like in books like *The Secret* (Byrne 2006) where we manifest what we're focusing on. And I remember somebody saying to me once that their mother worked for the Peace Corps. And you've never met anybody so surrounded by war. We're so focused on equality and injustice. And sometimes I can see how that is manifesting in my reality. That just gives me hope.

Every time I sit in a room with young people, I have hope. Because there's an energy. I was in Sweden recently and I met a very young woman who was doing her PhD on trees being sentient beings. This kind of stuff will change the world – if trees have the same rights and rivers have the same rights. I mean, this is the kind of stuff that young people are doing. I thought this is the world, my kids, who are tiny, are going to be living in, growing up in.

Camilla

I guess I'm going to start quite pessimistically. Often I think of what I knew as adult education that is gone now ... it's dead. It's been co-opted. That notion that if you want to control something or tame something, then you make it your own.

A lot of the hope for me now is outside of what's called FET but where the principles of adult education are alive. So ... there was a march in Dublin organized by the socialist–feminist group ROSA for International Women's Day. Thousands showed up.

And I went to listen to the author and academic Sara Ahmed last week and she was also talking about activism – I mean street activism. And I see adult education principles and practices in trade union spaces and in feminist spaces. Suzanne, your current research about how community education can respond to the rise of the alt-right there. That's hopeful. Maybe we should ignore what the government are telling us to do and focus on the principles, the reasons, the praxis.

Jane

I'd be a little bit more hopeful, I'm an optimist at heart. So I think of hope and kindness and the connection that we have with each other and the connection that we have with individuals in our professional and personal life. That is something that I hold on to, especially when you meet somebody who's dealing with so many different things ... from borders to homophobia and more. You know what they believe and who they love. You know where they're trying to get to ... developing their own potential, their own passions. Each one of those people is a change agent to the future and that's something that I hold on to every time I meet someone ... maybe I can say something that may help them ... ask them what they need or what they're looking for.

My worry is that people are getting tired, they're getting exhausted and they're turning inwards. They're turning just to themselves and their family because they're worn out trying to help others. So there's a huge need now for more kindness, more compassion and more connection.

Jerry

And I am going to bring Eilish in here... who couldn't be with us today but still has hope to share ... Eilish?

Eilish

Thanks Jerry. In terms of hope or the work that needs to be done in the area of Global Education. [...] My plea for the future is for more critical and postcritical

GE in adult, community and further education. At its most basic, this involves us as educators, no matter what type of education we are involved with, questioning our own assumptions about the world, the challenges we face and how they may need to be addressed; that we question the constraints on justice and equality etc. resulting from prevailing educational policy and institutional practices that we often take for granted; and that we really ask difficult questions about the challenges facing the world, and the people we work with, and the kinds of education we need to be supporting to address them.

Jerry

… I like the way that we're all thinking about hope differently and I do like the idea of hope that is wrapped up in some kind of critical action upon the world – a hope with teeth … but I also like how Jane sees hope in all the connections we make in our work – all the possibilities in our encounters. We've embodied a bit of that today. The academy and institutions can often pitch us against each other so … We need to be doing more of this.

Brendan

… in terms of hope when you hear the views that students have and the energy they have, everything that's going on for them, about the future, where they want to go, what they want to do ….

Jerry

Lilian … how about you?

Lilian

I want just to echo what Jane said. I have felt hopeless, even in the last week or so. But sitting down to reflect, I actually do have hope, and I do have hope in individuals, because just looking at this space, I can see Bríd and I know the impact she has had in Camilla's life – and I can see Camilla and I know the impact she has had on my life – and I know what I am giving to my students.

I know that love is transformative, so we might not be able to change the world. But we can do things one student at a time, one person at a time, one educator at a time and … and I have hope that we can keep lighting little fires … we need to keep lighting the little fires ….

ABOUT THE AUTHORS

Leo Casey

In my capacity as director of the Centre for Education and Lifelong Learning at the National College of Ireland, I am fortunate to be involved in a wide range of teaching, research and innovative education projects. When I look back on my career, I realize the prevailing theme is the intersection between new technology and learning. This is still the case today. My scholarly interests are learning across the lifespan, teacher professional development and how the digital world impacts our lives. I am excited to be principal investigator for PIKT, an Irish Research Council funded project on building teacher professional identity in Cambodia. I am also involved in P-TECH, a new approach to provide learning pathways for school and college students in disadvantaged areas. I have great colleagues; love my work and I'm still learning.

Eve Cobain

Eve Cobain is Senior Research Officer at AONTAS, the National Adult Learning Organisation. She supports the delivery of the organization's research, with a particular focus on community education. In 2021, Eve led the development of the first census to examine the state of community education in Ireland; she is currently conducting similar research in Northern Ireland.

Bríd Connolly

I came to adult and community education by accident when I was a young mother, looking for a tribe. It was the makings of me, much more than formal, accredited education. In my forty years of work with adult learners, I've seen the power of this alternative to mainstream education change people's lives individually and socially. Additionally, I've also observed the essential role it plays in social critique. In these troubling times, I'm completely convinced that it contains the crucial response to the crises that we're facing, through critical group work, curriculum, pedagogy and consciousness raising.

Sarah Coss

I began working in this sector by chance when I covered a short period of maternity leave in a Youthreach centre following my undergrad studies in Social Science. I left to take my own maternity leave but returned soon after to work with a group of young parents – a role I occupied myself. I pursued a Higher Diploma in Adult and Community Education in 2005 with Maynooth University and learned theories and practices that expanded my view of education, (in)equality and liberation. From here, I started working with MU on their Certificate in Adult and Community Education, got married, had two more children and returned to MU for a master's in education, all the while continuing my work leading to my current role in an Adult Education Service. That three-month maternity cover led to a life of work and personal fulfilment in a sector I continue to thoroughly enjoy being a part of.

Susan Cullinane

Susan works as a Community Education Facilitator with Kildare and Wicklow Education and Training Board. She is interested in how community education can contribute to individual and social transformation by responding to the pressing issues of our time.

Eilish Dillon

Eilish is a lecturer at the Maynooth University, Department of International Development. She has been involved in global education in different capacities over many years, conducting doctoral research in this area in 2016. She has recently led the development of a Certificate in global citizenship education for educators at Maynooth University and is currently co-editing a book on Global Education in Ireland.

Camilla Fitzsimons

I work as an associate professor at the Department of Adult and Community Education at Maynooth University. I'm told I'm a bit of a troublemaker because I always question the way things are and constantly ask 'why'. I see universities as elitist spaces that do more to keep people out than let people in. I see great potential of education in alternative spaces such as community gatherings, trade unions and campaign groups. But it's not so much about where we are, it is more the ideas that are brought to any space including within FET. The ideas I like are disruptive, anti-capitalist and radical. As well as many peer-reviewed articles, I've written two other books, *Community Education and Neoliberalism* (2017) and *Repealed: Ireland's Unfinished Fight for Reproductive Rights* (2021), and I am currently working on my third book called *Reframing Feminism in Ireland* which, all going well, will be published in 2024.

Brendan Kavanagh

Brendan Kavanagh has a background in pre-hospital emergency care and is working as a second-career teacher within the City of Dublin ETB. Brendan is currently studying for a professional doctorate in education at Dublin City University.

Suzanne Kyle

Suzanne has worked in the area of community education for over twenty years. She is currently a PhD student in the Department of Adult and Community Education at Maynooth University. Her research interests include the role of community education in times of social crisis and the factors which enable or constrain the ability of practitioners to embed social justice principles in their practice.

Francesca Lorenzi

Francesca is a lecturer, is based in the School of Policy and Practice, DCU and is a researcher with FETRC (Further Education and Training Researcher Centre). A concern for the democratization of educational practices, the promotion of divergence and creativity in education and the inclusion of older learners and of people from diverse cultural backgrounds are core themes that inform and underpin her research and teaching.

Elaine McDonald

I work as a lecturer and teacher educator in the School of Policy and Practice, DCU Institute of Education. Education disadvantage, inclusion, teacher identity and widening participation in higher education are core to my teaching and research interests.

Lilian Nwanze

My name is Lilian Nwanze. I am a Black Nigerian-Irish woman. I qualified and practised as a Barrister and Solicitor of the Federal Republic of Nigeria before I migrated to Ireland. I have experienced first hand what it feels like to be in classrooms where there is no prior thought about racism and its attendant manifestations. Consequently, when I became a teacher in Ireland, I made it a priority to not only centre issues of race in my practice, but to also speak out and write about race and racism and the impact they can have on students in the classroom. When I am not writing and speaking about race, I am interested in practical ways that classrooms at every level of Irish education can truly become transformative spaces for those who attend.

Jane O'Kelly

My name is Jane and I'm passionate about people, their potential and access to opportunities. I have been lucky to find support and encouragement through my family, my work and my friends. I followed a diverse path from a secretarial course, through administration, training and now working in DCU as a lecturer and researcher. I believe that people are fundamentally good. I think that the generalized systems that we live within are necessary but need to serve the people and not the other way around. I care about people who are not served by the system and I want to listen to, and work with, learners and practitioners.

Jerry O'Neill

I often think that my first really positive educational experience was as a student on a sound engineering course in Ballyfermot Senior College (now College of Further Education) back in the late 1980s. That one-year course ignited something in me about the value of FE that burned away slowly over the years. Those embers stayed with me on my subsequent crooked life paths until I found myself returning as a mature student to university in Belfast about ten years later. I eventually qualified as a teacher and worked for several years in FE in Scotland before returning to Ireland where, after years of surviving on the scraps of precarious work in adult, community, work-based and higher education, I now seem to find myself as a lecturer in Maynooth University coordinating, among other things, a further education ITE programme. I'm interested in reflexive, creative and perambulatory approaches to pedagogy and research.

Sarah Sartori

I have worked in adult, further and higher education contexts for over fifteen years, and am particularly interested in creative, inclusive and participatory methods that disrupt traditional modes of practice and amplify voice. I received my PhD in Adult and Community Education from Maynooth University in 2020, which was a creative exploration of educational exclusion from the perspective of people in prison and youth. I'm a mum to three small people, who motivate me to want to make the world a better place. I have strong opinions, that usually change, and I love dancing and chocolate ... occasionally at the same time.

BIBLIOGRAPHY

Accenture. 2020. "BRIDGING THE GAP: Ireland's Digital Divide." *Accenture*. Accessed March 20, 2023. https://www.accenture.com/ie-en/insights/local/digital-divide.
AHEAD. 2021. *UDL for FET Practitioners, Summary Version*. SOLAS. Accessed March 30, 2023. https://www.solas.ie/f/70398/x/0dc582f3c2/udl-for-fet-practitioners-summary.pdf.
———. 2023. "Funding and Finance." *AHEAD*. Accessed March 30, 2023. https://www.ahead.ie/financefaqs.
Ahmad, A. S. 2020. "Why You Should Ignore All That Coronavirus-Inspired Productivity Pressure." *The Chronicle of Higher Education*, 26 March. Accessed March 20, 2023. https://www.chronicle.com/article/why-you-should-ignore-all-that-coronavirus-inspired-productivity-pressure/.
Ahmed, S. 2021. *Complaint!* London: Duke University Press.
———. 2017. *Living a Feminist Life*. Durham and London: Duke University Press.
Akinborowa, V., C. Fitzsimons, and P. Obasi. 2020. "Nothing about us without us – Reflections on the Experiences of Nigerian and Irish Women Working Together." In *I am a Man of Peace: Writings Inspired by the Maynooth University Ken Saro-Wiwa Collection*, by H. Fallon, 128–135. Québec: Daraja Press.
Alkhaldi, R. S., E. Sheppard, and P. Mitchell. 2019. "Is There a Link Between Autistic People Being Perceived Unfavorably and Having a Mind That Is Difficult to Read?" *Journal of Autism and Developmental Disorders* 49: 3973–3982. https://doi.org/10.1007/s10803-019-04101-1.
Allais, S. 2014. *Selling Out Education: National Qualifications Frameworks and the Neglect of Knowledge*. Rotterdam: Sense Publications.
Allen, K. 2013. *Austerity Ireland: The Failure of Irish Capitalism*. New York and London: Pluto Press.
Ambrose, D. 2014. "Seeking Chaotic Order: The Classroom as a Complex Adaptive System." In *A Critique of Creativity and Complexity*, by D. Ambrose, B. Sriraman and K. M. Pierce, 157–183. Leiden: Brill.
Anderson, A. H., J. Stephenson, M. Carter, and S. Carlon. 2019. "A Systematic Literature Review of Empirical Research on Postsecondary Students with Autism Spectrum Disorder." *Journal of Autism and Developmental Disorders* 49 (4): 1531–1558.
Anderson, M. L., J. Goodman, and N. Schlossberg. 2011. *Counseling [sic] Adults in Transition: Linking Schlossberg's Theory with Practice in a Diverse World*. New York: Springer.
Andreotti, V. 2006. "Soft versus Critical Global Citizenship Education." *Policy & Practice: A Development Education Review* 3 (Autumn): 40–51.
Andreotti, V. 2011. *Actionable Postcolonial Theory in Education*. London: Palgrave Macmillan.
Andreotti, V. 2014. "Critical Literacy: Theories and Practices in Development Education." *Policy & Practice: A Development Education Review* 19 (Autumn): 12–32.

Andrews, K. 2018. *Back to Black Retelling Black Radicalism for the 21st Century*. London: Zed books.

Anthony, G., and K. Ord. 2008. "Change-of-Career Secondary Teachers: Motivations, Expectations and Intentions." *Asia-Pacific Journal of Teacher Education* 36 (4): 359–376.

Antoine, A., R. Mason, R. Mason, S. Palahicky, and C. Rodriguez de France. 2018. *Pulling Together: A Guide for Curriculum Developers*. Victoria, BC: BC Campus. Accessed November 30, 2022. https://opentextbc.ca/indigenizationcurriculumdevelopers/.

AONTAS. 2004. *Community Education*. Dublin: AONTAS. Accessed March 20, 2023. https://www.aontas.com/assets/resources/Community-Education/community_ed_04%20publication%20for%20website.pdf.

———. 2011. *The AONTAS Community Education Network Position paper on creating an effective funding mechanism for community education*. AONTAS CEN. Accessed April 6, 2023. https://www.aontas.com/assets/resources/Policy/Position%20Paper%20-%20Effective%20Funding%20for%20Community%20Education%20Feb%202011.pdf.

———. 2020. *Mitigating Educational Disadvantage (Including Community Education Issues)*. Dublin: AONTAS.

———. 2023. *Annual Report 2022*. Dublin: AONTAS. Accessed December 6, 2023. Available at: https://www.aontas.com/Annual%20Report%20Spread%202023_FINAL%202%20AW.pdf.

Aronowitz, S. 1993. "Paulo Freire's Radical Democratic Humanism." In *Paulo Freire a Critical Encounter*, by P. McLaren and P. Leonard, 8–23. London: Routledge.

Arruzza, C., T. Bhattacharya, and N. Fraser. 2019. *Feminism for the 99%*. New York: Verso Books.

AsIAm. 2023. 'Child Diagnosis'. Available at: https://asiam.ie/autism-child-diagnosis/ Accessed December 7, 2023.

Avis, J., and A. M. Bathmaker. 2004. "Critical Pedagogy, Performativity and a Politics of Hope: Trainee Further Education Lecturer Practice." *Research in Post-Compulsory Education* 9 (2): 301–316.

Bacalja, A., C. Beavis, and A. M. O'Brien. 2022. "Shifting Landscapes of Digital Literacy." *The Australian Journal of Language and Literacy* 45 (2): 253–263.

Baeten, M., and W. Meeus. 2016. "Training Second-career Teachers: A Different Student Profile, A Different Training Approach?" *Educational Process: International Journal* 5 (3): 173–201.

Bailey, G., and H. Colley. 2015. "Learner-centred' Assessment Policies in Further Education: Putting Teachers' Time under Pressure." *Journal of Vocational Education & Training* 67 (2): 153–168.

Bailey, N. 2009. *Integrating Development Education into Adult Education Using Active Citizenship as a Focus*. Dublin: AONTAS.

Bar-Tal, S., and L. Biberman-Shalev. 2022. "Reverberations of a Previous Career as Reflected in Personal Blogs of Career Switchers into Teaching." *International Education Studies* 15 (2): 172–181.

Bar-Tal, S., N. Chamo, D. Ram, Z. Snapir, and I. Gilat. 2020. "First Steps in a Second Career: Characteristics of the Transition to the Teaching Profession among Novice Teachers." *European Journal of Teacher Education* 43 (5): 660–675.

Barton, D., M. Hamilton, and I. Roz. 2000. *Situated Literacies: Reading and Writing in Context*. London & New York: Routledge.

Bates Evoy, S. 2017. "Professional Identity and the Irish Further Education and Training Practitioner." *ESREA /LHBN 2017*. Tuborgvej. 1–15. Accessed March 14, 2023.

https://conferences.au.dk/fileadmin/user_upload/ESREA-LBHN2017_Filer/1_lbhn_17_batesevoy_fetpractitionerid.pdf.
Baumgartner, L. M. 2010. "White Whispers: Talking about Race in Adult Education." In *The Handbook of Race and Adult Education*, by V. Sheared, J. Johnson-Bailey, III S. A. J. Colin, E. Peterson and Stephen Brookfield and Associates, 105–117. San Francisco: John Wiley and Sons.
Bawden, D. 2008. "Origins and Concepts of Digital Literacy." *Digital Literacies: Concepts, Policies and Practices* 30: 17–32.
Beardon, L., and G. Edmonds. 2007. "ASPECT consultancy report. A national report on the needs of adults with Asperger syndrome." Accessed March 30, 2023. www.shu.ac.uk/theautismcentre.
Beardon, L., N. Martin, and I. Woolsey. 2009. "What Do Students with AS and HFA Want at College or University – in their Own Words." *Good Autism Practice (GAP)* 10 (2): 35–43.
Beauvoir, S. de. 1953. *The Second Sex*. Harmondsworth: Penguin.
Becker, J. C., L. Hartwich, and S. A. Haslam. 2021. "Neoliberalism Can Reduce Well-being by Promoting a Sense of Social Disconnection, Competition, and Loneliness." *British Journal of Social Psychology* 60 (3): 947–965. doi: 10.1111/bjso.12438.
Beijaard, D., P. C. Meijer, and N. Verloop. 2004. "Reconsidering Research on Teachers' Professional Identity." *Teaching and Teacher Education* 20 (2): 107–128.
Berger, J. L., and Y. D'Ascoli. 2012. "Becoming a VET Teacher as a Second Career: Investigating the Determinants of Career Choice and their Relation to Perceptions about Prior Occupation." *Asia-Pacific Journal of Teacher Education* 40 (3): 317–341.
Biesta, G. 2006. "What's the Point of Lifelong Learning if Lifelong Learning has No Point? On the Democratic Deficit of Policies for Lifelong Learning." *European Educational Research Journal* 5 (3&4): 169–180.
Biggs, J. 2012. "What the Student Does: Teaching for Enhanced Learning." *Higher Education Research & Development* 31 (1): 39–55.
Bilgrami, A. 2006. "Notes toward the Definition of 'Identity'." *Daedalus* 135 (4): 5–14.
Bissett, J. 2008. *Regeneration: Public Good or Private Profit*. Bristol: Policy Press.
———. 2015. "Defiance and Hope: Austerity and the Community Sector in the Republic of Ireland." In *Ireland under Austerity, Neoliberal Crisis, Neoliberal Solutions*, by C. Coulter and A. Nagle, 171–191. Manchester and New York: Manchester University Press.
Blaisdell, B. 2015. "Schools as Racial Spaces: Understanding and Resisting Structural Racism." *International Journal of Qualitative Studies in Education* 29 (2): 248–272.
Boal, A. 2002. *Games for Actors and Non-Actors, Second Edition*. London and New York: Routledge.
Bobek, A., S. Pembroke, and J. Wickham. 2018. *Living with Uncertainty: Social Implications of Precarious Work*. Dublin: TASC.
Boland, T., and E. Hazelkorn. 2022. *Strengthening the Sustainability, Quality and Competitiveness of Irish Higher Education: Trends and Propositions to Provoke Debate*. Shannon: BH Associates.
Bolton, G. 2014. *Reflective Practice: Writing and Professional Development (4th Ed.)*. London: Sage.
Bonilla-Silva, E. 2015. "The Structure of Racism in Color-Blind, 'Post-Racial' America." *American Behavioural Scientist* 59 (11): 1358–1376. doi: 10.1177/0002764215586826.
Botha, M., and D. M. Frost. 2020. "Extending the Minority Stress Model to Understand Mental Health Problems Experienced by the Autistic Population." *Society and Mental Health* 10 (1): 20–34.
Botha, M., B. Dibb, and D. M. Frost. 2022. "'Autism is me': An Investigation of How Autistic Individuals Make Sense of Autism and Stigma." *Disability & Society* 37 (3): 427–453.

Boud, D., and R. Soler. 2016. "Sustainable Assessment Revisited." *Assessment & Evaluation in Higher Education* 41 (3): 400–413.

Bourn, D. 2014. "The Theory and Practice of Global Learning." *Development Education Research* (Paper no. 11): 1–52. Accessed March 20, 2023. https://discovery.ucl.ac.uk/id/eprint/1492723/.

———. 2020. "Global and Development Education and Global Skills." *Educar* 56 (2): 279–295.

Bracken, M. 2020. "The Power of Language and the Language of Power: Exploring Discourses on Development Education in Policies Underpinning Adult and Community Education." *Policy & Practice: A Development Education Review* 31 (Autumn): 55–76.

Bradley, M. G., and L. De Noronha. 2022. *Against Borders. The Case for Abolition*. London: Verso Books.

Brannan, D., and T. Bleistein. 2012. "Novice ESOL Teachers' Perceptions of Social Support Networks." *TESOL Quarterly* 46 (3): 519–541.

Brian, D. J., and O. Elbert. 2005. "Learning at Highlander: A Template for Transformative Adult Education." *Adult Education Research Conference*. Accessed February 10, 2023. https://newprairiepress.org/aerc/2005/papers/66.

Brookfield, S. D. 1998. "Critically Reflective Practice." *The Journal of Continuing Education in the Health Professions* 18: 197–205.

———. 2015. *The Skillful Teacher: On technique, Trust and Responsiveness in the Classroom*. San Francisco: Jossey-Bass.

———. 2017. *Becoming a Critically Reflective Teacher*. 2nd. New York: John Wiley & Sons.

———. 2018. *Teaching Race: How to Help Students Unmask and Challenge Racism*. Newark: John Riley and Sons Incorporated.

Brookfield, S., and L. Nwanze. 2022. "Becoming an Anti-Racist Adult Education Practitioner." *Podcast*. EPALE Ireland. Accessed March 27, 2023. https://epale.ec.europa.eu/en/blog/becoming-anti-racist-adult-education-practitioner-podcast.

Brookfield, S., and M. Hess. 2021. *Becoming a White Antiracist. A Practical Guide for Educators, Leaders, and Activists*. Sterling: Stylus Publishers LLC.

Brownlow, C., H. B. Rosqvist, and L. O'Dell. 2015. "Exploring the Potential for Social Networking among People with Autism: Challenging Dominant Ideas of 'friendship'." *Scandinavian Journal of Disability Research* 17 (2): 188–193.

Bryan, A. 2020. "Affective Pedagogies: Foregrounding Emotion in Climate Change Education." *Policy and Practice: A Development Education Review* 30 (Spring): 8–30.

———. 2022. "From 'the conscience of humanity' to the Conscious Human Brain: UNESCO's Embrace of Social-Emotional Learning as a Flag of Convenience." *Compare: A Journal of Comparative and International Education*. https://doi.org/10.1080/03057925.2022.2129956.

Bryan, A., and M. Bracken. 2011. *Learning to Read the World: Teaching and Learning about Global Citizenship and International Development in Post-Primary Schools*. Dublin: Irish Aid.

Buchanan, J. 2020. *Challenging the Deprofessionalisation of Teaching and Teachers*. Singapore: Springer.

Bunn, G., and D. Wake. 2015. "Motivating Factors of Nontraditional Post-baccalaureate Students Pursuing Initial Teacher Licensure." *The Teacher Educator* 50 (1): 47–66.

Burgstahler, S. 2009. "Universal design of instruction (UDI): definition, principles, guidelines, and examples. DO -IT." Accessed February 20, 2023. https://www.washington.edu/doit/sites/default/files/atoms/files/UD_Instruction_06_15_20.pdf.

Butler, J. 1990. *Gender Trouble*. New York: Routledge.

Byrne, R. 2006. *The Secret*. New York: Atria Books.

Cai, R. Y., and A. L. Richdale. 2016. "Educational Experiences and Needs of Higher Education Students with Autism Spectrum Disorder." Journal of Autism Developmental Disorders 46 (1): 31–41. doi: 10.1007/s10803-015-2535-1.

Cage, E., J. Di Monaco, and V. Newell. 2018. "Experiences of Autism Acceptance and Mental Health in Autistic Adults." *Journal of Autism Development Disorders* 48: 473–484.

Cage, E. and J. Howes. 2020. "Dropping Out and Moving On: A Qualitative Study of Autistic People's Experiences of University." *Autism* 24 (7): 1664–1675.

Casey, L. 2009. *Pathways to Competence and Participation in the Digital World*. PhD Thesis, Maynooth University. http://eprints.nuim.ie/1545/.

———. 2015. "Participation as Telos for Learning." In *International Handbook of Progressive Education*, by M. Y. Eryaman and B. C. Bruce, 401–418. New York: Peter Lang.

CAST. 2018. Universal Design for Learning Guidelines version 2.2. Available at: http://udlguidelines.cast.org. Accessed March 9, 2023.

Chambers, D. 2002. "The Real World and the Classroom: Second-career Teachers." *The Clearing House* 75 (4): 212–217.

Chancel, L., T. Piketty, E. Saez, and G. Zucman. 2022. *World Inequality Report 2022*. World Inequality Lab. Accessed April 7, 2023. https://wir2022.wid.world/www-site/uploads/2023/03/D_FINAL_WIL_RIM_RAPPORT_2303.pdf.

Chilcoat, J. N. D. "Fair Isn't Always Equal: The Band Aid Lesson." Accessed December 28, 2021. https://www.hol.edu/uploads/essays/Fair-Isnt-Always-Equal-59821ca0e2e81.pdf.

Citizen's Information Board. 2023. "Types of residence permission for non-EEA nationals." *Citizen's Information*. 23 February. https://www.citizensinformation.ie/en/moving_country/moving_to_ireland/rights_of_residence_in_ireland/types_residence_permission_non_eea_nationals.html.

Cixous, H. 1976. "The Laugh of the Medusa." Edited by Keith Cohan and Paula Cohan. *Signs* 1 (4): 875–893.

Clance, P. R., and S. A. Imes. 1978. "The Imposter Phenomenon in High Achieving Women: Dynamics and Therapeutic Intervention." *Psychotherapy: Theory, Research and Practice* 15 (3): 241–247.

Clark, M. C. 1993. "Transformational Learning." *New Directions for Adult and Continuing Education* 1993 (57): 47–56.

Clouder, L., M. Karakus, A. Cinotti, et al. 2020. "Neurodiversity in Higher Education: A Narrative Synthesis. *Higher Education* 80: 757–778. https://doi.org/10.1007/s10734-020-00513-6.

Cobain, E., L. Dowdall, N. O'Reilly, and S. Akisato. 2020. *Community Education in a Time of Covid*. Dublin: AONTAS. Accessed February 28, 2022. https://www.aontas.com/assets/resources/AONTAS-Research/AONTAS_CEN_Census_REPORT_FINAL.pdf.

Cobain, E., L. Dowdall, N. O'Reilly, and A. Suzuki. 2021. CEN Census 2020: Community Education in a Time of COVID-19. Available at: 15525_AONTAS_CEN_Census_V12-Sept.pdf.

Coffey, C., P. Espinoza Revello, R. Harvey, M. Lawson, A. Parvez Butt, K. Piaget, D. Sarosi, and J. Thukkdan. 2020. *Time to Care, Unpaid and Underpaid Care Work and the Global Inequality Crisis*. Oxford: Oxfam.

Cole, M. 2009. "Critical Race Theory Comes to the UK: A Marxist Response." *Ethnicities* 9 (2): 246–284.

———. 2020. "A Marxist Critique of Sean Walton's Defence of the Critical Race Theory Concept of 'White supremacy' as Explaining All Forms of Racism, and Some

Comments on Critical Race Theory Black Radical and Socialist Futures." *Power and Education* 12 (1): 95–109.

Colley, H. 2012. "Not Learning in the Workplace: Austerity and the Shattering of Illusion in Public Service Work." *Journal of Workplace Learning* 24 (5): 317–337.

Combat Poverty Agency. 2000. *The Role of Community Development in Tackling Poverty*. Dublin: The Irish Health Repository. Accessed March 20, 2023. https://www.lenus.ie/handle/10147/297172.

Commission on Adult Education. 1984. *Lifelong Learning: Report on the Commission on Adult Education*. Dublin: The Stationary Office.

Committee on Adult Education. 1973. *Adult Education in Ireland*. Dublin: The Stationary Office.

Committee on the Rights of Persons with Disabilities. 2021. *Initial Report of Ireland under the Convention on the Rights of Persons with Disabilities*. Ireland: Department of Children, Equality, Disability, Integration and Youth. Accessed March 30, 2023. https://www.gov.ie/en/publication/75e45-irelands-first-report-to-the-united-nations-committee-on-the-rights-of-persons-with-disabilities/.

Connolly, B. 2001. *Women's Community Education in Ireland*. Dublin: One Step Up. http://www.onestepup.ie/assets/files/pdf/womens_community_education_in_ireland.pdf.

———. 2005. "Learning from the Women's Community Education Movement in Ireland." In *Popular Education, Engaging the Academy, International Perspectives*, by J. Crowther, V. Galloway, and I. Martin, 204–213. Leicester: NAICE.

———. 2006. "Adult and Community Education: A Model for Higher Education? In: from the National University of Ireland, Maynooth." In *What Price the University? Perspectives on the Meaning and Value of Higher Education*, by A Special Issue of Maynooth Philosophical Papers, 36–46. Maynooth: National University of Ireland, Maynooth, Maynooth.

———. 2008. *Adult Learning in Groups*. Manchester: Manchester University Press.

Connolly, B., C. Fitzsimons, and M. Shaw. 2021. "Reasserting the Politics of Community Education." *The Community Education Webinar Series Part 1*. Epale, 28 May. Accessed March 20, 2023. https://epale.ec.europa.eu/en/blog/reasserting-politics-community-education.

Conway, P. F. and R. Murphy. 2013. "A Rising Tide Meets a Perfect Storm: New Accountabilities in Teaching and Teacher Education in Ireland." *Irish Education Studies* 32 (1): 11–36.

Conway, P., R. Murphy, A. Rath, and K. Hall. 2009. *Learning to Teach and its Implications for the Continuum of Teacher Education: A Nine-country Cross-national Study. Maynooth*. Maynooth: The Teaching Council.

Cooper, K., L. G. E. Smith, and A. Russell. 2017. "Social Identity, Self-Esteem, and Mental Health in Autism. *European Journal of Social Psychology* 47: 844–854. doi: 10.1002/ejsp.2297.

Coppe, T., V. März, L. Coertjens, and I. Raemdonck. 2021. "Transitioning into TVET Schools: An Exploration of Second Career Teachers' Entry Profiles." *Teaching and Teacher Education* 101: 1–13. doi: 10.1016/j.tate.2021.103317.

Coss, S. 2022. "Measuring Success in Adult Education: Recognising Diverse Outcomes from a Diverse Sector." *The Adult Learner: The Irish Journal of Adult and Community Education* 141–162.

Courtois, A., and T. O'Keefe. 2015. "Precarity in the Ivory Cage: Neoliberalism and Casualisation of Work in the Irish Higher Education Sector." *Journal for Critical Education Policy Studies* 13 (1): 43–66.

Crenshaw, K. 1991. "Mapping the Margins: Intersectionality, Identity Politics, and Violence against Women of Color." *Stanford Law Review* 43 (6): 1241–1299.

Crow, G. M., L. Levine, and N. Nager. 1990. "No More Business as Usual: Career Changers who Become Teachers." *American Journal of Education* 98 (3): 197–223.

Crowther, J. 2018. "The Contradictions of Populism: Reasserting Adult Education for Democracy." *Andragoška spoznanja* 24 (1): 19–34. doi: 10.4312/as.24.1.19-34.

Cullinane, S., and J. O'Neill. 2020. *'We make the Path by Walking: Community Education Walking Dialogues' AONTAS CEN Conversation Series 2*. Dublin: AONTAS.

Cush, M. 2016. *Report to the Minister for Education and Skills of the Chairperson of the Expert Group on Fixed-term and Part-time Employment in Lecturing in Third Level Education in Ireland*. Dublin: Department of Education and Skills. Accessed July 09, 2021. https://www.tui.ie/_fileupload/Cush%20Report.pdf.

Dabiri, E. 2021. *What White People Can Do Next*. Dublin: Penguin.

Daft, R. L., and D. Marcic. 2013. *Building Management Skills: An Action-First Approach*. International Edition: Cengage Learning.

Danish Folk High Schools. 2022. *A Brief History of the Folk High School*. Accessed February 10, 2023. https://danishfolkhighschools.com/about-folk-high-schools/history.

Darder, A., and R. D. Torres. 2003. *The Critical Pedagogy Reader*. London: Routledge.

Davies, H. 2022. "Autism Is a Way of Being: An 'insider perspective' on Neurodiversity, Music Therapy and Social Justice." *British Journal of Music Therapy* 36 (1): 16–26.

Davies, P. L., C. L. Schelly, and C. L. Spooner. 2013. "Measuring the Effectiveness of Universal Design for Learning Intervention in Postsecondary Education." *Journal of Postsecondary Education and Disability* 26 (3): 195–220.

Davis, R. 2020. "UK must compel Amazon to improve worker conditions." *The Guardian*, 12 October. Accessed September 25, 2021. https://www.theguardian.com/technology/2020/oct/12/uk-must-compel-amazon-to-improve-worker-conditions-say-unions.

Day, C. 2007. "School Reform and Transitions in Teacher Professionalism and Identity." In *Handbook of Teacher Education: Globalization, Standards and Professionalism in Times of Change*, by T. Townsend and R. Bates, 597–612. Dordrecht: Springer.

———. 2012. "New Lives of Teachers." *Teacher Education Quarterly* 39 (1): 7–26.

Dean, M., R. Harwood, and C. Kasari. 2016. "The Art of Camouflage: Gender Differences in the Social Behaviors of Girls and Boys with Autism Spectrum Disorder." *Autism*. doi: 10.1177/1362361316671845.

Delgado, R., and J. Stefancic. 2017. *Critical Race Theory: An introduction*. New York: New York University Press.

Dempsey, M. 2023. "Curriculum: The Great Public Project." In *The New Publicness of Education: Democratic Possibilities after the Critique of Neo-Liberalism*, by C. A. Säfström and G. Biesta, 40–54. London/New York: Routledge.

Denzin, N. K. 2014. *Interpretive Autoethnography*. 2nd. London: Sage.

Department of Education and Science. 1995. *Charting Our Education Future, the White Paper on Education*. Dublin: Government of Ireland. Accessed March 14, 2023. https://assets.gov.ie/24448/0f3bff53633440d99c32541f7f45cfeb.pdf.

———. 1998. *Green Paper: Adult Education in an Era of Lifelong Learning*. Dublin: Government Publications.

———. 2000. *The White Paper: Learning for Life*. Dublin: Government Publications.

———. 2020. Educational Provision for Learners with Autism Spectrum Disorder in Special Classes Attached to Mainstream Schools in Ireland. Dublin: Inspectorate. Available at file:///Users/janemurnaghan/Desktop/75048_0e5a1e59-45e7-44c3-95be-ffb722d9bfe5%20(1).pdf. Accessed March 8, 2023.

Department of Further and Higher Education, Research, Innovation and Science. 2022. *Progressing a Unified Tertiary System for Learning, Skills and Knowledge.* Dublin: DFHERIS.

Department of Health. 2018. *Estimating Prevalence of Autism Spectrum Disorders (ASD) in the Irish Population: A review of data sources and epidemiological studies.* Accessed March 8, 2023. Available at: https://www.gov.ie/pdf/?file=https://assets.gov.ie/10707/ce1ca48714424c0ba4bb4c0ae2e510b2.pdf#page=null.

Dewey, J. 1997. *Experience and Education.* New York: Touchstone.

Dillon, E. 2017. "How critical is talk? Discourses of development education among facilitators in Ireland." Unpublished Doctoral Thesis:, Maynooth University. Accessed March 20, 2023. http://mural.maynoothuniversity.ie/9558/.

———. 2019. "Connecting the Personal and the Political: Feminist Perspectives on Development Education." *Policy and Practice: A Development Education Review* 29 (Autumn): 11–30.

———. 2022. "Making Connections in Challenging Times: The Transformative Potential of Poetry for Critical Global Education." *Journal of Transformative Education* 20 (4): 396–413.

Done, E., H. Knowler, M. Murphy, T. Rea, and K. Gale. 2011. "(Re)writing CPD: Creative Analytical Practices and the 'continuing professional development' of Teachers." *Reflective Practice* 12 (3): 389–399.

Doody, P., M. Wang, S. Scarlett, A. Hever, and A. M. O'Mahoney. 2020. *Internet access and use among adults aged 50 and over in Ireland: Results from Wave 5 of The Irish Longitudinal Study on Ageing.* Tilda. Accessed March 20, 2023. https://tilda.tcd.ie/publications/reports/pdf/Report_Covid19HealthcareUtilisation.pdf.

Dorman, P. 2007. *Things can be Different: The Transformation of Fatima Mansions.* Dublin: CAN Publications.

Doyle, A., C. Mc Guckin, and M. Shevlin. 2017. "'Close the door on your way out': Parent Perspectives on Supported Transition Planning for Young People with Special Educational Needs and Disabilities in Ireland." *Journal of Research in Special Educational Needs* 17 (4): 274–281.

Dublin City University Neurodivergent Society Constitution. 2019. Accessed March 20, 2023. https://cdn.dcuclubs.ie/user_files/constitution/10221/c9c55d4341801360c8d2efb1d78de819.pdf.

Dulee-Kinsolving, A., and S. Guerin. 2020. "FET IN Numbers 2019: Learners with Disabilities." Accessed February 1, 2023. https://www.solas.ie/f/70398/x/c1aa6d09ff/disabilities-fet-report-2019.pdf.

Dwyer, P., E. Mineo, K. Mifsud, C. Lindholm, and T. C. Waisman. 2020. "Building Neurodiversity-Inclusive Postsecondary Campuses: Recommendations for Leaders in Higher Education." *Autism in Adulthood* 5 (1): 1–14.

Dwyer, P., J. G. Ryan, Z. J. Williams, and D. L. Gassner. 2022. "First Do No Harm: Suggestions Regarding Respectful Autism Language." *Pediatrics*: 149.

Eddo-Lodge, R. 2017. *Why I'm No Longer Talking to White People about Race.* London: Bloomsbury Publications.

Edwards, J. 2009. *Language and Identity.* Cambridge: Cambridge University Press.

Elias, R, A. D. Muskett, and S. W. White. 2017. "Educator Perspectives on the Postsecondary Transition Difficulties of Students with Autism." *Autism* 21 (3): 260–264.

Elias, R., and S. W. White. 2018. "Autism Goes to College: Understanding the Needs of a Student Population on the Rise." *Journal of Autism Development Disorders* 48: 732–746.

ETBI. 2017. *Further Education and Training Professional Development Strategy: 2017–19*. Dublin: SOLAS & Education and Training Boards Ireland.

———. 2021. "The Special Educational Needs Initiative (SENI) in Youthreach." Accessed March 8, 2023. Available at: https://www.etbi.ie/wp-content/uploads/2021/06/Overview-of-the-SEN-Initiative-in-Youthreach.pdf?x16306.

———. 2022. "Stronger Together: Further Education and Training Conference Looks to the Future of FET." Athlone.

Etherington, K. 2004. *Becoming a Reflexive Researcher: Using Our Selves in Research*. London: Kingsley Publishers.

European Commission. 2022. "Digital Economy and Society Index (DESI) Thematic Chapters." *European Commission – Shaping Europe's Digital Future*. Accessed March 20, 2023. https://digital-strategy.ec.europa.eu/en/policies/desi.

European Commission. 2022. *The Digital Economy and Society Index (DESI)*. European Commission. Accessed March 30, 2023. https://digital-strategy.ec.europa.eu/en/policies/desi.

Evaristo, B. 2019. *Girl, Women, Other*. London: Penguin.

———. interview by BBC Radio 4. 2022. *Point of View: The War with Words, Essay* (15 May).

Fagan, P. 2008. *Migrant Women and Domestic Violence in Ireland: The Experience of Domestic Violence Service Providers*. Adaptservices.ie. Accessed April 1, 2023. https://adaptservices.ie/file_uploads/Migrant_Women_and_Domestic_Violence_in_Ireland-The_Experience_of_Domestic_Violence_Service_Providers.pdf.

Falchikov, N. 2006. *Improving Assessment Through Student Involvement: Practical Solutions for Aiding Learning in Higher and Further Education*. New York: Routledge.

Fanjoy, M., and B. Bragg. 2019. "Embracing Complexity: Co-creation with Retired Immigrant Women." *International Journal of Community Research and Engagement* 12 (1). https://doi.org/10.5130/ijcre.v12i1.6342.

Fanning, B. 2002. *Racism and Social Change in Ireland*. Manchester: Manchester University Press.

Farrell, T. S. 2007. "Failing the Practicum: Narrowing the Gap between Expectations and Reality with Reflective Practice." *Tesol Quarterly* 41 (1): 193–201.

Fausto-Sterling, A. 2000. *Sexing the Body*. New York: Basic Books.

Ferguson, S. 2019. *Women and Work Feminism, Labour, and Social Reproduction*. London: Pluto Press.

Finnegan, F., S. Valadas, J. O'Neill, A. Fragoso, and L. Paulos. 2019. "The Search for Security in Precarious Times: Non-traditional Graduates Perspectives on Higher Education and Employment." *International Journal of Lifelong Education* 38 (2): 157–170. doi: 10.1080/02601370.2019.1567613.

Finnegan, F., and J. O'Neill. 2016. "Building Critical Visions on Employability in European Higher Education: Listening to Students' Voices." *ESREA 8th Triennial European Research Conference*. Maynooth University.

———. 2020. "Spalpeens on the Isle of Wonder: Reflections on Work, Power and Collective Resistance in Irish Further Education." In *Caliban's Dance: FE after the Tempest*, by M. Daley, K. Orr and J. Petrie, 148–159. London: Institute of Education Press.

Fishbach, A., and K. Woolley. 2022. "The Structure of Intrinsic Motivation." *Annual Review of Organizational Psychology and Organizational Behavior* 9 (1): 339–363.

Fisher, J., R. Viscusi, A. Ratesic, and A. Johnston. 2018. "Clinical Skills Temporal Degradation Assessment in Undergraduate Medical Education." *Journal of Advances in Medical Education & Professionalism* 6 (1): 1–15. Accessed February 22, 2022. https://web.archive.org/web/20180410134230id_/http://jamp.sums.ac.ir/index.php/JAMP/article/viewFile/919/168.

Fitzsimons, C. 2017a. *Community Education and Neoliberalism: Philosophies, Practices and Policies in Ireland*. Zurich: Palgrave-Macmillan.

———. 2017b. "Rhetoric and Reality: The Irish Experience of Quality Assurance." *The Adult Learner: The Irish Journal of Adult and Community Education* 15–32.

———. 2019. "Working as a White Adult Educator, Using Our Own Life Stories to Explore Asymmetries of Power and Privilege." *Studies in the Education of Adults* 52 (1): 88–100. https://doi.org/10.1080/02660830.2019.1587876.

———. 2021. *Repealed, Ireland's Ongoing Struggle for Reproductive Rights*. London: Pluto Press.

———. 2022. "Critical Perspectives on Education in the Irish Repeal Movement." *Studies in the Education of Adults*. 54 (2): 128–144.

Fitzsimons, C., and L. Nwanze. 2022. "Towards Critical, Engaged, Antiracist Learning Environments." *The Adult Learner: The Irish Journal of Adult and Community Education* 163–181.

———. 2023. "Can Critical Education Help Address Racial Discrimination in Irish Maternity Settings?" *Journal of Critical Education Policy Studies* 20 (3): 215–242.

Fitzsimons, C., and P. Dorman. 2013. "Swimming in the Swamp – Inquiry into Accreditation, Community Development and Social Change." *The Adult Learner: The Irish Journal of Adult and Community Education* 44–58.

Fitzsimons, C., S. Henry, and J. O'Neill. 2022. "Precarity and the Pandemic: An Inquiry into the Impact of Covid19 on the Working Lives of Non-permanent Educators in Post-compulsory Education in Ireland." *Research in Post-Compulsory Education* 27 (4): 622–642.

Fletcher, L. 2023. "Numbers in Direct Provision Double to 20,000 in a Year." *RTÉ news*. 13 March. Accessed April 6, 2023. https://www.rte.ie/news/ireland/2023/0312/1361762-direct-provision/#:~:text=There%20are%20a%20total%20of,people%20on%2027%20March%202022.

Fletcher-Watson, S., J. Adams, K. Brook, T. Charman, L. Crane, J. Cusack, S. Leekam, D. Milton, J. R. Parr, and E. Pellicano. 2019. "Making the Future Together: Shaping Autism Research through Meaningful Participation." *Autism* 23 (4): 943–953.

Flowers, D. A. 2010. "Mammies, Maids, and Mamas: The Unspoken Language of Perceptual and Verbal Racism." In *The Handbook of Race and Adult Education*, by V. Sheared, J. Johnson-Bailey, III S. A. J. Colin, E. Peterson and Stephen Brookfield and Associates, 271–282. San Francisco: John Wiley and Sons.

Flynn, S. 2012. "Quinn Promises Training Sector Boost." *The Irish Times*, 14 September. Accessed January 3, 2023. https://www.irishtimes.com/news/quinn-promises-training-sector-boost-1.530135.

Formenti, L., and L. West. 2018. *Transforming Perspectives in Lifelong Learning and Adult Education: A Dialogue*. Cham: Palgrave Macmillan.

Frawley, M. 2013. "Quinn dissolves scandal-hit FÁS." *The Irish Independent*, 30 October: 15. Accessed March 20, 2023. https://www.independent.ie/irish-news/quinn-dissolves-scandal-hit-fas-29709817.html.

Freire, P. 1972. *Pedagogy of the Oppressed*. London and New York: Penguin.

———. 1994. *Pedagogy of Hope*. New York: Continuum.

———. 1996. *Pedagogy of the Oppressed*. London: Penguin.

Freire, P., and D. Macedo. 1987. *Reading the Word and the World*. Westport: Bergin and Garvey.
Gallagher, A. 2022. *Web of Lies: The Lure and Danger of Conspiracy Theories*. Dublin: Gill Publishers.
Gannon, S. 2006. "The Im(Possibilities) of Writing the Self-Writing: French Poststructural Theory and Autoethnography." *Cultural Studies <=>Critical Methodologies* 6 (4): 474–495.
Garner, S. 2004. *Racism in the Irish Experience*. London: Pluto Press.
Gaynor, N. 2016. "Shopping to Save the World? Reclaiming Global Citizenship within Irish Universities." *Irish Journal of Sociology* 24 (1): 78–101.
Gee, J. 1999. "The New Literacy Studies and the "Social Turn" Opinion Paper." *Institute of Education Sciences*. Accessed March 20, 2023. https://eric.ed.gov/?id=ED442118.
GENE. 2015. *Global Education in Ireland*. Dublin: GENE. Accessed March 20, 2023. https://www.irishaid.ie/news-publications/publications/publicationsarchive/2015/november/2015genereport/.
———. 2022. "The European Declaration on Global Education to 2050." *Final Congress Version, Adopted 4th November 2022*. Accessed March 20, 2023. https://www.gene.eu/ge2050-congress.
Gill-Peterson, J. 2018. *Histories of the Transgender Child*. London: University of Minnesota Press.
Gilster, P. 1997. *Digital Literacy*. New York: Wiley Computer Publishing.
Giri, A., J. Aylott, P. Giri, S. Ferguson-Wormley, and J. Evans. 2021. "Lived Experience and the Social Model of Disability: Conflicted and Interdependent Ambitions for Employment of People with a Learning Disability and their Family Carers." *British Journal of Learning Disabilities* 50 (1): 98–106.
Giroux, H. 2004. "Critical Pedagogy and the Postmodern/Modern Divide: Towards a Pedagogy of Democratization." Teacher Education Quarterly 31 (1): 31–47.
———. 2020. *On Critical Pedagogy*. 2nd. London: Bloomsbury.
———. 2021. *Race, Politics and Pandemic Pedagogy; Education in a Time of Crisis*. London: Bloomsbury Academic.
Gódány, Z., R. Machová, L. Mura, and T. Zsigmond. 2021. "Entrepreneurship Motivation in the 21st Century in Terms of Pull and Push Factors." *TEM Journal* 10 (1): 334–342.
Goodall, C. 2020. *Understanding the Voices and Educational Experiences of Autistic Young People*. Oxon: Routledge.
Gosepath, S. 2021. *Equality, in The Stanford Encyclopaedia of Philosophy*. Stanford: Stanford University. Accessed February 10, 2023. https://plato.stanford.edu/archives/sum2021/entries/equality/.
Government of Ireland. 1998. *Green Paper: Adult Education in an Era of Lifelong*. Dublin: Government Publications.
———. 2020. *Referendum Results 1937–2019*. Accessed February 10, 2023. https://www.gov.ie/en/publication/32ea7-1937-2019-referendum-results/.
———. 2021. *Adult Literacy for Life: A 10-year Adult Literacy, Numeracy and Digital Literacy Strategy*. Dublin: Government publications. Accessed March 30, 2023. https://www.gov.ie/en/publication/655a4-adult-literacy-for-life-a-10-year-literacy-strategy/.
———. 2022. "Autism Good Practice Guidance for Schools Supporting Children and Young People." Accessed February 5, 2023. https://www.gov.ie/en/publication/8d539-autism-good-practice-guidance-for-schools-supporting-children-and-young-people/.
Griffin, E., and D. Pollack. 2008. "Neurodiversity in Higher Education: Insights from Qualitative Research by the BRAINHE Project." Accessed February 10, 2023. bdabrainheproceedings2008.com.

Grummell, B. 2014. "FET: Responding to Community Needs or Shaping Communities to Suit a Global Market Place Crisis." In *Further Education and Training: History, Politics, Practice*, by M. Murray, B. Grummel and A. Ryan, 122–135. Maynooth: Mace Press.

Grummell, B., and F. Finnegan. 2020. *Doing Critical and Creative Research in Adult Education: Case Studies in Methodology and Theory*. The Netherlands: Brill.

Grummell, B., and M. Murray. 2015. "A Contested Profession: Employability, Performativity, and Professionalism in Irish Further Education." *Journal of Educational Administration and History* 47 (4): 432–450.

Habermas, J. 1984. *The Theory of Communicative Action*. Translated by T. McCarthy. 2 vols. Boston: Beacon Press.

Hamad, R. 2021. *White Tears, Brown Scars: How White Feminism Betrays Women of Colour*. London: Orion Publishing Company.

Hardiman, F. 2011. "Finding a voice, the experience of mature students in a college of further education." *PhD thesis*. Maynooth University eprints. Accessed January 1, 2022. https://mural.maynoothuniversity.ie/3908/.

Harvey, L. 2004. "The Power of Accreditation: Views of Academics." *Journal of Higher Education Policy and Management* 26 (2): 207–223.

———. 2012. *Downsizing the Community Sector: Changes in Employment and Services in the Voluntary and Community Sector in Ireland 2008–2012*. Dublin: Irish Congress of Trade Unions.

———. 2015. "Local and Community Development in Ireland: An Overview." In *The Changing Landscape of Local and Community Development in Ireland: Policy and Practice*, by C. Forde, D. O'Byrne, R. O'Connor, F. Ó hAdhmaill and C. Power, 7–14. Cork: University College Cork.

Healy, R., D. Ryder, and C. McGuckin. 2022. *Students with Disabilities Engaged with Support Services in Higher Education in Ireland 202/2021*. Dublin: AHEAD. Accessed March 30, 2023. https://www.ahead.ie/userfiles/files/Students%20with%20Disabilities%20Engaged%20with%20Support%20Services%20in%20Higher%20Education%20in%20Ireland%2020%2021.pdf.

Hearn, M. 2009. "Color-Blind Racism, Color-Blind Theology, and Church Practices." *Religious Education* 104 (3): 272–288.

———. 2023. "Elon Musk joins call for pause in creation of giant AI 'digital minds'." *The Guardian*, 29 March. Accessed April 2, 2023. https://www.theguardian.com/technology/2023/mar/29/elon-musk-joins-call-for-pause-in-creation-of-giant-ai-digital-minds.

Hearne, R. 2022. *Gaffs. Why No One Can Get a House and What We Can Do about It*. London: Harper-Collins.

Hebron, J. and N. Humphrey. 2014. "Mental Health Difficulties among Young People on the Autistic Spectrum in Mainstream Secondary Schools: A Comparative Study." *Journal of Research in Special Educational Needs* 14: 22–32.

Heron, J. 1999. *The Complete Facilitator's Handbook*. London: Kogan Page.

Hickey, G., S. Smith, L. O'Sullivan, and L. McGill. 2020. "Adverse Childhood Experiences and Trauma Informed Practices in Second Chance Education Settings in the Republic of Ireland: An Inquiry-Based Study." *Children and Youth Services Review* 118: 1–16. doi: 10.1016/j.childyouth.2020.105338.

Higher Education Authority. 2022. "4. Geographic Profile." *Higher Education Authority: Statistics*. Accessed April 6, 2023. https://hea.ie/statistics/data-for-download-and-visualisations/students/widening-participation-for-equity-of-access/dis-2020/4-geographic-profile-dis-2020/.

Highlander Research and Education Centre. 2020. *Our History.* Accessed February 10, 2023. https://highlandercenter.org/our-history-timeline/.

Hodge, C. 2017. "The Coal Operator's Daughter: Zilphia Horton, Folk Music, and Labour Activism." *The Arkansas Historical Quarterly* 27 (4). Accessed February 10, 2023. https://www.jstor.org/stable/26384778.

Hoggan, C., K. Mälkki, and F. Finnegan. 2017. "Developing the Theory of Perspective Transformation: Continuity, Intersubjectivity, and Emancipatory Praxis." *Adult Education Quarterly* 67 (1): 48–64.

Hong, J., L. Bishop-Fitzpatrick, L. E. Smith, et al. 2016. "Factors Associated with Subjective Quality of Life of Adults with Autism Spectrum Disorder: Self-Report versus Maternal Reports." *Journal of Autism Developmental Disorders* 46: 1368–1378.

hooks, b. 1984. *Feminist Theory from Margins to Center.* Boston: South End Press.

———. 1992. "Bell Hooks Speaking about Paulo Freire, the Man, His Work." In *Paulo Freire: A Critical Encounter,* by P. Leonard, & P. McLaren, 145–152. London: Taylor and Francis Group.

———. 1994. *Teaching to Transgress: Education as the Practice of Freedom.* New York: Routledge.

———. 2000. *All about Love New Visions.* New York: Harper Collins.

———. 2000. *Feminism Is for Everyone: Passionate Politics.* London: Pluto Press.

———. 2002. *Communion, the Female Search for Love.* New York: Perennial, HarperCollins books.

———. 2003. *Teaching Community: A Pedagogy of Hope.* London: Routledge.

———. 2010. *Teaching Critical Thinking: Practical Wisdom.* New York and London: Routledge.

———. 2015. *Talking Back: Thinking Feminist, Thinking Black.* New York: Routledge.

Hoover, D. W., and J. Kaufman. 2018. "Adverse Childhood Experiences in Children with Autism Spectrum Disorder." *Current Opinion in Psychiatry* 31 (2): 128–132.

Horgan, A. 2021. *Lost in Work: Escaping Capitalism.* London: Pluto Press.

Horgan, F., N. Kenny, and P. Flynn. 2023. "A Systematic Review of the Experiences of Autistic Young People Enrolled in Mainstream Second-level (Post-primary) Schools." *Autism* 27 (2): 526–538.

Horton, M. 1998. *The Long Haul: An Autobiography.* New York: Teachers' College, Columbia University.

Howlin, P., and I. Magiati. 2017. "Autism Spectrum Disorder: Outcomes in Adulthood." *Current Opinion in Psychiatry* 3 (2): 69–76.

Hull, L., K. V. Petrides, C. Allison, P. Smith, S. Baron-Cohen, M. C. Lai, and W. Mandy. 2017. "Putting on My Best Normal: Social Camouflaging in Adults with Autism Spectrum Conditions." *Journal of Autism and Development Disorders* 47: 2519–2534. DOI 10.1007/s10803-017-3166-5.

Hurley, K. 2014. "Taking Shape, Shaping Up, Changing Shape: Equality and Human Capital." In *Further Education and Training, History Politics and Practice,* by M. Murray, B. Grummell, and A. Ryan, 52–78. Kildare: MACE Publications.

Husserl, E., and D. Moran. 2001. *Logical Investigations.* London: Routledge.

Hussey, T., and P. Smith. 2008. "Learning Outcomes: A Conceptual Analysis." *Teaching in Higher Education* 13 (1): 107–115.

Ibarra, H. 2006. "Career Change." In *Encyclopedia of Career Development,* by J. H. Greenhaus and G. A. Callanan, 77–83. Thousand Oaks: Sage.

IDEA. 2013. *Leaflet introducing Development Education.* Dublin: IDEA.

Illeris, K. 2003. "Towards a Contemporary and Comprehensive Theory of Learning." *International Journal of Lifelong Education* 22 (4): 396–406.

Inglis, T., K. Bailey, C. Murray, and National Association Adult Education. 1993. *Liberating Learning: A Study of Daytime Education Groups in Ireland*. Dublin: AONTAS.

International Labour Organisation. 2019. *Decent Work*. International Labour Organisation. Accessed January 1, 2022. https://www.ilo.org/global/topics/decent-work/lang--en/index.htm.

Irish Refugee Council. 2020. *AIDA Country Report: Ireland. Asylum Information* Database. Accessed September 1, 2021. https://asylumineurope.org/wp-content/uploads/2021/04/AIDA-IE_2020update.pdf.

Irvine, A. and N. Rose. 2022. "How Does Precarious Employment Affect Mental Health? A Scoping Review and Thematic Synthesis of Qualitative Evidence from Western Economies." *Work, Employment and Society* 00 (0): 1–22.

Iyall Smith, K. E. 2008. "Hybrid Identities: Theoretical Examinations." In *Hybrid Identities: Theoretical and Empirical Examinations*, by K. Iyall Smith and P. Leavy, 3–11. Leiden: Brill.

Jackson, S. 1997. "Crossing Boarders and Changing Pedagogies from Giroux and Freire to Feminist Theories of Education." *Gender and Education* 9 (4): 457–468.

Jaffe, S. 2021. *Work Won't Love You Back*. London: Hurst and Company.

Johnson, R. 1988. "Really Useful Knowledge 1790–1850: Memories for Education in the 1980s." In *Radical Approaches to Adult Education*, by T. Lovett, 3–58. London: Routledge.

Joint Committee on Justice and Equality. 2019. *Report on Direct Provision and the International Protection Application Process*. Dublin: Houses of the Oireachtas.

Jorissen, K. T. 2003. "Successful Career Transitions: Lessons from Urban Alternate Route Teachers Who Stayed." *The High School Journal* 86 (3): 41–51.

Joseph, E. 2020. *Critical Race Theory and Inequality in the Labour Market*. Manchester: Manchester University Press.

Kapp, S. K., K. Gillespie-Lynch, L. E. Sherman, and T. Hutman. 2013. "Deficit, Difference, or Both? Autism and Neurodiversity." *Developmental Psychology* 49 (1): 59–71. doi: 10.1037/a0028353.

Kearns, M. 2021. *A Review of Policy & Practice Developments in Development Education-Global Citizenship Education and the Implications for Adult & Community Education Practitioners*. Dublin: Saolta.

Kelleher, P., and C. Kelleher. 1999. *A Review of the Social Impact of Locally-based Community and Family Support Groups*. Dublin: Department of Social, Community and Family Affairs.

Kelleher, P., and C. O'Neill. 2018. *The Systematic Destruction of the Community Development, Anti-Poverty and Equality Movement (2002–2015)*. Cork: Kelleher Associates. Accessed March 20, 2023. https://www.drugsandalcohol.ie/31231.

Kelly, S. 2010. "Qualitative Interviewing Techniques and Styles." In *The SAGE Handbook of Qualitative Methods in Health Research*, by I. Bourgeault, R. Dingwall, and R. de Vries, 307–324. London: SAGE.

Kendall, F. 2013. *Understanding White Privilege; Creating Pathways to Authentic Relationships across Race*. 2nd Edition. New York: Routledge.

Kennedy, N., and D. O'Sullivan. 2022. "CNN." *CNN Web site*. 20 May. Accessed November 30, 2022. https://edition.cnn.com/2022/05/20/europe/ireland-ukraine-refugees-controversy-intl-cmd/index.html.

Kenny, L., C. Hattersley, B. Molins, C. Buckley, C. Povey, and E. Pellicano. 2016. "Which Terms Should Be Used to Describe Autism? Perspectives from the UK Autism Community." *Autism* 20 (4): 442–462. doi: 10.1177/1362361315588200.

Kenny, M., and S. O'Malley. 2002. *Development Education in Ireland: Challenges and Opportunities for the Future*. Dublin: Dóchas.
Khechen, M. 2013. "Social Justice Concepts, Principles, Tools and Challenges." *ECONOMIC AND SOCIAL COMMISSION FOR WESTERN ASIA*. Accessed February 10, 2023. https://www.unescwa.org/sites/default/files/pubs/pdf/social-justice-concepts-principles-tools-challenges-english.pdf.
Khoo, S. M. 2006. "Development Education, Citizenship and Civic Engagement at Third Level and Beyond in the Republic of Ireland." *Policy and Practice: A Development Education Review* 3 (Autumn): 26–39.
Kincheloe, J., and K. Tobin. 2009. "The Much Exaggerated Death of Positivism." *Cultural Studies of Science Education* 4 (September): 513–528.
Kirylo, J. D., and A. A. Kirylo. 2011. "An Interview with Ana Maria Araújo Freire." *Childhood Education (Taylor and Frances Group)* 87 (3): 191–195.
Kitchenham, A. 2008. "The Evolution of John Mezirow's Transformative Learning Theory." *Journal of Transformative Education* 6 (2): 104–123.
Klaus, P. 2007. *The Hard Truth about Soft Skills: Workplace Lessons Smart People Wish They'd Learned Soon*. New York: Collins.
Klein, N. 2007. *The Shock Doctrine*. London: Allen Lane.
Kravetz, D. 1978. "Consciousness Raising Groups in the 1970s." *Psychology of Women Quarterly (Human Sciences Press)* 3 (2): 66–71.
Kyle, S. 2018. "Assessing the Health of Community Education: The Experience of Change from the Perspective of Community Education Practitioners." *The Adult Learner: The Irish Journal of Adult and Community Education* 50–67.
Laming, M., and M. Horne. 2013. "Career Change Teachers: Pragmatic Choice or a Vocation Postponed." *Teachers and Teaching: Theory and Practice* 19 (3): 326–343.
Lange, E. 2016. "Transforming Transformative Education through Ontologies of Relationality." *Journal of Transformative Education* 16 (4): 280–301.
Lankshear, C., and M. Knobel. 2008. *Digital Literacies: Concepts, Policies and Practices*. Vol. 30. New York: Peter Lang.
Lasky, S. 2005. "When the Best Maps Cannot Guide Us: Exploring and Understanding Teacher Vulnerability." In *Connecting Policy and Practice: Challenges for Teaching and Learning in Schools and Universities*, by P. Denricolo and M. Kompf, 191–196. New York: Routledge.
Lather, P. 1998. "Critical Pedagogy and Its Complicities: A Praxis of Stuck Places." *Educational Theory* 48 (4): 487–498.
Leahy, D., and D. Dolan. 2010. "History of the European Computer Driving Licence." *International Conference on History of Computing (HC) / Held as Part of World Computer Congress (WCC)*. Brisbane, Australia. IFIP WG 9.7.
Le Cornu, R. 2013. "Building Early Career Teacher Resilience: The Role of Relationships." *Australian Journal of Teacher Education* 38 (4): 1–16. http://ro.ecu.edu.au/ajte/vol38/iss4/1.
Ledwith, M. 2011. *Community Development: A Critical Approach*. Bristol: Policy Press.
Lee, D., and M. A. Lamport. 2011. "Non-traditional Entrants to the Profession of Teaching: Motivations and Experiences of Second-career Educators." *Christian Perspectives in Education* 4 (2): 1–39.
Lee, D. 2011. "Changing Course: Reflections of Second-career Teachers." *Current Issues in Education* 14 (2): 1–17. Accessed March 16, 2023. https://cie.asu.edu/ojs/index.php/cieatasu/article/download/683/172.

Leggo, C. 2005. "The Heart of Pedagogy: On Poetic Knowing and Living." *Teachers and Teaching* 11 (5): 439–455.

Le Master, B. 2019. "(Un) Becoming Ally: Trans at the Intersections of Difference." *Women and Language* 41 (1): 155–158.

Lentin, A. 2004. *Racism and Anti-Racism in Europe*. London: Pluto Press.

Lentin, R. 2007. "Ireland: Racial State and Crisis Racism." *Ethnic and Racial Studies* 30 (4): 610–627.

Lentin, R., and R. McVeigh. 2006. *After Optimism? Ireland, Racism and Globalization*. Dublin: Metro Eireann Publications.

Lin, Y., and A. S. Chen. 2021. "Experiencing Career Plateau on a Committed Career Journey: A Boundary Condition of Career Stages." *Personnel Review* 50 (9): 1797–1819.

Lopes, A., and I. A. Dewan. 2015. "Precarious Pedagogies? The Impact of Casual and Zero-Hour Contracts in Higher Education." *Journal of Feminist Scholarship*, 7 (Fall): 28–42.

Lord, C., J. B. McCauley, L. A. Pepa, M. Huerta, and A. Pickles. 2020. "Work, Living, and the Pursuit of Happiness: Vocational and Psychosocial Outcomes for Young Adults with Autism." *Autism* 24 (7): 1691–1703.

Luckritz Marquis, T. 2021. "Formative assessment and scaffolding online learning'. New Directions for Adult and Continuing Education." 51–60. doi: https://doi.org/10.1002/ace.20413.

Lynch, K., and J. Baker. 2005. "Equality in Education: An Equality of Condition Perspective." *UCD Research Repository*. Accessed February 10, 2023. https://researchrepository.ucd.ie/server/api/core/bitstreams/1f71c5c7-65b4-4598-945e-2613443a2e34/content.

Lynch, K., J. Baker, and M. Lyons. 2009. *Affective Equality: Love, Care and Injustice*. London: Palgrave Macmillan.

Lynch, K. 1989. *The Hidden Curriculum: Reproduction in Education, a Reappraisal*. London: The Falmer Press.

———. 2018. "Affective Equality, who cares?" *The Open College*. Accessed February 10, 2023. https://www.theopencollege.com/wp-content/uploads/2018/11/Lynch-2010-Affective-Equality.pdf.

Lynch, K. 2022. "Social Class Inequality in Ireland: What Role Does Education Play." In *There are Better Ways: Education, Class and Freethought FM*, by G. Phelan, 32–43. Dublin: The Douglas Hyde Gallery of Contemporary Art.

Lynch, K., B. Grummell, and D. Devine. 2012. *New Managerialism in Education*. London: Palgrave Macmillan.

Mac Leod, A. 2010. "'Welcome to my first rant!' Report on a Participatory Pilot Project to Develop the 'AS portal', an Online Peer Support Network for Higher Education Students on the Autism Spectrum." *Journal of Assistive Technologies* 4 (1): 14–24.

———. 2019. "Interpretative Phenomenological Analysis (IPA) as a Tool for Participatory Research within Critical Autism Studies: A Systematic Review." *Research in Autism Spectrum Disorders* 64: 49–62.

Magrath, C., and C. Fitzsimons. 2020. "Funding Community Education in Ireland – Making the Case for a Needs-based Approach." *Journal of Social Science Education* 18 (4): 38–50.

Maïano, C., C. L. Normand, M.-C. Salvas, G. Moullec, and A. Aimé. 2016. "Prevalence of School Bullying among Youth with Autism Spectrum Disorders: A Systematic Review and Meta-analysis." *Autism Research* 9 (6): 601–615.

Makdisi, S. 2010. *Palestine Inside Out, an Everyday Occupation*. New York: W. W. Norton and Company.

Matilla-Santander, N., E. Ahonen, M. Albin, S. Baron, M. Bolíbar, K. Bosmans, B. Burström, et al. 2021. "COVID-19 and Precarious Employment: Consequences of the Evolving Crisis." *International Journal of Health Services* 51 (2): 226–228.

Mayo, M. 2020. *Community-based Learning and Social Movements: Popular Education in a Populist Age*. Bristol: Policy Press.

McCammon, H. J., V. A. Taylor, and J. Einwohn Reger. 2017. *The Oxford Handbooks of US Women's Social Movement Activism*. Oxford: Oxford University Press.

McCormack, A. 2010. *The e-Skills Manifesto A Call to Arms*. Brussels: European Schoolnet (EUN Partnership AISBL). Accessed March 20, 2023. https://www.ademccormack.com/wp-content/uploads/2017/07/The-e-Skills-Manifeso.pdf.

McCormack, D. 2010. "The Transformative Power of Journaling: Reflective Practice as Self-Supervision." In *The Soul of Supervision: Integrating Practice and Theory*, by M. Benefiel and G. Holton, 26–37. New York: Morehouse Publishing.

———. 2014. "Trína chéile: Reflections on Journaling in the Border Country of Doctoral Research." *Studies in the Education of Adults* 46 (2): 163–174.

Mc Cormack, D., J. O'Neill, M. Ryan, and T. Walsh. 2020. "Autoethnography in, and as, Adult Education: Eavesdropping on a Conversation' (2019)." In *Doing Critical and Creative Research*, by F. Finnegan and B. Grummell, 73–85. Leiden: Brill | Sense.

McDermott, S. 2023. "Asylum Seekers Sleeping Rough on the Streets of Dublin: 'I don't know what's next'." *The Journal.ie*, 27 January. Accessed April 1, 2023. https://www.thejournal.ie/asylum-seekers-rough-sleeping-dublin-citywest-closure-5980824-Jan2023/.

McGinnity, M., J. Nelson, P. Lunn, and E. Quinn. 2009. *Discrimination in Recruitment, Evidence from a Field Experiment*. Dublin: The Equality Authority.

Mc Guckin, C., M. Shevlin, S. Bell, and C. Devecchi. 2014. "Moving to Further and Higher Education: An Exploration of the Experiences of Students with Special Educational Needs." *NCSE RESEARCH REPORTS NO: 14*. Accessed February 20, 2023. https://ncse.ie/wp-content/uploads/2014/10/Report_14_Higher_Ed_09_04_14.pdf.

McGuinness, S., A. Bergin, E. Kelly, S. McCoy, E. Smyth, J. Banks, and A. Whelan. 2014. *Further Education and Training in Ireland: Past, Present and Future*. Dublin: ESRI Research Series 35. Accessed March 20, 2023. https://www.esri.ie/publications/further-education-and-training-in-ireland-past-present-and-future.

McGuinness, S., S. Bergin, E. Kelly, S. McCoy, E. Smith, D. Watson, and A. Whelan. 2018. *Evaluation of PLC Programme Provision*. Dublin: ESRI. Accessed March 1, 2023. https://www.esri.ie/system/files/publications/RS61_0.pdf.

McGuire, P. 2013. "Quinn Receives Frosty Reception at TUI Conference." *The Irish Times*, 3 April. Accessed November 4, 2022. https://www.irishtimes.com/news/quinn-receives-frosty-reception-at-tui-conference-1.1347578.

McLaren, P. 2000. *Che Guevara, Paulo Freire and the Pedagogy for Revolution*. Lanham, MD: Rowman and Littlefield.

———. 2009. "Critical Pedagogy: A Look at the Major Concepts." In *The Critical Pedagogy Reader*, by A. Darder, P. Darder, R. Baltodano, and D. Torres, 69–96. London and New York: Routledge.

———. 2020. "The Future of Critical Pedagogy." *Educational Philosophy and Theory* 52 (12): 1243–1248.

McLaren, P., and D. Houston. 2004. "Revolutionary Ecologies: Ecosocialism and Critical Pedagogy." *Educational Studies* 32 (1): 27–44.

Meaney-Sartori, S., and L. Nwanze. 2021. *A Community Needs Analysis with Refugees and People Seeking Asylum*. Dublin: Irish Refugee Council.

Menyhárt, A. 2008. "Teachers or Lecturers? The Motivational Profile of University Teachers of English." *Working Papers in Language Pedagogy* 43 (3): 119–137.

Mercille, J., and E. Murphy. 2015. "The Neoliberalization of Irish Higher Education under Austerity." *Critical Sociology* 43 (3): 1–17. doi: 10.1177/0896920515607074.

Meyler, A., L. Lovejoy, and L. Swan. 2023. *Lifelong Learning Participation in Ireland: A focus on Marginalised and Vulnerable Groups*. Dublin: AONTAS. Accessed March 27, 2023. https://www.aontas.com/assets/resources/Lifelong%20Learning/AONTAS_LLL%20Research%20Report_Final%20Digital%20Launch.pdf.

Mezirow, J. 1978a. "Perspective Transformation." *Adult Education* 28 (2): 100–110.

———. 1978b. *Education for Perspective Transformation: Women's Re-Entry Programs in Community Colleges*. New York: Teacher's College, Columbia University.

———. 1990. "A Transformation Theory of Adult Learning." *Adult Education Research Annual Conference May 18–20, Athens* (Georgia University). 141–146.

———. 1991. *Transformative Dimensions of Adult Learning*. San Francisco: Jossey-Bass.

Mezirow, J. 1994. "Understanding Transformation Theory." *Adult Education Quarterly* 44 (4): 222–232.

———. 1996. "Toward a Learning Theory of Adult Literacy." *Adult Basic Education* 6 (3): 115.

———. 2000. *Learning as Transformation: Critical Perspectives on a Theory in Progress*. The Jossey-Bass Higher and Adult Education Series. 1st ed. San Francisco: Jossey-Bass.

Michael, L. 2015. *Afrophobia In Ireland: Racism against people of African Descent*. European Network against Racism.

Migrant Rights Centre Ireland. 2015. *Workers on the Move*. Dublin: MRCI.

Mills, C. W. 2000. *The Sociological Imagination*. Oxford: Oxford University Press.

Milton, D. E. 2012. "On the Ontological Status of Autism: The 'Double Empathy Problem'." *Disability & Society* 27 (6): 883–887.

Milton, D., E. Gurbuz, and B. López. 2022. "The 'double empathy problem': Ten Years On." *Autism* 26 (8): 1901–1903.

Merriam Webster Dictionary. 2022. "Essentialism." *Merriam Webster Dictionary*. Accessed February 10, 2023. https://www.merriam-webster.com/dictionary/essentialism.

Mirsa, J., J. H. Lundquist, E. Holmes, and S. Agiomavritis. 2011. "The Ivory Ceiling of Service Work." *Academe* 97 (1): 22.

Moon, J. 2004. *A Handbook of Reflective and Experiential Learning: Theory and Practice*. London: Routledge.

Moser, C. 1999. *A Fresh Start: Improving Literacy and Numeracy*. The Report of the Working Group Chaired by Sir Claus Moser. DfEE. Accessed March 20, 2023. http://www.educationengland.org.uk/documents/pdfs/1999-moser-summary.pdf.

Mountz, A., A. Bonds, B. Mansfield, J. Loyd, J. Hyndman, and M. Walton-Roberts. 2015. "For Slow Scholarship: A Feminist Politics of Resistance through Collective Action in the Neoliberal University." *ACME: An International Journal for Critical Geographies* 14 (4): 1–23.

Murphy, H. 2015. "The Professionalisation of Adult Education in Ireland. An Exploration of the Current Discourse, Debate and Policy Developments." In *Professionalisation of Adult Educators: International and Comparative Perspectives*, by S. Lattke and W. Jütte, 25–43. Frankfurt am Main: Peter Lang: Peter Lang.

Murray, M., B. Grummell, and A. Ryan. 2014. *Further Education and Training, History, Politics and Practice*. Kildare: MACE Press.

Murtagh, L. 2015. "From Humble Beginnings to the Dawning of a New Era." In *Further Education & Training: History, Politics, Practice*, by M. Murray, B. Grummell and A. Ryan, 10–19. Maynooth: MACE Press.

NALA. 2022. "Literacy and Numeracy in Ireland." *National Adult Literacy Agency*. Accessed February 10, 2023. https://www.nala.ie/literacy-and-numeracy-in-ireland/.

National Council for Special Education. 2015. "Supporting Students with Autism Spectrum Disorder in Schools." *NCSE POLICY ADVICE PAPER NO. 5*. Meath: NCSE. Accessed February 20, 2023. https://ncse.ie/wp-content/uploads/2016/07/1_NCSE-Supporting-Students-ASD-Schools.pdf.

National Disability Authority and National Council for Special Education. 2017. "A qualitative study of how well young people with disabilities are prepared for life after school." Accessed March 15, 2023. https://ncse.ie/wp-content/uploads/2018/05/NDA-NCSE-Young-People-with-Disabilities-Preparedness-Report-v-final-publication-20180528.pdf.

Newton, K. J., E. Fornaro, and J. Pecore. 2020. "Program Completion and Retention of Career Changers Pursuing Alternative Teacher Certification: Who Drops, Who Commits, and Why?" *Journal of the National Association for Alternative Certification*. Accessed March 15, 2023. https://files.eric.ed.gov/fulltext/EJ1258648.pdf.

NFQ. 2015. *Making Connections for You*. Accessed August 1, 2021. https://nfq.qqi.ie/assets/qualifications_frameworks.pdf.

Noddings, N. 1992. *The Challenge to Care in Schools: An Alternative Approach to Education*. New York: Teachers College Press.

Oberdofer, H., M. Kearns, and R. O'Hallaron. 2022. *Report on the 2nd Mapping of Global Citizenship Education in the Adult and Community Education Sector*. Ireland: Saolta.

O'Grady, M. 2018. "Existence and Resistance: The Social Model of Community Education in Ireland." *Social Sciences* 7 (12): 1–12 Accessed March 20, 2023. doi: https://doi.org/10.3390/socsci7120270.

O'Halloran, M. 2019. "Ireland has 'worrying pattern' of racism, head of EU agency warns." *The Irish Times*, 27 September. https://www.irishtimes.com/news/politics/ireland-has-worrying-pattern-of-racism-head-of-eu-agency-warns-1.4032957.

O'Keefe, T., and A. Courtois. 2019. "'Not One of the Family': Gender and Precarious Work in the Neoliberal University." *Gender Work Organisation* 26: 463–479. doi: 10.1111/gwao.12346.

O'Leary, M., and J. Rami. 2017. "The Impact of Austerity in Further Education: Cross Cultural Perspectives from England and Ireland." In *International and Comparative Education*, by B. Bartram, 74–86. Abingdon: Routledge.

Olende, K. 2018. "Marxism and Anti-racism." *Critical and Radical Social Work* 6 (2): 159–177.

Oliver, M. 1981. "A New Model of the Social Work Role in Relation to Disability." In *The handicapped Person: A New Perspective for Social Workers*, by J. Campling, 19–32. London: RADAR.

O'Mara, S. 2019. *In Praise of Walking*. London: Vintage.

O'Neill, G. 2015. *Curriculum Design in Higher Education: Theory to Practice*. Dublin: UCD Teaching and Learning.

O'Neill, J. 2015. "Ar Lorg na Slí, (et cetera)." *PhD Thesis*. Maynooth University. Accessed February 10, 2023. https://mural.maynoothuniversity.ie/7587/1/joneill%20-%20submission%20copy%20-%20sep%202016.pdf.

O'Neill, J., and C. Fitzsimons. 2020. "Precarious Professionality: Graduate Outcomes and Experiences from an Initial Teacher (Further) Education Programme in Ireland." *Research in Post-Compulsory Education* 25 (1): 1–22. doi: doi.org/10.1080/13596748.2020.1720143.

O'Neill, J., and S. Cullinane. 2017. "Holding the Line: A Slow Movement Towards a Critical Professional Development for Community Educators." *The Adult Learner* 113–129.

O'Neill, M., L. Martell, H. Mendick, and R. Muller. 2014. "Slow Movement/Slow University: Critical Engagements." *Forum: Qualitative Social Research* 15 (3). Accessed September 29, 2014. doi: https://doi.org/10.17169/fqs-15.3.2229.

Orsmond, G. I., P. T. Shattuck, B. P. Cooper, P. R. Sterzing, and K. A. Anderson. 2013. "Social Participation among Young Adults with an Autism Spectrum Disorder." *Journal of Autism Developmental Disorders* 43: 2710–2719.

O'Sullivan, R. 2018. "From the 'Cinderella' to the 'Fourth Pillar' of the Irish Education System – A Critical Analysis of the Evolution of Further Education and Training in Ireland." *Unpublished PhD thesis.* Trinity College Dublin.

Oxfam International. 2021. *Not all Gaps are Created Equal: The True Value of Care Work.* Accessed April 18, 2022. https://www.oxfam.org/en/not-all-gaps-are-created-equal-true-value-care-work.

Oxfam Ireland. 2023. "Ireland's Two Richest People have more Wealth – €15 billion than half of the Irish Population who have €10.3 billion." *Oxfam Ireland.* Accessed April 6, 2023. https://www.oxfamireland.org/blog/ireland-two-richest-people-have-more-wealth-50-percent-population-poorest-end#:~:text=By%20using%20Credit%20Suisse's%20Global,wealth%20(%E2%82%AC10.3%20billion).

Palinkas, L A., S. M. Horwitz, C. A. Green, J. P. Wisdom, N. Duan, and K. Hoagwood. 2015. "Purposeful Sampling for Qualitative Data Collection and Analysis in Mixed Method Implementation Research." *Administration and Policy in Mental Health* 42 (5): 533–544.

Papen, U. 2005. *Adult Literacy as Social Practice: More than Skills.* New York: Routledge.

Pashby, K., M. da Costa, S. Stein, and V. Andreotti. 2020. "A Meta-review of Typologies of Global Citizenship Education." *Comparative Education* 56 (2): 144–164.

Pelias, R. J. 2019. *The Creative Qualitative Researcher.* London: Routledge.

Pembrook, S. 2019. "Foucault and Industrial Schools in Ireland: Subtly Disciplining or Dominating through Brutality?" *Sociology* 53 (2): 385–400.

Pesonen, H. V., M. Waltzb, M. Fabric, M. Lahdelmaa, and E. V. Syurinab. 2020. "Students and Graduates with Autism: Perceptions of Support When Preparing for Transition from University to Work." *European Journal of Special Needs Education* 36 (4): 531–546.

Phillips, S. D. 2015. "Lifespan Career Development." In *APA Handbook of Career Intervention, Vol. 1. Foundations*, by P. J. Hartung, M. L. Savickas, and W. B. Walsh, 99–113. Washington: American Psychological Association.

Plummer, K. 2022. "What Is Critical Humanism?" *Ken Plummer Sociology Humanism Narrative Sexualities.* Accessed February 10, 2023. https://kenplummer.com/cosmosexualities/what-is-critical-humanism/.

Pollack, S. 2020. "'Frustrated and Angry': Thousands March in Dublin to Protest Death of George Floyd." *The Irish Times.* 1 June. https://www.irishtimes.com/news/ireland/irish-news/frustrated-and-angry-thousands-march-in-dublin-to-protest-death-of-george-floyd-1.4268066.

Powell, A. B., and M. Frankenstein. 1997. *Ethnomathematics: Challenging Eurocentricism in Mathamatics Education.* New York: State University of New York Press.

Power, S. 2002. *A Problem from Hell: America and the Age of Genocide.* New York: Basic Books.

Priestley, M., S. Philippou, D. Alvunger, and T. Soini. 2022. *Curriculum Making in Europe: Policy and Practice within and across Diverse Settings.* Bradford: Emerald Publishing Limited.

QQI. 2012. *Component Specification NFQ Level 5 Communications 5N0690 (PDF)*. QQI. Accessed March 31, 2023. https://qsdocs.qqi.ie//sites/docs/AwardsLibraryPdf/5N0690_AwardSpecifications_English.pdf.

———. 2018a. *Green Paper on Assessment of Learners and Learning*. QQI. Accessed December 2021. https://www.qqi.ie/sites/default/files/media/file-uploads/Green%20Paper%20Assessment%20of%20Learners%20and%20Learning%20March%202018.pdf.

———. 2018b. *Quality Assuring Assessment Guidelines for Providers – Version 2*. QQI. Accessed March 31, 2023. https://www.qqi.ie/sites/default/files/2021-10/quality-assuring-assessment-guidelines-for-providers-revised-2013.pdf.

———. 2019. "Professional Award-type Descriptors at NFQ Levels 5 to 8: Annotated for QQI Early Learning and Care (ELC) Awards Professional Award Type Descriptors at NFQ Levels 5–8 (Annotated for QQI ELC Awards).pdf." *Quality and Qualifications Ireland*. Accessed March 13, 2023. https://www.qqi.ie/sites/default/files/media/file-uploads/Professional%20Award%20Type%20Descriptors%20at%20NFQ%20Levels%205-8%20%28Annotated%20for%20QQI%20ELC%20Awards%29.pdf.

———. 2021. *National Framework of Qualifications*. QQI. Accessed December 1, 2023. Available at: https://www.qqi.ie/what-we-do/the-qualifications-system/national-framework-of-qualifications.

———. 2022. "Implementation Guidelines for using Broad Award Standards at NFQ Levels 1–4." *Quality and Qualifications Ireland*. Accessed March 13, 2023. https://www.qqi.ie/sites/default/files/2022-10/Guidelines%20for%20using%20broad%20award%20standards%20at%20NFQ%20levels%201-4.pdf.

Quirk, M., and P. McCarthy. 2020. *A Conceptual Framework for the Universal Design of Learning for the Irish Further Education and Training Sector*. SOLAS and AHEAD. Accessed March 30, 2023. https://www.solas.ie/f/70398/x/b1aa8a51b6/a-conceptual-framework-of-universal-design-for-learning-udl-for-the-ir.pdf.

Rawls, J. 1971. *A Theory of Justice*. Cambridge: Harvard University Press.

Rehab Group. 2023. *Disability Support Service*. Accessed March 2023. https://rehab.ie/national-learning-network/info-and-support/supports-for-students/disability-support-service/.

Research voor Beleid (Alpine). 2008. *The ALPINE Report– Adult Learning Professions in Europe*. Zoetermeer: European Commission.

Richardson, L. 1994. "Writing: A Method of Inquiry." In *Handbook of Qualitative Research*, by N. Denzin and Y. Lincoln, 923–948. Thousand Oaks: Sage.

Richardson, P. W., and H. M. Watt. 2010. "Current and Future Directions in Teacher Motivation Research." *Advances in Motivation and Achievement* 16 (Part B): 139–173.

Richardson, P. W., and H. M. Watt. 2018. "Teacher Professional Identity and Career Motivation: A Lifespan Perspective." In *Research on Teacher Identity*, by P. A. Schutz, J. Hong and D. Cross Francis, 37–48. Cham: Springer.

Robison, J. E. 2015. *Neurodiversity: What Does It Mean for 2015?* Accessed February 10, 2023. https://www.psychologytoday.com/gb/blog/my-life-aspergers/201503/neurodiversity-what-does-it-mean-2015.

Rogers, A., and N. Horrocks. 2010. *Teaching Adults*. 4th ed. Berkshire: Open University Press.

Rogers, C. 1970. *Encounter Groups*. London: Penguin.

———. 1989. *The Carl Rogers Reader, Selections from the Lifetime Work of America's Preeminent Psychologist, Author of on Becoming a Person and a Way of Being*, by H. Kirschenbaum and V. L. Henderson. Boston: Houghton Mifflin Harcourt.

———. 1995. *On Becoming a Person: A Therapist's View of Psychotherapy*. Boston: Houghton Mifflin.

Rosenthal, N. B. 1984. "Consciousness Raising: From Revolution to Re-Evaluation." *Psychology of Women* (Human Sciences Press/Sage). 8 (4): 309–326.

Roser, M., and E. Ortiz-Ospina. 2016. "Global Education-Online Resource." *OurWorldInData.org*. Accessed February 10, 2023. https://ourworldindata.org/global-education.

Rubenson, K. 2011. *Adult Learning and Education*. Elsevier: Oxford Academic Press.

Ruitenburg, S. K., and A. E. Tigchelaar. 2021. "Longing for Recognition: A Literature Review of Second-Career Teachers' Induction Experiences in Secondary Education." *Educational Research Review* 33: 1–20. doi: 10.1016/j.edurev.2021.100389.

Ruohotie–Lyhty, M. 2018. "Identity–agency in Progress: Teachers Authoring their Identities." In *Research on Teacher Identity*, by P. A. Schutz, J. Hong and D. Cross Francis, 25–36. Cham: Springer.

Russell, G., S. K. Kapp, D. Elliott, C. Elphick, R. Gwernan-Jones, and C. Owens. 2019. "Mapping the Autistic Advantage from the Accounts of Adults Diagnosed with Autism: A Qualitative Study." *Autism in Adulthood* 1 (2): 124–133.

Ryan, A. B. 2001. *Feminist Ways of Knowing: Towards Theorising the Person for Radical Adult Education*. Leicester: NIACE.

Salem, S. 2018. "Intersectionality and Its Discontents: Intersectionality as Traveling Theory." *European Journal of Women's Studies* 25 (4): 403–418.

Sandberg, S. 2013. *Lean in: Women, Work, and the Will to Lead*. New York: Knopf Doubleday Publishing Group.

Sartori, S., and D. Demir Bloom. 2023. *A Community Needs Analysis with FET Students*. College Connect. Accessed March 27, 2023. https://collegeconnect.ie/a-community-needs-analysis-with-fet-students/.

Schön, D. A. 2003. *The Reflective Practitioner: How Professionals Think in Action*. Aldershot: Ashgate.

Sennett, R. 1998. *The Corrosion of Character: The Personal Consequence of Work in the New Capitalism*. London: W. W. Norton & Company.

Seth, A. 2021. *Being You: The New Science of Consciousness*. London: Faber and Faber.

Shannon, D. 2019. "A Tale of a Discursive Shift: Analysing EU Policy Discourses in Irish Adult Education Policy – From the White Paper to the Further Education and Training Strategy." *The Adult Learner: The Irish Journal of Adult and Community Education* 98–117.

Shaw, M., and J. Crowther. 2014. "Adult Education, Community Development and Democracy: Renegotiating the Terms of Engagement." *Community Development Journal* 49 (3): 390–406.

Sheehy, M. 2001. *Partners Companion to Training for Transformation*. Dublin: Partners.

Shor, I. 2021. "Making Hope Practical, a Dialogue on the Life, Legacy and Continuing Relevance of Paulo Freire to Adult Education in Ireland and Internationally." Maynooth, 27 November. https://www.maynoothuniversity.ie/adult-and-community-education/news/making-hope-practical-dialogue-freire.

Shor, I., and P. Freire. 1987. *A Pedagogy for Liberation: Dialogues on Transforming Education*. Westport, CT, London: Bergin & Garvey.

Sidebottom, K. 2021. "Rhizomes, Assemblages and Momad War Machines – Re-imagining Curriculum Development for Posthuman Times." *PhD Thesis*. Lancaster University.

Siew, C.T., T. G. Mazzucchelli, R. Rooney, and S. Girdler. 2017. "A Specialist Peer Mentoring Program for University Students on the Autism Spectrum: A Pilot study." *PLoS One* 12 (7): 1–18.

Silberman, S. 2015. *Neurotribes: The Legacy of Autism and How to Think Smarter about People Who Think Differently*. Crows Nest, NSW, Australia: Allen & Unwin.

Singer, J. 1999. "Why can't you Be Normal for Once in your Life? From a Problem with No Name to the Emergence of a New Category of Difference." In *Disability Discourse*, by M. Corker and S. French, 59–70. Buckingham: Open University Press.

Smith, M. 2008. "What Is Group Work?" *The Encyclopedia of Pedagogy and Informal Education*. Accessed February 10, 2023. https://infed.org/mobi/group-work/.

Sneddon, F. 2021. "The Value and Appeal of Further Education and Training: Shining a light on FET in Ireland in 2021." *Ireland's Education Yearbook*. Accessed March 20, 2023. https://irelandseducationyearbook.ie/downloads/IEYB2021/YB2021-FET-07.pdf.

SOLAS. 2014. *Further Education and Training Strategy 2014–2019*. Dublin: SOLAS. Accessed April 09, 2022. https://www.solas.ie/f/70398/x/920e2fa0b6/fetstrategy2014-2019.pdf.

———. 2019. "This is FET: Facts and Figures 2019." Accessed February 10, 2023. https://www.solas.ie/f/70398/x/1ba83e5971/15429_solas_facts_report_2019_web.pdf.

———. 2020. *Future FET: Transforming Learning. The National Further Education and Training (FET) Strategy 2020–2024*. Dublin: SOLAS.

———. 2022. *The Reach Fund*. Accessed March 27, 2023. https://www.solas.ie/reach-fund/.

Solnit, R., and A. T. Fernandez. 2014. *Men Explain Things to Me (Updated)*. Chicago: Haymarket Books.

Sosnowy, C., C. Silverman, and P. Shattuck. 2018. "Parents' and Young Adults' Perspectives on Transition Outcomes for Young Adults with Autism." *Autism* 22 (1): 29–39.

Soto, N., and R. Moriana. 2020. *Employability of Migrant Women in Ireland*. Dublin: New Community Partnerships.

Springgay, S., and S. E. Truman. 2019. *Walking Methodologies in a More-than-Human World: Walking Lab*. London: Routledge.

St. Pierre, E. A. 2013. "The Posts Continue: Becoming." *International Journal of Qualitative Studies in Education* 26 (6): 646–657.

Stein, S. 2021. "Reimagining Global Citizenship Education for a Volatile, Uncertain, Complex, and Ambiguous (VUCA) World." *Globalisation, Societies and Education* 19 (4): 482–495.

Stein, S., and V. Andreotti. 2016. "Decolonization and Higher Education." In *Encyclopedia of Educational Philosophy and Theory*, by M. Peters. Singapore: Springer Science and Business Media. doi: 10.1007/978-981-287-532-7_479-1.

Sterzing, P. R., P. T. Shattuck, S. C. Narendorf, M. Wagner, and B. P. Cooper. 2012. "Bullying Involvement and Autism Spectrum Disorders: Prevalence and Correlates of Bullying Involvement Among Adolescents with an Autism Spectrum Disorder." *Archives of Pediatrics & Adolescence* 166 (11): 1058–1064.

Stopper, A. 2006. *Monday at Gaj's: The Story of the Irish Women's Liberation Movement*. Dublin: The Liffey Press.

Sutin, A. R., M. Luchetti, Y. Stephan, and A. Terracciano. 2022. "Sense of Purpose in Life and Motivation, Barriers, and Engagement in Physical Activity and Sedentary Behavior: Test of a Mediational Model." *Journal of Health Psychology* 27 (9): 2068–2078.

Sweeney, J. 2016. "Raising the Status of FET: the Labour Market as an Ally." *National Economic and Social Council*. Accessed February 1, 2023. https://www.nesc.ie/assets/files/Presentations/Raising-the-Status-of-FET_the-Labour-Market-as-an-Ally.pdf.

Sweeney, M. R., T. Burke, K. Quinn, and A. Harris. 2018. Living with Autism as a University Student at Dublin City University: Developing an Autism Friendly University. Available at: https://doras.dcu.ie/23340/1/Final%20Report%20autism%20friendly%20university%20project.pdf. Accessed March 10, 2023.

Sweetman, R. 2020. *Feminism Backwards*. Cork: Mercier Press.

Táíwò, O. O. 2022. *Elite Capture How the Powerful Took Over Identity Politics and Everything Else*. London: Pluto Press.

Tebbutt, C. 2022. "Thinking about Queer-Inclusive Teaching and Learning" | InspirED. www.academic-practice.com.

Tett, L., M. Hamilton, and Y. Hillier. 2006. *Adult Literacy, Numeracy and Language: Policy, Practice and Research*. Columbus: Open University Press.

Thamar, M. H., S. S. Finnborg, and E. Thorgerdur. 2017. "Academic Career Making and the Double-Edged Role of Academic Housework." *Gender and Education* 29 (6): 764–780.

The New London Group. 1996. "A Pedagogy of Multiliteracies: Designing Social Futures." *Harvard Educational Review* 66 (1): 60–93.

Thompson, J. 1996. "Really Useful Knowledge' Linking Theory and Practice." In *Radical Learning for Liberation*, by T. Fleming, D. McCormack, A. Ryan, and B. Connolly, 25–36 Maynooth: MACE Occasional Series.

Tigchelaar, A., N. Brouwer, and F. Korthagen. 2008. "Crossing Horizons: Continuity and Change During Second–career Teachers' Entry into Teaching." *Teaching and Teacher Education* 24 (6): 1530–1550.

Tigchelaar, A., N. Brouwer, and J. D. Vermunt. 2010. "Tailor–made: Towards a Pedagogy for Educating Second–career Teachers." *Educational Research Review* 5 (2): 164–183.

Tisdell, E. J., and D. E. Tolliver. 2009. "Transformative Approaches to Culturally Responsive Teaching: Engaging Cultural Imagination." In *Transformative Learning in Practice: Insights from Community, Workplace, and Higher Education*, by J. Mezirow and E. W. Taylor, 89–99. San Francisco: Jossey Bass.

Todd, S. 2009. *Towards an Imperfect Education: Facing Humanity, Rethinking Cosmopolitanism*. London/Boulder: Paradigm Publishers.

Trent, J. 2018. "'It's Like Starting All over Again'. The Struggles of Second–career Teachers to Construct Professional Identities in Hong Kong Schools." *Teachers and Teaching* 24 (8): 931–950.

Trent, J., and X. Gao. 2009. "'At Least I'm the Type of Teacher I Want to be': Second–career English Language Teachers' Identity Formation in Hong Kong Secondary Schools." *Asia–Pacific Journal of Teacher Education* 37 (3): 253–270.

Tubbett, C. 2022. "Thinking about Queer-inclusive Teaching and Learning." *InstpirED*. 14 July. Accessed August 27, 2022. https://academic-practice.com/2022/07/14/thinking-about-queer-inclusive-teaching-and-learning/.

UCU. 2016. *Precarious Work in Higher Education: A Snapshot of Insecure Contracts and Institutional Attitudes*. London: University and College Union.

United Nations. 2007. "Convention on the Rights of Persons with Disabilities [A/RES/61/106]." Accessed March 6, 2023. https://www.un.org/development/desa/disabilities/resources/general-assembly/convention-on-the-rights-of-persons-with-disabilities-ares61106.html.

———. 2023. "Sustainable Development Goal 4." *United Nations Department of Economic and Social Affairs, Sustainable Development*. Accessed March 20, 2023. https://sdgs.un.org/goals/goal4.

van Manen, M. 1991. *The Tact of Teaching: The Meaning of Pedagogical Thoughtfulness*. New York: State University of New York.

Vergès, F. 2022. *A Feminist Theory of Violence*. London: Pluto Press.

Vuorikari, R., S. Kluzer, and Y. Punie. 2022. *DigComp 2.2: The Digital Competence Framework for Citizens – With New Examples of Knowledge, Skills and Attitudes*. European Commission, Luxembourg: Publications Office of the European Union. Accessed March 20, 2023. https://publications.jrc.ec.europa.eu/repository/handle/JRC128415.

Walker, N. 2012. "Throw away the Master's Tools: Liberating ourselves from the Pathology Paradigm." In *Loud Hands: Autistic People, Speaking*, by J. Bascom, 225–237. Washington, DC: Autistic Self-Advocacy Network.

Walker-Donnelly, K., D. A. Scott, and T. Cawthon. 2019. "Introduction: Overview and Application of Career Development Theories." *New Directions for Student Services* 166: 9–17.

Walsh, S. C. 2004. "Troubling Experience through an Art-Informed Research Process: Presentation for British Educational Research Association." September. Accessed November 01, 2013. http://www.leeds.ac.uk/educol/documents/00003948.pdf.

Walton, S. 2020. "Why the Critical Race Theory Concept of 'White supremacy' Should not be Dismissed by Neo-Marxists: Lessons from Contemporary Black Radicalism." *Power and Education* 12 (1): 78–94.

Ward, F., and P. Ayton. 2019. *A Short History of the Adult Literacy Service and the Foundation of the Adult Literacy Organisers Association*. Adult Literacy Organisers Association. Accessed March 20, 2023. http://www.aloa.ie/wp-content/uploads/2019/05/A-Short-History-of-the-Adult-Literacy-Service-and-ALOA-4.pdf.

Waterman, A. S. 2004. "Finding Someone to Be: Studies on the Role of Intrinsic Motivation in Identity Formation." *Identity* 4 (3): 209–228.

Watson, N., A. Roulstone, and C. Thomas. 2012. "The Social Model of Disability: Valuable or Irrelevant?" In *The Routledge Handbook of Disability Studies*, by C. Barnes, 12–29. London: Routledge.

Watson, N. 2018 "Enabling Identity: Disability, Self and Citizenship," In *The Disability Reader: Social Science Perspectives*, by T. Shakespeare, 147–162. London, UK: Continuum.

Wener, L. 2021. "John Rawls." In *The Stanford Encyclopaedia of Philosophy*, by Stanford University. Accessed February 10, 2023.

Western States Resource Center. 2003. Dismantling Racism: A Resource Book. Oregon: Western States Center.

Whelan, J. 2021. "Tales of Precarity: A Reflexive Essay on Experiencing the Covid Pandemic as a Social Work Educator on a Precarious Contract." *Qualitative Social Work* 20 (1–2): 579–586.

Williams, J. 2010. "Constructing a New Professional Identity: Career Change into Teaching." *Teaching and Teacher Education* 26 (3): 639–647.

———. 2013. *Constructing New Professional Identities. Career Changes in Teacher Education*. Rotterdam: Sense Publishers.

Wilson, M. E., D. L. Liddell, A. S. Hirschy, and K. Pasquesi. 2016. "Professional Identity, Career Commitment, and Career Entrenchment of Midlevel Student Affairs Professionals." *Journal of College Student Development* 57 (5): 557–572.

Wilson, N. 2022. "Thinking Together: A Feminist Collaborative Inquiry into Pedagogical Approaches for Domestic Violence Work in Ireland." *PhD thesis*. Maynooth University. Accessed October 27, 2022. https://mural.maynoothuniversity.ie/15844/.

Wood, C., and M. Freeth. 2016. "Students' Stereotypes of Autism." *Journal of Educational Issues* 2 (2): 131.

Worth, N. 2016. "Feeling Precarious: Millennial Women and Work." *Environment and Planning D: Society and Space* 34 (4): 601–616.

Wray, M., and A. M. Houghton. 2019. "Implementing Disability Policy in Teaching and Learning Contexts – Shop Floor Constructivism or Street Level Bureaucracy?" *Teaching in Higher Education* 24 (4): 510–526.

Wrigley, T. 2017. "Canonical Knowledge and Common Culture: In Search of Curricular Justice." *European Journal of Curriculum Studies* 4 (1): 536–555.

Yu, N. 2018. *Consciousness-Raising: Critical Pedagogy and Practice for Social Change*. London: Routledge.

Zakaria, R. 2021. *Against White Feminism*. London: Penguin Books.

Zeidan, J., E. Fombonne, J. Scorah, A. Ibrahim, M. S. Durkin, S. Saxena, A. Yusuf, A. Shih, and M. Elsabbagh. 2022. "Global Prevalence of Autism: A Systematic Review Update." *Autism Research* 15 (5): 778–790.

Zembylas, M. 2007. "Risks and Pleasures: A Deleuzo-Guattarian Pedagogy of Desire in Education." *British Educational Research Journal* 33 (3): 331–347.

INDEX

access courses 5
accreditation 17, 40, 146, 176
active citizenship 10
activism 5, 45, 60, 61, 88, 99, 102, 104
administrative burdens 139, 145, 148, 150
Adult Literacy for Life 124, 126
anti-immigration 81
anti-intellectual 86
anti-racism 57, 62, 94, 150
AONTAS 137–39, 142, 148, 149
apprenticeships 7
assumptions 83, 97–99, 102, 104, 105, 113
asylum seekers 47, 49, 50
authoritarian 8, 82

banking 18, 19, 46, 80
behaviourism 19, 83
binary 22, 25, 82, 83, 88
Brookfield 31, 43, 51, 52, 55, 56, 60, 107, 111, 112, 114, 195
bureaucratic 143, 145

care 9, 19, 21, 23, 24, 61, 79, 80, 89, 115, 118, 138, 144, 147, 148, 173, 174
CEFA 138, 139, 149
CEN 138, 139, 148, 149
childcare 22, 141
CID (Contract of Indefinite Duration) 172
citizenship 14, 47, 80, 88, 94, 95, 100
civil rights 84
communities of practice 27, 148
community development 5, 15, 93, 138, 142, 143
Community Development Programme 142
community education 4, 5, 8, 13, 14, 81–83, 85, 87, 88, 90, 91, 171, 172, 179
Community Education Facilitators 7

conscientization 27, 79, 85–87, 98, 99
consciousness raising 79, 82, 85–89, 138, 145, 149
conservative 81, 82, 90
constitution 87
Contraceptives Train protest 87
Covid 138, 148, 150, 174
CPD 177, 178
critical pedagogy 18, 19, 23, 24, 26, 85, 87
critical reflection 57, 79, 82, 98, 109, 111, 112, 144, 145
critical thinking 19, 43, 80, 84, 86, 88, 89
curriculum 17, 23, 31, 34–37, 41, 42, 44, 80, 89, 96, 113, 116, 173
Cush report 180

deficit 15, 23, 81
democratic 50, 82, 142, 145, 149
Department of Education 7, 12n3, 74, 80, 81, 85, 137, 141, 142, 143, 145, 152, 176–78
Department of Education and Science 7, 81, 85, 137, 141–43, 146, 152, 176
Department of Education and Skills 143, 177
DFHERIS 10
digital literacy 15
direct action 27, 87
disability 22, 58, 88, 90
disorientation 111, 117, 120, 148
disruptive 4, 116, 149

economy 10, 21, 47, 80, 88
emancipation 25, 79, 81, 87, 90
emancipatory 14, 79, 88, 89, 144, 150
employability 5, 8, 15, 176
engaged pedagogy 18, 19, 24, 27

Equality Studies Centre 81
equality/inequality 20, 26, 27, 79, 81, 83, 87, 89–91
ETB 169, 174
ETBi 177
EU 14, 41n3, 45, 47, 48, 55

family 21, 42, 83, 93, 144, 147
feminism 86, 90
FET strategy 10
Folk High Schools 84, 90
Freire 3, 18, 19, 20, 22, 23, 27, 45, 46, 56, 61, 62, 79–81, 83, 85–87
Freirean 18, 24, 39, 42, 46, 109, 112, 141, 144, 149, 150
funding cuts 8, 143
funding systems 144

Global South 23
grassroots 86, 99, 149, 150
Green Paper 38, 40, 176
groupwork 14, 29, 39, 79, 81–85, 88, 89

Harris, Simon 10
hidden curriculum 14, 32, 39
hierarchies 22, 82–84, 90
higher education 10, 11, 13, 180
Highlander 84, 89
homophobia 25
hooks 18–20, 22–26, 51, 52, 54, 56, 59, 61, 85, 86, 89, 99, 114
hope 55, 61, 89, 93, 98, 101, 103, 105, 113, 114, 121, 170
housing 5, 20, 149, 181
humanism 90

imperialist white-supremacist capitalist patriarchy 20, 27
Irish Travellers 23
Irish Women's Liberation Movement 87

job security 148, 150

labour market activation 143
language 9, 22, 24, 30, 46, 50, 174
leadership 5, 82, 86, 140
learner enrolment forms 145
LGBTQI+, 81, 90

lifelong learning 10, 15
literacy 5, 15, 82, 172
lived experience 58, 85, 86, 99, 114, 140, 141, 149, 150
lockdown 148
love 14, 46, 61, 62, 89, 172, 174, 181
Lynch, Kathleen 81, 89, 90

meritocracy 88
migrant rights 149

NALA 90
naming 5, 150
neoliberalism 20
networks 148, 149, 178
NFQ (National Framework of Qualifications) 13, 34n1, 35, 38, 40, 41n3
non-accredited 96, 150

pandemic 11, 79, 93, 111, 117, 118, 148, 149, 170, 174
participation 43, 80, 83, 87, 107, 141, 142
policy 5, 10, 13, 27, 46, 59, 176
post-compulsory education 7, 171
poverty 15, 81, 88, 98, 141–43
power 5, 13, 20, 22, 24, 41, 51, 52, 57, 59, 61, 62, 83, 84, 91, 173, 180
precarious/precarity 22, 27, 170, 171, 173–75, 178, 179, 181
productivity 148
professional identity 15, 172, 177
progression 90, 144, 173, 176, 178

QQI 29, 30, 33–40, 55
quality 5
quality assurance 30, 36

racism 14, 20, 21, 45–47, 51–58, 60–62
radicalism 23, 24, 46, 90
really useful knowledge 82
recession 144
reflexivity 98, 102, 103, 105, 112, 116, 148
refugees 49, 50, 150
rights 5, 47, 49, 50, 52, 81, 84, 94, 95, 98, 100, 101, 104, 172, 175
Rogers, Carl 19, 42, 84, 90
route 3, 177

second career 15
social exclusion 141, 143
social inclusion 139, 143, 145
social inequality 81
social justice 8, 10, 27, 60, 81
social movements 14, 81, 87, 100, 141
soft skills 14, 79, 83
SOLAS 10, 177
solidarity 79, 82, 100, 101, 104, 105, 149, 150
standardization 5

TASC 179
Teaching Council 170, 172, 176, 178
technology 15, 29, 79, 80

The Three Pillars 139
trade union 20, 179, 180
transphobia 25
trust 27, 40, 41, 61, 85, 89, 117
TUI 179

vocational 5–10, 41n3, 82, 96
VTOS 171

The White Paper 137, 138, 141, 142, 144, 150
women's groups 4, 93, 141, 142
women's movement 8, 86–88

Youthreach 70, 171

Printed in the USA
CPSIA information can be obtained
at www.ICGtesting.com
JSHW022139180224
57433JS00006B/1